Risk Management for Operational Technology (OT) Systems

Risk Management for Operational Technology (OT) Systems highlights the importance of applying risk assessments specifically tailored to OT environments, rather than relying solely on traditional IT-focused approaches.

Conventional IT and enterprise risk management methods often fail to adequately address OT systems—despite their critical role in sustaining and maintaining the operational status of essential infrastructure. As such, OT environments demand greater attention and specialized frameworks.

Historically, industries such as petrochemical refining and nuclear power generation have implemented comprehensive safety and risk assessments, covering every aspect of operations. These rigorous processes, refined over decades, have proven highly effective in ensuring safe, stable, and optimized production. OT computing systems within these facilities were traditionally isolated from corporate IT networks, making their performance and risk profile well-understood and reliably managed through engineered specifications.

However, the situation has changed. Modern requirements for integration, interoperability, and remote accessibility mean that formerly isolated OT systems are now increasingly interconnected with IT networks and, in many cases, the wider Internet. This connectivity introduces new vulnerabilities, exposing once-secure operational systems to external threats and sophisticated adversaries.

The authors propose a modern approach to risk management in OT, one that recognizes these new realities. This approach emphasizes proactive measures to operationally protect legacy and modern OT systems alike from tampering, intrusion, and cyberattack—ensuring that critical infrastructure can remain resilient, safe, and reliable in a connected world.

Risk Management for Operational Technology (OT) Systems

Robert Radvanovsky
Steve Mustard

CRC Press
Taylor & Francis Group
Boca Raton London New York

CRC Press is an imprint of the
Taylor & Francis Group, an **informa** business

Front cover image: Photography by Robert Radvanovsky

First edition published 2026
by CRC Press
2385 NW Executive Center Drive, Suite 320, Boca Raton FL 33431

and by CRC Press
4 Park Square, Milton Park, Abingdon, Oxon, OX14 4RN

CRC Press is an imprint of Taylor & Francis Group, LLC

ISBN: 978-1-041-00682-4 (hbk)
ISBN: 978-1-041-00576-6 (pbk)
ISBN: 978-1-003-61055-7 (ebk)

DOI: 10.4324/9781003610557

Typeset in Sabon
by SPi Technologies India Pvt Ltd (Straive)

From Robert

This book is dedicated to my loving wife, Tammy, who has always supported and been patient with me, especially while this book was being written. She continues encouraging me with my research.
She is my rock

From Steve

To Charlotte, Benjamin, Jeanette, and Toby—my family and my constant source of love, encouragement, and support.

Contents

About the Authors

Robert Radvanovsky is an active professional in the United States with over 50 years of knowledge in security, engineering, risk management, business continuity, and disaster recovery planning and remediation. He has numerous degrees in business administration, engineering, and computer science. He has significantly contributed to establishing several certification programs, specifically in the areas of critical infrastructure protection (utilizing a holistic/all-hazards approach to CIP, rather than NERC CIP), cyber forensics, cybersecurity (encompassing IT, OT, and control systems), and incident response management. He has a special interest and knowledge in matters of critical infrastructure and has published numerous articles and research papers and is considered a world-renowned expert regarding this topic. Although he has been significantly involved in establishing security training and awareness programs through his company, Infracritical, his extracurricular activities include working with several professional accreditation and educational institutions on topics such as homeland security, critical infrastructure, and cybersecurity. He is the owner of the SCADASEC mailing list for SCADA and control systems security discussion forums, while working as an active participant with several industry-related as well as U.S. government-related special interest groups pertaining to critical infrastructure protection, cybersecurity (specifically OT and control systems), and incident response management. Additionally, he has written numerous books pertaining to critical infrastructure protection and assurance, homeland security, policy management, information security and privacy, infrastructure protection law, regulatory and compliance standards for cybersecurity (specifically OT and control systems), cybercrime, transportation systems security, and more. He has authored *Critical Infrastructure: Homeland Security and Emergency Preparedness* (First Edition), co-authored with Allan McDougall on the *Critical Infrastructure: Homeland Security and Emergency Preparedness* (Second, Third, Fourth, and Fifth Editions), and the *Transportation Systems Security* books, as well as co-authored/co-edited, with Jacob Brodsky, the *Handbook of SCADA/Control Systems Security* (First and Second Editions) books; and has written several chapters in numerous books pertinent to cybercrime, cyber forensics, cyber e-discovery, cybersecurity law, international cybersecurity law, international cybersecurity policy (both NATO and private-sectored), risk and governance management, and incident response management.

Steve Mustard is an industrial automation consultant with extensive technical and management experience across multiple sectors. He is a licensed Professional Engineer in Texas and Kansas, ISA Certified Automation Professional®, UK registered Chartered Engineer, European registered Engineer, GIAC Global Industrial Cyber Security Professional, and Certified Mission Critical Professional. Backed by more than 35 years of engineering experience, Steve Mustard specializes in the development and management of real-time embedded equipment and automation systems and cybersecurity risk management related to those systems. He serves as president of National Automation, Inc. Steve Mustard is a member of the Water Environment Federation (WEF) Safety and Security Committee. He was the 2021 President of the International Society of Automation (ISA) and is a Liveryman of the Worshipful Company of Engineers. Steve Mustard writes and presents on a wide array of technical topics and is the author of *Industrial Cybersecurity: Case Studies and Best Practices* and *Mission Critical Operations Primer*, both published by ISA, and *A Guide to Cybersecurity for Water and Wastewater Utilities*, published by WEF. He has also contributed to other technical books, including WEF's *Design of Water Resource Recovery Facilities, Manual of Practice No.8, Sixth Edition* and *The Digital Twin* book, published by Springer. Steve Mustard's previous and current client list includes: the UK Ministry of Defense; NATO; major utilities, such as Anglian Water Services and Sydney Water Corporation; major oil and gas companies, such as bp, BG Group, and Shell; Fortune 500 companies, such as Quintiles Laboratories; and other leading organizations.

Additional Information

Due to the ongoing and rapidly changing nature of Internet resources, the authors have provided a secondary source of reference material in case the primary web page URL is no longer available. The entire purpose of this is to maintain a sense of consistency throughout the publication, as well as to provide information as a "snapshot in time," providing helpful resources at the time while writing this book.

We hope that you find these alternative resources useful and informative. An example of the alternate reference material may be as follows:

http://riskbook.infracritical.com/book1/<chapter_number>/<reference_number>.pdf

For example, the URL http://riskbook.infracritical.com/book1/chapter12/ch12ref1.pdf is the first publicly accessible reference for Chapter 12. As this is the first edition of our book, "book1" is the first subdirectory representing the beginning of the documentation tree. Please refer to the specific reference text, as there is no viewable website; only website documentation is available in Adobe PDF format.

Authors' Note

This publication offers an in-depth examination of risk management and its application to operational technology (OT) systems. Traditional risk management methods currently do not cover these systems. As they are critically important and vital to sustaining and maintaining the operational status of our critical infrastructures, additional and more focused attention should be given to these systems and their environments.

In the past, comprehensive safety and risk assessments were conducted in highly critical operational environments. Environments such as petrochemical refineries or nuclear power generation facilities require a thorough inspection of every aspect of these production sites; one potential error could mean the difference between a normal, fully functional, and operational environment and a total disaster. This approach has been well-founded, adopted, and refined over many decades. It has proven highly effective in ensuring that safe and optimal production at these facilities continues without significant issues.

Many operational computing systems at these facilities have remained virtually isolated and detached from the remainder of corporate networked environments; their levels of performance and risk were well-known and maintained at optimal safety and production levels based on a suite of engineered specifications. These specifications have been refined gradually over several decades of operation, and their outcomes have been consistently the same.

However, as newer technologies emerged, so did the need for interconnectivity and the increased demand for more products within faster periods of time. This meant that operational technology must now be interconnected with other OT, as well as the remainder of the corporate network, to ensure the best possible performance levels. However, the assessment methods used originated from corporate cultures, utilizing vulnerability rather than risk analysis. Faster production meant faster analysis. This, however, does not mix well in critical environments where safety factors play an important and vital role. Since safety is included as part of these assessments, the use of traditional risk audits was substituted with vulnerability audits—two totally different approaches to reviewing safety and performance. The same is also true with automation systems, as their primary function is process, compared to information systems, whose primary function is data.

The book will examine the evolving importance of utilizing risk assessments in operational environments, rather than traditional IT assessments. While recognizing the underlying value of this technology, this work will provide a broader perspective on how our operational technologies impact and affect production and safety within automated environments.

The authors wish to examine the following emerging issues:

- The need for organizations to adopt risk evaluation assessments instead of IT-based vulnerability assessments in operational environments.
- Reintroduce the concept of post-regression analysis in automated environments.
- The need for organizations to adopt resilient planning, implementation, and decision-making processes in order to respond to changes within the threat environment, including reasoning to "de-IT-ify"[1] operational environments where safety should always be a priority.
- The changing role of what is risk, and why it is even more important today, now that all operations are interconnected between automated environments and corporate networks.

In an effort to keep the references available for the readers, we have provided a set of "snapshots of the website" links for all government and public domain website references. As these website references change, become deleted, and so on, it is important that readers know what the references were at the time of the writing of this book. This will ensure that those references are "frozen in time" and will not be changed or altered in any fashion whatsoever. We consider this a value-added feature to this book and invite you to review those website references now in case they become unavailable over time. You may access this information via a dedicated website at http://riskbook.infracritical.com.

NOTE

1 No, that's not a legitimate word.

Acknowledgments

FROM ROBERT

To Steve, for his collaborative efforts and industry expertise on this subject matter, and for his dedicated patience and humor in the face of my constant pestering. Writing this book with Steve has been an absolute pleasure.

To those who have collaborated with me, whom I trust with discretion during the writing of this manuscript, thank you; your feedback has been immeasurably helpful.

FROM STEVE

To Robert, for the original idea behind this book, for the countless hours spent writing and debating its direction, and for your lifelong dedication to safeguarding critical national infrastructure.

To Ricky Burns, Houston Green, and Andrew McDonald, whose clear-eyed view of risk and reward remains a constant source of inspiration.

To my International Society of Automation family—both members and staff—for working together to create a better world through the power of automation.

And to all those I have had the privilege to work with throughout my career, who have shaped the engineering profession and left the world better than they found it.

CHAPTER 1

Risk Management

1.1 INTRODUCTION

Risk is an inherent aspect of organizational decision-making and operations, impacting every industry and sector. Effective risk management requires understanding its dual components—likelihood and consequence—and applying this framework across various domains, including financial, legal, reputational, operational, safety, environmental, and cybersecurity.

In today's interconnected and asset-intensive environments, understanding and managing risk—especially cybersecurity risk—requires more than technical controls and compliance checklists. This chapter explores foundational concepts of risk, particularly as they apply to Operational Technology (OT) environments, which underpin critical infrastructure sectors. Starting with definitions and evolving models of risk—including insurance-based, logical, and volatility-based models—this chapter explains why context is essential to risk assessment. It introduces distinctions between qualitative and quantitative methods, outlines the cybersecurity risk chain from product design to fielded operations, and clarifies how OT cybersecurity risk differs significantly from that in traditional IT environments. Through real-world examples, structured tables, and integrated risk assessment models, such as bowtie diagrams, this chapter lays the groundwork for how organizations can develop practical, resilient, and context-specific approaches to assessing and mitigating cybersecurity risks.

1.2 WHAT IS RISK?

Risk is the possibility of an event occurring that could result in negative consequences for an organization. Risk is most commonly characterized by two primary factors:

- Likelihood—A measure of the possibility of the risk occurring. This could be measured as a probability or an estimated frequency.

DOI: 10.4324/9781003610557-1

- Consequence—The potential result if the risk materializes, for instance, the scale of the financial loss, the number of people harmed or killed, the scale of damage to the environment, etc.

There are, however, many definitions for risk, depending on its intended use. Ralph Langer identifies "three faces of risk":

- The insurance model defines risk as consequence × likelihood (or probability). This works well, as the insurance industry can use actuarial data to calculate a value for a particular unfavorable condition (e.g., an insured patient develops lung cancer). The volume of data available is so vast that calculations are statistically significant.
- The logical model defines risk as a threat and vulnerability leading to an incident. Unlike the insurance model, data on incidents is sparse. As Langer notes, this lack of data results in two extreme estimates of risk: for asset owners, the risk is low—the number of incidents over multiple years across all asset owner facilities results in a minuscule probability—and for security vendors and experts, the risk is high—often because of the intentional use of fear tactics. In both cases, the party estimating the risk benefits most from their conclusion.
- The financial model defines risk as volatility. This model recognizes that risk is due to *uncontrollable variations in factors that cannot be easily predicted*. Langer says this model is best suited for cybersecurity management in OT environments and encourages his readers to consider fragility and robustness.[1] The terms fragility and robustness come from Nicholas Taub's book *Black Swan*. The term black swan refers to unpredictable events that have severe consequences and are often explained away after they occur as if they were predictable.[2]

Langer's suggestion is a good one. Very few people truly understand risk assessments, and by relating it to well-understood engineering or operational terms like fragility and robustness, there is a chance to improve this understanding. As this book will frequently highlight, cybersecurity risk can only be effective when it becomes embedded in existing operational practices. If it is treated as a special discipline, it will continue to be ignored by those who can contribute most to managing the risk.

1.3 CONTEXT

As Langer indicates, what risk means depends on the context in which it is used. Different contexts alter how risk is measured, how that measurement is interpreted, and how it is acted upon.

Radvanovsky and McDougall identify three elements—safety, security, and economic well-being—as being critical deliverables of critical infrastructure, and so the objective is to protect that capability or capacity.[3] Every critical infrastructure organization uses OT to support its operations. Therefore, it makes sense to treat OT cybersecurity risk as something that can adversely affect safety, security, and economic well-being.

However, in critical infrastructure, context matters. Each sector contributes something different to the overall goals of safety, security, and economic well-being. Some may be more fundamental than others. Radvanovsky and McDougall consider energy, transportation, and finance to be the most critical, as nothing can function without these three sectors.[4]

Regardless of which sector is deemed more critical, the consequences of loss of capacity vary considerably depending on which asset owner is affected. The impact does not only vary by sector. Within sectors, the impact can vary based on the services and population served. Within the water and wastewater sector, water systems may serve anything from a few hundred people to millions.

Radvanovsky and McDougall make extensive reference to the term *interdependence*, and this is yet another factor to consider in the context of a risk assessment.[5] Critical infrastructure sectors are dependent on each other. Power stations need water for cooling and steam, but water treatment plants need power to run pumps and other equipment to treat that water.[6] Telecommunications companies need power to provide the communications that power stations and water treatment plants need to transfer operational data across sites.

Even within an asset owner, context matters. For example, at a nuclear power plant, cooling operations are less important than rod control of the nuclear reactor, and rod control is far more important than turbine control. This differentiation of various operations assists the assessor in determining which areas to focus their attention. Thus, rather than focusing on all aspects of a plant's site operations, which would clearly rank the assessment process as a flattened area of determination rather than an adjusted, ranked area of determination based on criticality, levels of importance, and most importantly, safety of the operation.

Table 1.1 is an example table of some of the more significant functions that are performed at a nuclear plant, along with their estimated safety risk ratings. This is defined using Safety Integrity Level, or SIL. A rating of "SIL-4" is the highest risk, and "SIL-1" is the lowest risk.

Table 1.1 shows that even if the same products or systems are used to operate these functions, the impact of a cybersecurity incident on the product or system can cause very different consequences. Therefore, when assessing cybersecurity risk, it is crucial to consider the context. This approach helps focus resources where they are most needed, in the response, recovery, restore, remediate, and reassess phases of a cybersecurity management system. It avoids the application of unnecessary controls to lower-risk elements. Perhaps most importantly, it shows the

TABLE 1.1 Safety Ratings for Nuclear Plant Functions

Function Group	Specific Function	SIL Rating
Reactor Operations	**Startup/Shutdown Management**	
	Startup Sequencing	SIL 2
	Shutdown Sequencing (Normal)	SIL 3
	Shutdown Sequencing (SCRAM)[a]	SIL 4
	Rod Control (Reactivity Management and Control)	SIL 4
	Power Management	SIL 3
	Fuel Management	SIL 2
Maintenance and Inspection	**Preventive/Corrective Management**	
	Refueling Management	SIL 1
	In-Service Inspections	SIL 3
	Lifecycle Management	SIL 1
Instrumentation and Control	**Device Monitoring**	
	Device Management (Calibration, Update, Configuration)	SIL 2
	Safety Control	SIL 4
Safety and Emergency Management	**Radiation Management**	
	Radiation Monitoring	SIL 4
	Waste Management	SIL 2
	Fire Management (Monitoring, Suppression, Operation)	SIL 4
	Emergency Management (Planning, Drills, Operations)	SIL 2
Regulatory Compliance		
	NRC Oversight	SIL 1
	Environmental Monitoring	SIL 3

[a] The acronym "SCRAM" was originally termed from the tests conducted at the first atomic pile, which operated in Chicago, and was (supposedly) referred to as "Safety Control Rod Axe Man" (SCRAM), in which a worker was assigned to cut a rope with an axe if the need to immediately deactivate the pile was necessary. A similar concept applies today, which is caused by dropping the control rods immediately into the core of the reactor, thereby causing an immediate emergency shutdown of the reactivity process, whether triggered automatically if certain thresholds are met, or (usually) if an operator were to depress the "Big Red Button" manually (which is generally locked and very highly protected).

connection between a cybersecurity incident (e.g., malware on an OT device) and the safe and reliable operation of the facility.

Determining risk generally amounts to answering the following questions:

- What can go wrong?
- What are the associated consequences?

- How likely will it happen?
- What could cause this to happen?

The first question will consider a set of accident scenarios. These scenarios may be derived from safety or operational assessments that have already been conducted. This is the most important question, as this is what helps define the context.

The second question estimates the consequence of each scenario. To answer this question, categories of risk are identified. Table 1.2 shows typical categories and example consequences in that category. This is the next most important question, because this will help quantify the severity of the risk.

The third question will evaluate the probabilities of each of these scenarios. The SIL ratings in Table 1.1 will have been derived from asking this question from a functional safety perspective. This is a well-defined process that involves assessing equipment failure rates and their impact on response demand (i.e., operating when needed).

The last statement in Table 1.2 is fundamental to understanding cybersecurity risk. Unlike the other organizational risks, cybersecurity risk has no specific consequences of its own. A common mistake is to identify consequences of a cybersecurity risk (e.g., loss of server(s)). This leads to a misinterpretation of cybersecurity risk, ultimately incorrect management of that risk. Instead, organizations must understand what financial, legal, reputational, operational, safety, or environmental consequences may occur in the case of a cybersecurity incident. This will be discussed further in subsequent chapters of this book.

TABLE 1.2 Risk Categories and Example Consequences

Risk	Example Consequences
Financial	Additional costs for emergency resources (e.g., overtime, backup supplies, etc.). Remediation costs.
Legal	Fines for non-compliance. Custodial sentences for company directors.
Reputational	Damage to public image or trust.
Operational	Loss of production. Damage to manufacturing equipment.
Safety	Harm to employees or members of the public.
Environmental	Damage to the ecosystem (e.g., chemical spill, fire, etc.)
Cybersecurity	Any of the above consequences could arise from a cybersecurity risk.

Note that all risks ultimately result in financial, reputational, and legal consequences due to interdependencies.

1.4 QUALITATIVE AND QUANTITATIVE RISK ASSESSMENTS

Qualitative and quantitative risk assessments are complementary approaches used to evaluate and prioritize risk. Risk assessments identify sources of risks, causes, and their consequences. These assessments help decision-makers produce informed choices, prioritize actions, and distinguish among alternative courses of action. Decisions are made to determine if existing risk controls need to be modified or if additional controls need to be added to provide further prevention or mitigation efforts of risk.

Choosing the appropriate assessment approach or combination of approaches is a key step in supporting decision-making processes, where various options are evaluated against any risks that are associated with each choice. Both qualitative and quantitative risk assessments provide decision-makers with meaningful information that can be used to control and communicate any risk effectively. Selecting the proper assessment approach should be based on evaluating the technical and operational challenges that decision-makers face.

Qualitative assessments using expert judgment may be sufficient for most environments, such as simplified operations in which the level of risk is dependent on a smaller number of variables and where uncertainties are relatively low. Quantitative assessments, on the other hand, may offer additional insight when either the operation or the technology is significantly more complex. Decisions concerning the effectiveness of risk controls applied and their associated consequences are dependent on quite a number of variables; multiple paths of failure may exist; and the magnitude of risk will be greater, or its uncertainties higher. Ultimately, selecting the best risk assessment method will also allow for proper communication of risk between the operator, the regulator, and other stakeholders.

Qualitative risk relies on descriptive analysis and expert judgment to assess the likelihood and impact of a threat, often using scales such as low, medium, and high. It is beneficial when data is limited or when an evaluation is needed immediately for decision-making.

Quantitative risk, on the other hand, assigns numerical values to enable a more precise comparison of risks. The insurance model described by Langer can use quantitative risk because vast amounts of actuarial data exist to provide reliable results. However, such data is not always readily available in the quantities required to produce reliable results. As a result, both methods have their place.

Qualitative assessments are commonly used in several critical infrastructure sectors and are considered valuable when taking the first steps of the risk analysis process. They provide some semblance of structure, as used in the standard risk assessment method, through brainstorming. These forms of assessments are highly effective in strategically identifying many risks and consequences associated with several critical infrastructure sectors and their respective industries. Organizations use results from these assessments to develop and implement both risk and operations management programs. While these types of evaluations may be effective at identifying hazards, any risk rating is considered subjective, based on the consensus expert view at the time of the assessment.

These assessments are typically represented using likelihood and consequence on a risk matrix. A generic example is shown in Figure 1.1. The specific details will vary for each organization.

In this example, five consequence categories are identified: health and safety, environmental, financial, reputation and public disruption, and regulatory. Organizations in other sectors may choose to use different categories. For instance, confidentiality breach, strategic impact, and operational disruption may be more suited to a financial organization than health and safety and environmental categories.

Four distinct levels of consequence are identified, from low to severe. For each category, there is a description of what low, moderate, high, or severe means. Four distinct levels of likelihood are also identified, and descriptions are provided in terms of frequency of occurrence (from once per month to greater than ten years between occurrences).

As noted above, there is no consequence description for cybersecurity because the consequences of a cybersecurity incident should be measured in terms of health and safety, environmental, financial, reputation and public disruption, or regulatory terms.

The risk matrix enables organizations to understand all the risks they face and where they must focus resources to manage these risks:

- It facilitates proactive planning and helps mitigate potential issues.
- It guides resource allocation to address high-priority risks.
- It ensures regulatory compliance and builds resilience against uncertainties.

In Figure 1.1, the four levels of likelihood and four levels of consequence are combined to produce a number from 1 to 16, with 1 representing the lowest risk and 16 representing the highest. Colors or shading can

							Likelihood			
Consequence							Improbable (> 10 years)	Remote (Once in 10 years)	Occasional (Once a year)	Frequent (Once a month)
		Health/Safety	Environmental	Financial	Reputation and Public Disruption	Regulatory	1	2	3	4
Low	1	Injury or illness without a loss of a work day; Event requiring First Aid	Unfavorable impact but without any environmental harm or nuisance	Less than $10k	Public not aware	Limited impact with less than $10k in fines or penalties	1	2	3	4
Moderate	2	Injury or illness resulting in treatment by a doctor or hospitalization; Long-term sickness over 3 days	Unreasonable impact resulting in environmental nuisance/cleanup	Between $10k and $100k	Local media coverage; Telephone complaints	Fines or penalties between $10k and $200k	2	4	6	8
High	3	Permanent injury or long-term sickness over 3 months; Multiple serious injuries	Significant impact with localized environmental harm but not in an environmentally sensitive area	Between $100k and $1m	Extended local adverse media campaign; State media coverage	Fines or penalties totaling between $200k and $500k	3	6	9	12
Severe	4	Single or multiple deaths; Multiple permanent injuries	Major environmental harm caused in environmentally sensitive areas; Environmental damage causing a violation of law or regulation	Over $1m	National adverse media coverage	Officer jailed Fine or penalty over $500k	4	8	12	16

FIGURE 1.1 Example of a qualitative risk matrix.

be used to indicate categorization of these risks, e.g., minor risks that require very little oversight, moderate risks that need additional attention, and extreme risks that must be the primary focus for any risk management activities.

Note, however, that even this simplified representation has an important nuance that needs to be understood. While the combination of likelihood and consequence results in a numeric risk, risks of the same value do not always exhibit the same characteristics. For example, in the risk matrix, a risk rating of four can indicate either a low-probability, high-consequence event, or a high-probability, low-consequence event. These are very different in terms of overall impact. The former could mean "single or multiple deaths" while the latter could mean "injury requiring first aid." Low probability and high-consequence events are, by definition, hard to predict. This is, in fact, the *black swan event* described by Taub. Organizations must consider their resilience and robustness in response to such a possibility, no matter how improbable it may seem.[7] Thus, even with its inherent limitations, qualitative assessment is an essential tool.

Quantitative risk assessments, on the other hand, involve the assignment of factual, data-supported numerical values for assessing probabilities and their consequences. Often, these types of evaluations are used in conjunction with an initial qualitative assessment, focusing on the critical and high-risk areas that have been identified.

These account for the compounded effects of multiple scenarios (or events). This method involves identifying compounding effects by quantifying possible outcomes and their associated probabilities, enabling more transparent risk-informed and risk-based decision-making in the face of uncertainty. As there are several methods for performing quantitative risk assessments, some of the more common approaches may involve basic probability calculations, or they may be as complex and as complicated as using multiple regression models and simulations.

While there may be exceptions, quantitative risk assessments' approaches typically use simplified versions of many analytical tools available through a plethora of software platforms, both commercially and open-sourced versions (primarily due to the unavailability of any publicly available safety-based or industry-specific data, mainly due to regulatory controls). As such, many quantitative approaches may not necessarily support much or any detailed analysis of uncertainty, common cause failures, or human reliability and performance.

Table 1.3 provides a summary of the two methods.

TABLE 1.3 Comparison of Quantitative and Qualitative Risk Assessments

Feature	Quantitative Risk Assessment	Qualitative Risk Assessment
Definition	Uses numerical data and mathematical models to estimate risk	Uses descriptive terms and expert judgment to assess risk
Output Format	Dollar values, probabilities, expected annual loss (e.g., \$500,000/year)	Ratings or rankings (e.g., low, medium, high)
Data Requirements	Requires reliable historical or empirical data	Can be done with limited or anecdotal data
Precision	High—provides measurable and traceable outcomes	Low to moderate—provides general understanding
Subjectivity	Less subjective (data-driven)	More subjective (based on experience and opinion)
Use Case	Budgeting, cost-benefit analysis, ROI on security investments	Initial risk triage, broad assessments, or rapid decision-making
Time and Resource Demand	Higher—requires specialized tools and expertise	Lower—quicker to perform with fewer resources
Tools Commonly Used	Monte Carlo simulation, FAIR, Bayesian models	Risk matrices, heat maps, expert workshops
Best For	High-value decisions, insurance modeling, detailed analysis	Early stage planning, when data is sparse or unavailable
Limitations	Difficult to apply without sufficient data; can give false precision	Lacks exactness; harder to justify funding or investment

1.5 WHERE DOES CYBERSECURITY RISK ORIGINATE?

Organizations within their facilities typically handle cybersecurity risks, but these risks often originate much earlier. The cybersecurity risk chain, shown in Figure 1.2, outlines all the stages in the process from product design to facility operation. This chain demonstrates how cybersecurity vulnerabilities in an operational facility develop throughout the entire system lifecycle, from initial product design and development to operational use.

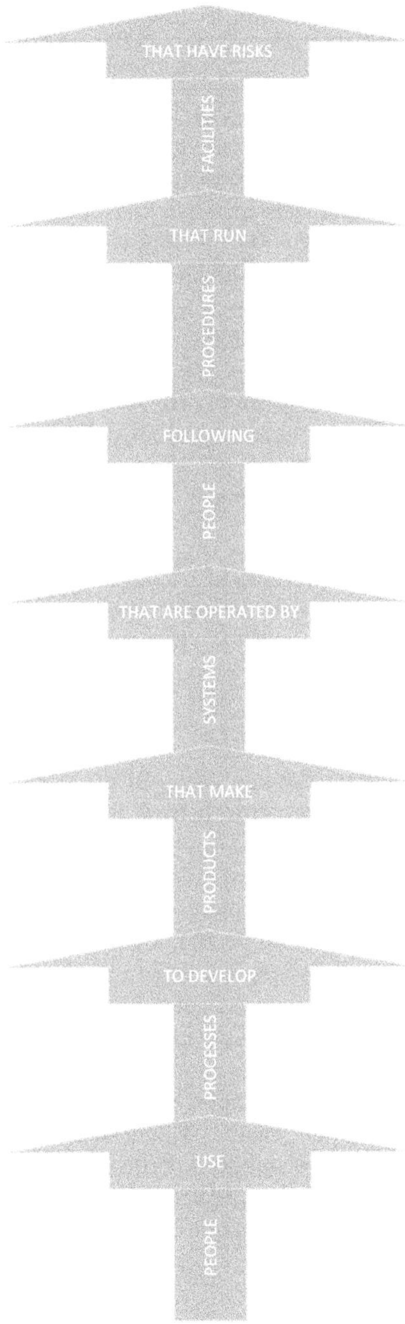

FIGURE 1.2 The cybersecurity risk chain.

TABLE 1.4 Issues in the Cybersecurity Risk Chain[8]

Stage	Issues
People	Lack of awareness of cybersecurity No training in secure-by-design concepts Limited prior experience in security
Processes	Lack of independence in development and testing Lack of rigor in development and testing process
Products	No common method to identify cybersecurity assurance
Systems	No common method to identify cybersecurity assurance Full assessment of each system required for each project
People	Lack of awareness of cybersecurity Lack of oversight of cybersecurity issues
Procedures	Lack of or poor cybersecurity management systems or documentation Adoption of minimum standards for regulatory compliance only Poor adherence to required cybersecurity safeguards Lack of oversight of cybersecurity issues
Facilities	Poor adherence to required cybersecurity safeguards Lack of oversight of cybersecurity issues

Table 1.4 summarizes the key stages in the risk chain. These issues, and recommendations to deal with them, will be discussed in subsequent chapters of this book.

The culmination of all these issues is that the cybersecurity of OT systems is often an afterthought, and in most cases, it is left to the asset owner to address. In her doctoral thesis report, Sarah Fluchs provides anecdotal evidence of this assertion, noting that, "[i]n the workflow drawn based on interviews with practitioners..., cybersecurity is not explicitly mentioned either," and that interviews with these practitioners highlighted that, while some may "consult an internal Automation Security Handbook as a checklist for the most important security configurations for the CPS they integrate," in most cases, "if cybersecurity considerations are made at all, they are usually initiated shortly before construction, after all other basic and detail engineering activities have been completed." She then states that "This situation matches the observations described in the state of research [in her thesis]."[9]

1.6 WHAT IS DIFFERENT ABOUT OT CYBERSECURITY RISK?

The consequences of a cybersecurity incident are very different in IT and OT environments.

In an IT environment, typical consequences include:

- Financial (or Reputational)—For example, the costs and brand damage resulting from the loss of sensitive information—whether it's personnel data (such as employee personally identifiable information—PII) or customer data (like banking or credit card details).
- Operational—The loss of proprietary information, like recipes or strategic plans, or a loss of business functions, such as billing, could impact business output.
- Regulatory—Stemming from one or more of the above consequences.

These consequences all relate to information. The consequences of a cybersecurity incident in an OT environment are very different, and in fact align with the safety consequences described earlier. Understanding this distinction is key to successfully managing risk effectively. OT environments are found in critical infrastructure, where a cybersecurity incident could result in the following:

- Death or injury—To personnel or, in some cases, to members of the public.
- Harm to the environment—For instance, a release of oil, gas, or chemicals due to a loss of containment.
- Equipment damage—Including expensive industrial plant machinery such as turbines or transformers that may take months—even years—to replace.
- Loss of production—Resulting from equipment damage or other process failures.
- Regulatory violations—Due to one or more of the above consequences.
- Brand damage—Due to one or more of the above consequences.

Note that the cybersecurity incident may be identical in IT and OT environments, but the consequences are very different. This is not to say that a cybersecurity incident in an IT environment is not serious. The costs associated with responding and recovering to a ransomware incident, for example, can be significant and the brand impact can be extremely damaging. The average cost of recovery from ransomware (excluding the ransom) is estimated by some studies as $2.73M.[10] The impact of the July 19, 2024, *CrowdStrike* incident[11] is estimated to have cost businesses $5.4, and CrowdStrike itself is forecasting a reduced annual rate of return, down 31% year on year, as a result.[12]

The financial and reputational impact of cybersecurity incidents can be affected by regulations. The U.S. Securities and Exchange Commission (SEC) has strict regulations regarding disclosure of cybersecurity programs and cybersecurity incidents. Companies under the remit of the SEC are required to include details of their cybersecurity programs in their annual SEC Form 10-K filings. Additionally, these companies must report cybersecurity incidents in a timely manner using a separate form, SEC Form 8-K. Failure to comply with these regulations can result in severe regulatory action, including fines.

However, consider cybersecurity incidents in OT environments, such as those shown in Table 1.5 with real-world examples of each.

TABLE 1.5 OT Cybersecurity Incidents and Real-World Examples

Incident	Real-world Example
Malicious modification of PLC code, causing machinery to operate outside of its normal envelope while reporting normal conditions to the operator occurred in an incident.	Stuxnet (2010) Malware operating in a nuclear enrichment facility in Iran modified PLC code to run centrifuges outside their normal operating envelope but report normal conditions to the operators. This malware caused millions of dollars of damage to centrifuge equipment and set back the Iranian nuclear enrichment program.[13]
Deployment of destructive malware or unauthorized remote access on a human-machine interface, which causes loss of view or control or enables remote control by an unauthorized user.	Ukraine (2015) Attackers took control of operator workstations in three Ukrainian power distribution companies and disabled power to over 225,000 customers for up to six hours and caused major disruption to operations for many months afterward.[14]
Safety controller disabled by malware or code modification, which results in failure to shut down a process in potentially unsafe conditions.	TRISIS (2017) An attack on a safety system in a petrochemical facility in the Middle East led to a plant shutdown, resulting in a loss of production as well as additional unscheduled time, cost, and risk involved with restarting the plant.[15]

1.7 MEASURING RISK POSTURE

Many critical infrastructure sectors have regulatory requirements that mandate risk assessments as part of compliance. In the U.S. healthcare sector, the Health Insurance Portability and Accountability Act mandates risk assessments for the protection of electronic protected health information, and in the U.S. financial sector, Sarbanes-Oxley Act mandates financial institutions to assess risks related to financial reporting.

In North America, the NERC CIP (North American Electric Reliability Corporation Critical Infrastructure Protection) requires risk assessments for cybersecurity in power systems. Other sectors in the United States have similar regulatory requirements.

The European General Data Protection Regulation mandates risk assessments for data processing activities that affect many organizations that operate in Europe and elsewhere. The NIS2 Directive, an EU regulation aimed at enhancing cybersecurity across Member States, mandates organizations to conduct risk assessments as part of comprehensive cybersecurity risk management across supply chains and various sectors, including energy, healthcare, digital infrastructure, and manufacturing.

While risk assessment is mandated in many regulations worldwide, the approach to assessing risk posture varies. For example, while both NERC CIP and NIS2 emphasize the importance of cybersecurity risk assessments, they represent fundamentally different regulatory philosophies. NERC CIP prioritizes prescriptive consistency, which ensures standardization and enforceability across the sector.

NIS2, on the other hand, adopts an outcomes-based approach. This favors adaptability and continuous improvement, aligning cybersecurity with business risk management and resilience goals. While NERC CIP identifies explicit controls and measures with auditable checklists, NIS2 looks for organizations to demonstrate they have implemented "appropriate and proportionate" technical and organizational controls.

The auditable checklist of NERC CIP has become a common practice in other sectors to assess cybersecurity posture. Checklists that define a set of security controls are used to conduct a gap assessment and identify necessary remediations.

The rationale for this approach is reasonable. Organizations need guidance on what to focus on. Many have limited resources and may lack the special skills and knowledge required to implement a comprehensive cybersecurity management system. A checklist could help them identify what things they should focus on.

Unfortunately, the outcome of using such checklists has been counterproductive to effective cybersecurity risk management. In many cases, organizations will follow such checklists without question. The result is that a single set of controls is implemented, irrespective of risk.

This creates challenges for low-risk systems that cannot support many of the technical controls, and on high-risk systems that may not be adequately protected by the minimal set of controls in the checklist.

Worse still, the terms *vulnerability assessment* and *risk assessment* are often used interchangeably, resulting in organizations failing to conduct a real risk assessment and thus being unaware of the potential consequences they might face if a cybersecurity incident occurs.

The most significant impact of using checklists in cybersecurity risk management is that it discourages critical thinking. Critical thinking is essential in any form of risk management because no two organizations, situations, or systems are the same. Interestingly, the negative impact of checklists on critical thinking is not limited to cybersecurity risk management. Marc Meola describes "a contextual approach to teaching undergraduates web-site evaluation" and in it states that "the checklist model ... encourages a mechanistic way of evaluating that is at odds with critical thinking."[16]

1.8 INCORPORATING CYBERSECURITY INTO RISK ASSESSMENTS

As previously discussed in this chapter, the implications of cybersecurity incidents are not isolated to the realm of digital security; instead, they act across various established organizational risk categories. These categories include financial, legal, reputational, operational, safety, and environmental risks. Understanding cybersecurity consequences through this lens allows organizations to appreciate the broader impact of such incidents, emphasizing that the fallout from an incident can extend far beyond immediate technical concerns.

This perspective encourages a more holistic view of risk management, where cybersecurity is seen as a critical component of overall organizational health; furthermore, it includes:

- Risks are interconnected—An integrated approach captures the interdependencies of cybersecurity incidents, such as financial loss, legal penalties, and safety or environmental impacts. The interconnected nature of risks necessitates an integrated approach to risk management, particularly in the context of cybersecurity. By recognizing the interdependencies among different risk categories, organizations can better understand how a cybersecurity incident might lead to financial losses, legal repercussions, and even safety or environmental hazards. This comprehensive understanding is essential for developing effective strategies that mitigate risks across the board.

- Regulatory compliance—Regulatory requirements specify an integrated risk management approach. Regulatory compliance often mandates such an integrated approach, as many regulations require organizations to consider the interplay of various risks when formulating their risk management framework.
- Resource efficiency—Integrating cybersecurity into existing risk assessments saves time and reduces redundancy, and ensures alignment with broader organizational goals. Incorporating cybersecurity into existing risk assessments not only enhances resource efficiency but also aligns with broader organizational objectives. By streamlining processes and reducing redundancy, organizations can allocate their resources more effectively, ensuring that they address the most pressing risks in a timely manner.
- Prioritization—An integrated approach enables the effective allocation of resources. Prioritization is crucial in a landscape where threats are constantly evolving, allowing organizations to respond proactively rather than reactively. Ultimately, an integrated risk management strategy fosters a more resilient organization, capable of navigating the complexities of today's risk environment while safeguarding its assets and reputation.

As a result, it is best practice to incorporate cybersecurity into organizational risk assessments. One example of this is found in the book *Security PHA Review for Consequence-Based Cybersecurity.*[17] The integrated methodology in the book utilizes the principles of safety risk assessment already in place, specifically the Process Hazard Analysis (PHA). As the authors note:

> The process industries have already established methods for risk assessment that have been successfully in use for decades. The optimal solution for assessment of cybersecurity risks is not to start from scratch with new studies but to extend the existing studies to incorporate new objectives and requirements.[18]

Sarah Fluchs's approach to formally incorporating cybersecurity into engineering workflows, such as risk assessment, is intended to "remind engineers of considering cybersecurity in their design." And the "coupling points should contain specific cybersecurity decisions to support the identification of required decisions."[19]

This approach to incorporating cybersecurity risk includes visualizing risk. Figure 1.3 shows a *bowtie diagram.* This type of diagram is used in safety risk assessment to help visualize the relationship between causes, hazards, and consequences.[20] In this example, the concept has been used to visualize cybersecurity risk.

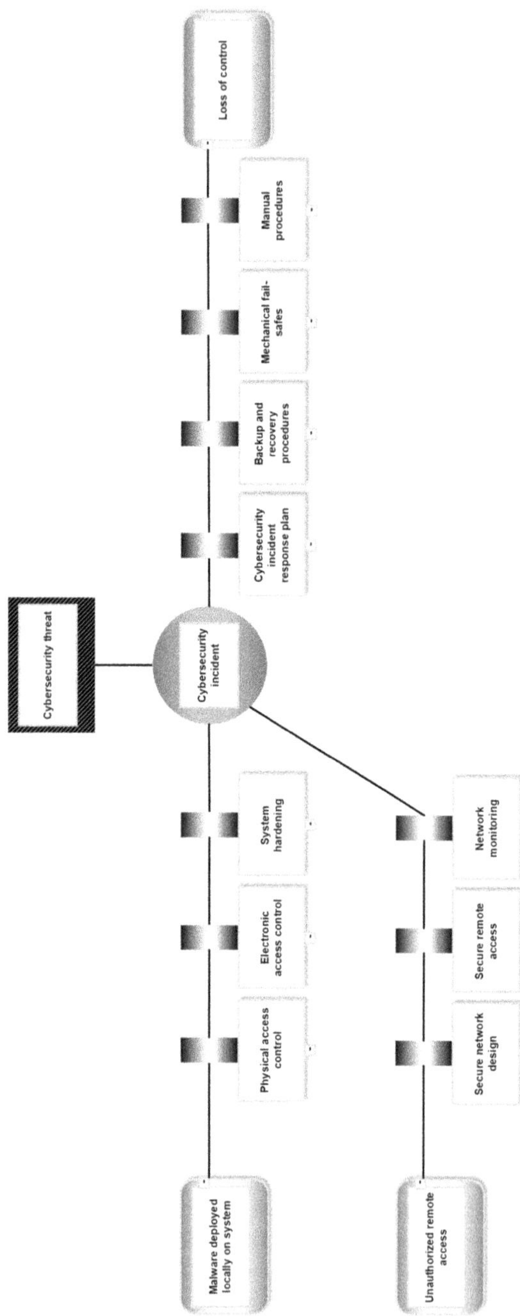

FIGURE 1.3 Example cybersecurity bowtie diagram.

In this case, the initiating cause (malware deployed on a system) leads to a generic hazard (cybersecurity threat), event (cybersecurity incident), and ultimately a consequence (loss of control). In this example, the impact on the process or operation is not described. Still, in an integrated safety and cybersecurity assessment, the objective is to identify what loss of control could lead to—for example, a loss of containment, fire, explosion, etc.

The items between the initiating cause and the hazard (on the left-hand side of the diagram) are called the *preventative* (or *preventive*) barriers or safeguards. These are individual controls that are required to reduce the likelihood of the initiating cause resulting in the hazard. For example, *physical access control* and *electronic access control* make it harder for someone to get to a machine to install malware, and *system hardening* reduces the likelihood that malware can run on the machine. The items between the hazard and the consequence (on the right-hand side of the diagram) are called the *mitigation* barriers or safeguards. These controls are required to reduce the consequences of a hazard when it occurs. For instance, if the malware is successfully deployed on a machine, these factors will reduce the impact of the loss of control situation that might occur. In this example, the factors include a *cybersecurity incident response plan* to isolate the machine and, possibly, to switch into a temporary manual mode, as well as *backup and recovery procedures* to remove the malware from the machine before it is restored to service. If these controls fail, there are *mechanical failsafes* (such as pressure release valves or independent shutdown devices) and *manual procedures* (such as switching equipment from *automatic* to *manual*) to mitigate any consequences.

One of the more important aspects to consider in cybersecurity risk management, especially for OT environments, is the *hackable* nature of the controls. In the integrated safety and cybersecurity described in this book, hackable means that "the scenario could be forced to occur by a malevolent actor who has taken control of the ICS [industrial control system]."[21] The assumption is that computer-related causes can be hacked, but mechanical-related causes cannot. If a cause can be hacked (i.e., it is a cybersecurity-related cause), the controls should be reviewed to determine if they can also be hacked.

These non-hackable controls are non-intuitive to conventional cybersecurity practitioners. Sarah Fluchs notes that "cybersecurity solutions that are implemented in the physical world ... often do not appear on cybersecurity requirements or best practices lists."[22]

Each sector tends to have its own preferred methods for assessing and managing operational risk. Cybersecurity should always be incorporated into the appropriate method.

For example, the oil and gas sector uses PHA, while the nuclear industry uses the design-basis threat (DBT) approach. This approach requires the definition of nuclear security requirements "based on the capabilities of a potential insider and external adversaries who might attempt unauthorized removal of nuclear and other radioactive material or sabotage."[23] This definition fits well with Taub's and Langer's approach of identifying robustness and resilience by incorporating safeguards into the operation, preventing incidents with serious consequences. Even if the systems used in the nuclear sector are identical to those in oil and gas, many of the safeguards will be different.

1.9 ABOUT THIS BOOK

This book presents a comprehensive exploration of cybersecurity risk assessment within OT environments, emphasizing the unique characteristics, challenges, and emerging considerations of asset-intensive industries.

This chapter establishes a vital foundation for the remainder of the book by clarifying what risk means, how it is measured, and why OT cybersecurity must be integrated into broader organizational risk frameworks. It underscores that risk is context-dependent and varies not just across sectors, but also within a facility, where different functions carry vastly different consequence ratings. It distinguishes between qualitative and quantitative risk assessments, emphasizing the need for both, depending on the availability of data and the decision-making requirements. The chapter emphasizes that cybersecurity is not an isolated discipline, but rather a catalyst that can trigger consequences across existing risk categories, such as safety, finance, operations, and the environment. It introduces the concept of the cybersecurity risk chain, highlighting how vulnerabilities accumulate throughout the lifecycle—from design through operation. Finally, it presents best practices for integrating cybersecurity into conventional risk assessments, utilizing familiar safety tools such as PHAs and bowtie diagrams. The message is clear: cybersecurity must be embedded in operational thinking, not bolted on as an afterthought.

This book is intended for practitioners, asset owners, policymakers, and engineers who seek to enhance the security and resilience of their systems. This book will not offer a single, one-size-fits-all "silver bullet" for managing OT cybersecurity risk, because such a solution simply does not exist. Every organization's operations, assets, and threat landscape are unique, and risk management is as much about context and judgment as it is about tools and checklists. Instead, this book will guide the reader through the principles, processes, and practical considerations needed to build a risk management approach that works for their environment. Each chapter will help with understanding what OT cybersecurity risk means, how to measure it, how to select and apply frameworks, and how to incorporate risk thinking into daily operations—so users can move beyond compliance checklists and toward meaningful, defensible risk management.

The chapters that follow are designed to take the reader on a progression from foundational concepts to practical application, from common pitfalls to advanced strategies

Chapter 2 defines Operational Technology and explains why protecting OT environments is essential—especially when safety and continuity are at stake. It introduces the need for a cybersecurity-centric risk model suited to OT.

Chapter 3 addresses common misunderstandings about risk assessments, particularly the flawed assumptions that "one size fits all" or that vulnerability assessments equate to risk assessments. It distinguishes IT and OT risk assessment approaches and stresses the importance of focusing on operational processes rather than just data.

Chapter 4 explains how to measure risk by contrasting cybersecurity risk with process risk and advocating for a hybridized model that combines both. It includes a three-layered view of risk—cyber, process, and societal—highlighting the interconnected nature of modern infrastructures.

Chapter 5 surveys key risk assessment frameworks, examining their core purposes, the differences between cyber-OT security-inclusive models and traditional models, and the criteria that make some frameworks more suitable for OT contexts.

Chapter 6 turns to the practice of risk assessment. It outlines processes for performing OT cybersecurity risk assessments, explores reasons behind them, and examines when to use full assessments versus checklists. The chapter also questions the long-term value of assessments if knowledge is lost through turnover or reduced to merely checking boxes for compliance.

Chapter 7 examines emerging risks in OT, including the increasing role of artificial intelligence and how financial pressures can influence risk perception and prioritization. It emphasizes why dedicated OT cybersecurity risk assessments are increasingly critical.

Chapter 8 examines the role of regulation, organizational culture, and governance. It challenges the over-reliance on regulatory compliance as a proxy for security and calls for greater honesty and self-awareness in evaluating proper risk postures.

Chapter 9 addresses the complexities of incident response and recovery in OT environments, where sabotage, accidents, and cyber events may produce similar symptoms. It highlights the need for forensic capabilities in control systems and proposes a multi-phase recovery framework: response, recovery, restoration, remediation, and reassessment.

Chapter 10 introduces post-regression analysis—an often-overlooked component of the risk lifecycle. It explores what we can learn from historical events, such as the Oldsmar incident, and how lessons from the past can (or should) inform future risk assessments.

Chapter 11 closes the main content by discussing continuous improvement. It introduces the concept of OT-specific OPSEC, the role of after-action reviews, and the importance of ensuring oversight and accountability in monitoring processes and technologies.

The appendices provide valuable reference material, including comparisons of risk frameworks and standards and a catalog of OT cybersecurity standards (Appendix A), and case studies analyzing both attack and non-attack operational disruptions in critical infrastructure systems (Appendix B).

Together, these chapters aim to shift the focus from checkbox compliance to meaningful risk understanding of risk, helping organizations enhance both their cybersecurity posture and operational resilience.

NOTES

1 Langer, Ralph. *Robust Control System Networks: How to Achieve Reliable Control after Stuxnet*, Momentum Press, 2012.
2 Taub, Nicholas. *Black Swan: The Impact of the Highly Improbable*, Random House, 2010.
3 Radvanovsky, Robert, & McDougall, Allan. *Critical Infrastructure, Homeland Security and Emergency Preparedness*, Fifth Edition, (pp. 8–18). CRC Press, 2024.
4 Radvanovsky, Robert, & McDougall, Allan. *Critical Infrastructure, Homeland Security and Emergency Preparedness*, Fifth Edition, (pp. 8–18). CRC Press, 2024.
5 Radvanovsky, Robert, & McDougall, Allan. *Critical Infrastructure, Homeland Security and Emergency Preparedness*, Fifth Edition, (pp. 8–18). CRC Press, 2024.
6 In most cases, power stations treat their own water.
7 Taub, Nicholas. *Black Swan: The Impact of the Highly Improbable*, Random House, 2010.
8 Mustard, S. *Industrial Cybersecurity: Case Studies and Best Practices*. In *International Society of Automation*, (pp. 81–83), 2022.
9 Fluchs, Sarah. *Cybersecurity Decision Diagrams, A Visual, Model-Based Concept for Making, Documenting, and Communicating Cybersecurity Decisions during and after the (re-)design of Industrial Cyber-Physical Systems*, Helmut Schmidt Universität, 2024.

10 Ransomware Payments Increase 500% In the Last Year, Finds Sophos State of Ransomware Report, https://www.sophos.com/en-us/press/press-releases/2024/04/ransomware-payments-increase-500-last-year-finds-sophos-state, retrieved November 30, 2024.
11 Analyzing the Market Impact of the CrowdStrike Outage, https://polygon.io/blog/analyzing-the-market-impact-of-the-crowdstrike-outage, retrieved November 30, 2024.
12 CrowdStrike 'Not Yet Out Of The Woods' Amid IT Outage, Says Analyst, https://www.investors.com/news/technology/crowdstrike-stock-crowdstrike-earnings-news-q32024/, retrieved November 30, 2024.
13 Langer, Ralph. *To Kill a Centrifuge: A Technical Analysis of What Stuxnet's Creators Tried to Achieve*, Arlington, VA: The Langner Group, November 2013, accessed June 21, 2021. https://www.langner.com/wp-content/uploads/2017/03/to-kill-a-centrifuge.pdf.
14 Krugman, Amy. "Cyber Autopsy Series: Ukrainian Power Grid Attack Makes History," GlobalSign Blog, October 22, 2020, accessed June 21, 2021, https://www.globalsign.com/en/blog/cyber-autopsy-series-ukranian-power-grid-attack-makes-history.
15 Dragos, "TRISIS Malware: Analysis of Safety System Targeted Malware," version 1.20171213, accessed June 21, 2021, https://www.dragos.com/wp-content/uploads/TRISIS-01.pdf.
16 Meola, Marc. *Chucking the Checklist: A Contextual Approach to Teaching Undergraduates Web-Site Evaluation*, Libraries and the Academy, The Johns Hopkins University Press, Vol. 4, No.3, (pp. 331–334), 2004. https://muse.jhu.edu/pub/1/article/170687/pdf.
17 Marszal, Edward, & McGlone, Jim. *Security PHA Review for Consequence-Based Cybersecurity*, Research Triangle Park, NC: ISA [International Society of Automation], 2019.
18 Marszal and McGlone, *Security PHA Review for Consequence-Based Cybersecurity*, p.14.
19 Fluchs, Sarah. *Cybersecurity Decision Diagrams, A Visual, Model-Based Concept for Making, Documenting, and Communicating Cybersecurity Decisions during and after the (re-)design of Industrial Cyber-Physical Systems*, Helmut Schmidt Universität, 2024.
20 It is not the aim of this book to describe the bowtie diagram in detail. The "Further Reading" section provides references for more details on this subject.
21 Marszal and McGlone, *Security PHA Review for Consequence-Based Cybersecurity*, p. 9.
22 Fluchs, Sarah. *Cybersecurity Decision Diagrams, A Visual, Model-Based Concept for Making, Documenting, and Communicating*

Cybersecurity Decisions during and after the (re-)design of Industrial Cyber-Physical Systems, Helmut Schmidt Universität, 2024.

23 Design Basis Threat (DBT), International Atomic Energy Agency, https://www.iaea.org/topics/security-of-nuclear-and-other-radioactive-material/design-basis-threat, retrieved January 22, 2025.

CHAPTER 2

What Is Operational Technology (OT)?

2.1 INTRODUCTION

Operational technology (OT) refers to a diverse array of programmable systems and devices that engage with the physical world or oversee devices that do so. These technologies are designed to detect or instigate direct changes by monitoring and controlling various devices, processes, and events. Common examples of OT include industrial control systems, building automation systems, transportation management systems, physical access control systems, and systems for monitoring and measuring the physical environment.

OT systems are typically composed of various control elements, including electrical, mechanical, hydraulic, and pneumatic components, which work in unison to fulfill specific objectives, such as manufacturing or transporting materials and energy. Within these systems, the segment focused on generating an output is known as the "process," while the segment dedicated to ensuring adherence to established specifications is termed the "controller." The control components are integral to the system, as they define the desired output or performance specifications.

A control system offers three distinct configuration options:

- Open-loop configurations allow system or process output to be regulated based on predefined settings, ensuring a straightforward operational approach.
- Closed-loop configuration, on the other hand, enables output to influence the input, thereby facilitating the achievement of specific control objectives through feedback mechanisms.
- Lastly, manual mode provides complete control to human operators, allowing them to manage the system entirely without automated assistance. This is especially useful if production-ready configurations are being performed within testing environments.

DOI: 10.4324/9781003610557-2

The contemporary landscape of OT has emerged primarily from the integration of information technology (IT) capabilities into pre-existing physical systems, frequently substituting or enhancing traditional control mechanisms. A notable instance of this transformation is the transition from analog to embedded digital controls in electrical generation.

These advancements provide additional cost-effectiveness and performance, which have caused this paradigm shift, leading to the development of numerous modern (so-called) "smart technologies," including the smart electric grid, intelligent transportation systems, smart buildings, advanced manufacturing processes, and the Internet of Things (IoT). While these innovations enhance connectivity and its importance in operational environments, they significantly heighten the necessity for safety, reliability, and performance.

2.2 WHY DO WE NEED TO PROTECT OT?

Our infrastructures operate in OT environments, both old and new.

OT plays a crucial role in the functioning of critical infrastructures (CIs) worldwide, not just in the United States. These systems are frequently characterized by their intricate interconnections and dependencies, both in physical terms and through a wide array of information and communication technologies; if you will, a hybridized system.

It is essential to recognize that while several government organizations manage several of these CIs in their respective countries, a significant portion is owned and operated by private entities. Furthermore, infrastructures are often described as a "system of systems" due to the complex interdependencies that exist among various industrial sectors and the connections between different business partners.

More importantly, OT and control systems are integral parts of a much more critical set of operations often associated with specific industries considered vital to society.

Called "critical infrastructure," this concept refers to assets of physical and logical systems that are essential to the minimum operations of the economy and government. This much, at least, has not changed. They include, but are not limited to, telecommunications, energy, banking and finance, transportation, water systems, and emergency services, both governmental and private. As these systems become further interconnected, we see two major trends becoming apparent.

The first trend involves the pace at which technology evolves. This is not a constant around the world. As time progresses, we continue to see examples of particular societies and communities progressing at different rates, along with the emerging challenges associated with replacing aging infrastructure.

The second trend involves understanding that specific elements making up a CI are not constant across all communities and may be subject to physical, sociological, and cultural factors; thus, risk levels will most undoubtedly vary. Advances in cyber technology and efforts to improve efficiencies in these systems and their infrastructures have become increasingly automated and interlinked. These improvements have created new risks relating to equipment failure, human error, weather, and other natural causes, as well as physical and computer-related attacks.[1]

It is these differences that create one or multiple interdependencies, which further exacerbate the need to reduce risk as low as possible. However, before we can reduce our risk, we first need to understand how interdependencies play such a critical anti-force against reducing our risk. What has been apparent is that an increasing number and frequency of infrastructure issues are highlighting the fact that infrastructure, and even whole communities, can be impacted through interdependencies and disruptions within the networked environment. Interdependency is where the level of one system's product is reduced, and this reduction causes an impact on another system.

Interdependencies flowing out of one system (host) and impacting an independent system, in that the impact does not cycle back onto itself (host)—henceforth, this would be more of a dependency rather than an interdependency. The number of dependencies that were purely linear in this respect now actually appears to be relatively few. These impacts would now relate more to a disruption of non-critical services. For example, if a doctor's cellular service were to become unavailable, but the service overall remains available, this would not impact the critical services provided by the healthcare service.

Interdependencies flowing out of one system (host) and impacting a system that provides a direct good or service back into the host system, leading to an elevated rate of deterioration attributable to the initial disruption. A recently observed scenario that supports this factor is a present-day disruption of an entire communications network servicing multiple CI sectors and their services. This outage resulted in the unavailability of critical services, such as 911 emergency call centers. The disruption of the entire telecommunications system, affecting 911 emergency centers in certain areas, is one that has both linear and cross-sectoral impacts. The 911 service being impacted creates a looping effect that is singular mainly in nature (i.e., once the impact happens, it stays at about the same level until it is fixed).

Interdependencies flow out of one system (host) and impact a system that then provides a service to another sector, which then influences the host. This form of impact has evolved to reveal four primary sectors: transportation, energy, communications, and finance/banking. When an event impacts a sector or industry, it begins to cascade within the four key infrastructure sectors, making recovery a complex issue. This interdependency involves other sectors that are co-dependent on at least one of the four key infrastructure sectors. Other almost equally important

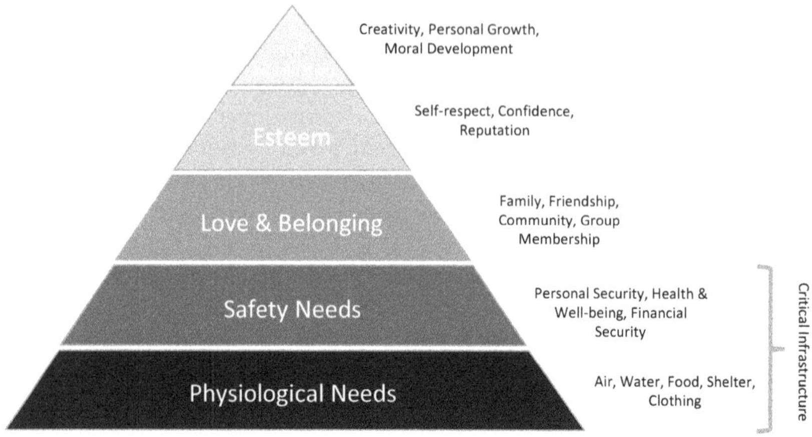

FIGURE 2.1 The significance of critical infrastructure in Maslow's Hierarchy of Needs.

infrastructure sectors include food and agriculture, as well as water, which fulfill the physiological and safety needs, the most critical elements in *Maslow's Hierarchy of Needs*, as shown in Figure 2.1.[2]

One contentious statement is that the term "critical infrastructure" refers to (logical) network architectures that support operations, not the operations themselves. This fails a key test. While the logical infrastructure (including information networks) has become increasingly important, it does not feed people, generate electricity, purify water, or ship goods. It is certainly incontestable that information networks supporting CIs play a significant and vital role; however, it is essential to clearly understand that this is just one function among many.

Thus, the other part, the operations themselves, represents the supporting side of CIs which interactively control and operate physical "things"; that is, these systems maintain, manage, and control physical devices that are part of a greater system, such as an electricity plant or a water treatment facility. These systems are just as, if not more so, critically important, as they are the mechanisms that regulate the processes that produce our food, water, and electricity (etc.).

Between regulations, controls imposed by the country (especially true for multinational organizations), and how financial budgeting is performed, will dictate how that organization views risk. In almost all cases today, theft of information and intellectual property runs rampant throughout the world; yet, with processed operations, although the risks are real and critically high, the level of importance and criticality depends on both the organization and, if regulated, how data is controlled.

A cybersecurity risk audit in OT focuses on ensuring the availability and safety of physical systems and processes, emphasizing the importance of operational continuity over data confidentiality, integrity, and availability.

In contrast, an IT cybersecurity risk audit is primarily concerned with the protection of data of systems, whereby the prevention of data breaches is a significant focus. Consequently, the fundamental distinction lies in the fact that OT prioritizes the safety and operational uptime of physical equipment, whereas IT is predominantly focused on securing data.

The issue here, however, is that processes aren't being as tightly controlled as many have indicated, as opposed to its data. Thus, the emphasis continues focusing solely on the data—and not the process(es)—of these operations. This is why cybersecurity risk audits regularly fail.

2.3 SYSTEM VERSUS PROCESS VERSUS FUNCTION

An accident or incident affecting one infrastructure often leads to consequences that result in both direct and indirect impacts on other infrastructures, which can lead to a series of cascaded failures.

There are models (and their methodologies) that define how systems are described. As such, there needs to be some clarification regarding terms and definitions. For this book, these terms and their definitions are reviewed from a holistic perspective, rather than a computing or informational one.

To begin with, a system can be defined as a structured collection or arrangement of resources and methodologies that are interconnected and governed by their interactions or through mutual dependencies, all aimed at achieving a defined (sometimes predefined) set of instructions to meet specific objectives. It is important to note that, as a whole, systems encompass a variety of specialized types, some of which include, but are not limited to, the following:

- automation and process control systems' environments;
- telephony, RF (wireless), and networked communication environments;
- safety and fire suppression environments; and,
- building and environmental control systems

But, the term "system" doesn't just apply to cyber systems, but the holistically defined version of "system," which can be both logical (as defined through an operation and its processes) and/or physical. Some of these systems include, but are not limited to, the following:

- financial systems (banking, trading, FOREX);
- healthcare systems (out-patient care, immediate care, doctor-patient); and,
- supply chain systems (railroad, maritime, truck)

Comparing the two types of systems above (logical versus process), cyber systems (logical) provide information and digital assets. In contrast, healthcare systems (process) provide critical care to patients (at critical care units, such as oxygen and intravenous drips).

Cybersecurity serves to safeguard an organization's data and resources against various cyber threats. The effectiveness of cybersecurity is assessed by evaluating the strengths and vulnerabilities inherent in an organization's protective measures against cyber risks. OT and control systems cybersecurity extends its function beyond just data, focusing primarily on process instead of data.

Healthcare systems are responsible for delivering medical care to patients while prioritizing the safety and well-being of individuals within healthcare environments. The concept of healthcare efficiency involves evaluating the results produced by a healthcare delivery system, such as the number of physician consultations, in relation to the resources utilized, which may include financial expenditures, time invested, or materials consumed. Cybersecurity serves to safeguard not only patient data, but financial data, projected forecasts, and, of course, control of patient care. It should be noted that OT cybersecurity is equally an integral part of healthcare systems through control systems used for critical care patients (O_2 and CO_2 flow rate monitors, heart monitors, etc.).

These are just a few of the numerous systems that exist. Simply put, a system represents a collective suite of smaller sub-systems, processes, and functions. A sub-system is a smaller encapsulation of a complete system, but on a smaller scale, often consisting of a specific role for its parent or overall operation. For example, an electrical generation facility has a multitude of collective systems. The overall system's primary function is to produce electricity; however, its smaller sub-systems control specific aspects that are comprised of several of these smaller systems that, when orchestrated together, consist of the homogenized collective of the site's overall system and its primary objective.

Given that an electrical generation facility has several key-critical aspects to work cohesively together to product electricity, failure in one or more of these sub-systems will result in a catastrophic collapse of the systems' operational integrity, sometimes resulting in destruction or damaged equipment, or worse, human causalities and/or fatalities.

In a given power plant, some of these sub-systems (not complete, merely an example) include functions such as:

- safety systems (to control and regulate key-critical sub-systems, processes, and their functions); these systems are vital to ensure that an operational site continues operating as per design specifications efficiently and as safely as possible;
- cooling systems (to generate steam, to turn turbines that create electricity);
- power regulators (stabilize electricity so power remains equalized as possible); and,
- turbine control (to prevent turbine trips, or worse, spindle decoupling)

Another example may be applied to transportation systems, in this case, rail systems, in which some of these sub-systems (not complete, either) include functions such as:

- safety systems (to control and regulate key-critical sub-systems, processes, and their functions); these systems are vital to ensure that an entire rail system continues operating; and, as some rail lines share roles for both freight and human transport, the need for near-zero risk is even more important; such systems exist to prevent train collisions, and include both collision alerting and control mechanisms, as well as emergency stop;
- signaling systems (including rail crossing, as well as rail traffic control and diversion);
- engine power regulators (used to stabilize rail locomotive performance); and,
- and recently, autonomous (remote) train control

These functions pertain only to a rail systems' operation for safe train locomotive transportation. This does not include other functions that are not considered as part of a rail systems' operation, which include building and environmental controls. Thus, the terms system and sub-system are utilized from a two-fold perspective, such that both the functionality as well as regulating the cyber systems are used to maintain the operations.

The next level down as part of a given system (and its sub-systems) are processes which represent a collection of connected or interconnected actions that utilize resources to achieve a desired outcome. These, then, are broken even further down into specific functions, such as opening or closing a valve (Figure 2.2).

Combined, there may be tens of thousands of processes which comprise a single system (or sub-system). The larger the scale, the more complex the system. In large manufacturing facilities, refineries, electric generation facilities, there are usually libraries with rows of engineering designs detailing each and every system, process, and function.

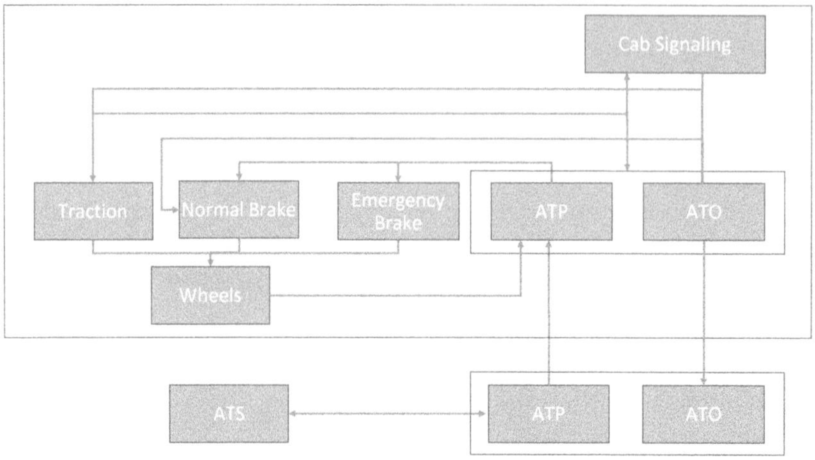

FIGURE 2.2 Automatic train control system functions.[3]

So where does the word "control" fit into the overall equation?

The word "control," used in this context of a holistic system, represents a suite of policies and procedures that ensure that the operation continues running smoothly—without interruption, without failure, and without casualties. More specifically, to control a system, its sub-systems, and its processes and functions means performing active and regular checks to ensure that the overall system is performing as designed per specifications. If not, then additional measures or countermeasures must be implemented to counteract whatever sub-system or process has failed or is failing. The overall objective, outside of production output, is to prevent system failure. It should be noted that an unintentional, non-malicious interruption of a given production may be considered also as a system failure. Note that if one sub-system of the collective system fails, the collective system as a whole does not fail; rather, its operation is merely interrupted. For example, with a nuclear power generation plant, if the main pump to a feedwater system were to fail, along with its backup, this would cause the reactor to SCRAM; thus, electricity would no longer be generated for transmission use. The pump (or pumps) failed, but the remainder of the collective system was simply interrupted.

This is the objective of controlling an operation—a careful manipulation of measures and countermeasures utilized to maintain the "status quo" of the site's operation. Change any of the parameters, and there is a failure. Change any of the parameters drastically or set these parameters to extreme settings, and it will result in a catastrophic failure, and, depending on the severity of the failure, will determine whether it is equipment damage, site-wide destruction of assets, or even worse, loss of life. Controls are implemented to prevent those scenarios from occurring, and thus, it is imperative that they must be adhered to exactly as designed and implemented.

The enforcement of that control is relegated to a "controller," which is the mechanism by which measures and countermeasures may be implemented in maintaining the "status quo" of the overall operation. This, too, must be adhered to exact requirements; otherwise, varied consequences will occur.

It is exactly for this reason why automation and process control systems are so critically vital in operating and maintaining our CIs. Those infrastructures which heavily rely upon control systems include, but are not limited to, the following:

- transportation (signaling, switching, traffic control);
- energy (separate from nuclear);
- nuclear (which relies completely on automation required for its precision);
- water and wastewater management;
- maritime (a plethora of ship management systems onboard a single ship keep the ship moving in the right direction and does not sink while doing so); and,
- healthcare (critical care units, in which patients rely on machines to keep them alive)

One issue that should be explained is that the terms "control" and "controller" are synonymous to both physical and cyber-related mechanisms. Additionally, they provide and service the same functions, too. Except with cyber-related mechanisms, these are digital computing devices used to impose and enforce the operation aspects of controlling a production operation.

2.4 IS IT SECURITY, OR IS IT "SECURITY"?

As it continues to evolve, the terms "security," "operational security," and "cybersecurity" have different connotations and meaning depending on how and where they are applied. These terms are deeply rooted within their respective communities of interest and have overlapping objectives; and, each one is defined with distinctive concepts consisting of varying focuses and applications.

Operational security (OPSEC) is a strategic framework that initially emerged from within the military community but has since been adopted by several CI sectors. Frequently mistaken for OT, OPSEC fundamentally necessitates that organizations view their activities through the lens of potential adversaries. This perspective enables the recognition of essential operations that may be vulnerable to exploitation, not just merely cyber-related. After pinpointing these operations, along with their associated processes and assets, organizations utilize established principles to evaluate the risks linked to each operation and formulate strategies aimed at effectively reducing those risks. The core objective of OPSEC is to safeguard sensitive assets from unauthorized access and potential exploitation. This process entails identifying critical information that, if exposed to adversaries, could jeopardize the integrity of missions or operations. OPSEC encompasses a comprehensive approach to information protection that transcends well beyond cybersecurity, incorporating elements such as physical security protocols, personnel vetting, and overall safeguarding practices.

In practical application, this entails the integration of operational, procedural, physical, and cybersecurity measures and countermeasures, alongside fostering a culture among personnel that emphasizes adherence to established operational best practices and standards. The ultimate goal of OPSEC is to thwart adversaries from uncovering vital operational details and strategies. This involves a thorough understanding of potential threats, a meticulous analysis of vulnerabilities, a careful assessment of associated risks, and the implementation of effective countermeasures to ensure the confidentiality of information. Thus, OPSEC prioritizes the management of information dissemination and the protection of sensitive secrets over the mere fortification of networks or technological systems.

In the expansive realm of risk management frameworks, OPSEC plays a crucial role. It extends beyond simple preventive measures, emphasizing the importance of building resilience against espionage threats, ensuring reliability in the face of process or procedural breakdowns, and facilitating the restoration of operations when necessary. By fostering a culture of continuous vigilance and adjusting countermeasures to meet the changing dynamics of threats, OPSEC guarantees the seamless continuation of operations, thus protecting the organization's integrity and overall security.

As hinted previously, OPSEC is a continuous and systematic approach designed to identify and mitigate various risks associated with processes and procedures, as well as physical and cyber threats, with the ultimate goal of improving the predictability of outcomes. This comprehensive framework includes several key components such as hazard identification, risk assessment, the implementation of control measures, safeguarding operations, and the ongoing monitoring of risk management strategies. By employing these procedures, organizations can make informed decisions that are grounded in a thorough understanding of the associated risks.

Risk management fundamentally involves presenting options and making decisions in situations characterized by uncertainty. It requires a systematic approach to identify, assess, and prioritize risks, followed by the application of resources to minimize, monitor, and control the probability or impact of unfortunate events. This process is crucial for organizations as it enables them to navigate potential challenges and seize opportunities, ensuring that they can achieve their objectives while maintaining a balance between risk and reward. Effective risk management not only enhances decision-making capabilities but also fosters a proactive culture that prepares organizations to respond to unforeseen circumstances.

A risk management process is essential for facilitating decision-making in organizations confronted with uncertainties regarding their ability to achieve established objectives. This process serves as a framework that assists organizations in identifying and prioritizing significant risks that require attention. By promoting a comprehensive evaluation process consisting of all potential risks that could impact an organization's overall goals, this would provide a more refined and thorough understanding of the existing risk landscape. It is systematic in nature, relying on insights gained from earlier stages, enabling informed judgments and decisions, and allowing for the integration of new data and information as it emerges.

And finally, the primary problem with cybersecurity risk is that the terms "security" and "operation" have completely different meanings and objectives; yet, both are used within the same context interchangeably. One is used for protecting logical assets and data, whereas the other is used for protecting the operation(s) and its processes.

2.5 THE GREAT CONVERGENCE

The term "convergence" serves as a significant descriptor for one of the most critical trends currently shaping the landscape of industrial control systems. This concept does not refer to a specific new technology or a recent development within the industry; rather, it has been a topic of discussion and analysis for several decades.

Thus, "The Great Convergence" of IT and OT represents a significant transformation that has the potential to enhance both efficiency and innovation within organizations. This integration facilitates the optimization of operational processes, fosters improved decision-making based on data analytics, and enables the development of novel services. By bridging the gap between these two domains, organizations can achieve a more cohesive operational framework that not only streamlines workflows but

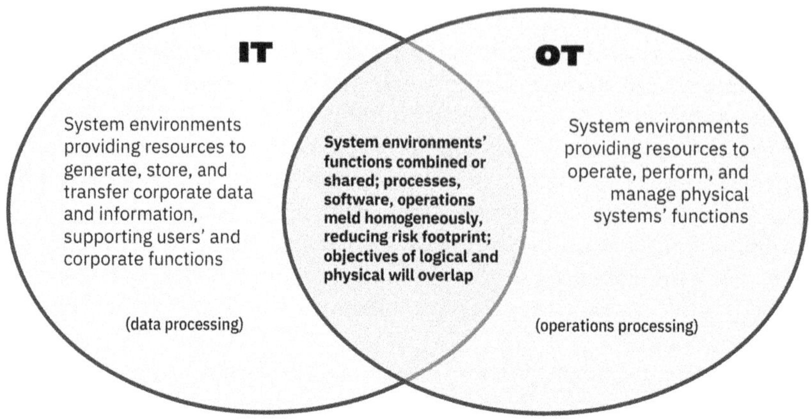

FIGURE 2.3 IT/OT convergence.

also drives strategic growth and adaptability in an increasingly competitive landscape. This is shown in Figure 2.3.

The convergence of IT and OT presents several advantages that can significantly enhance organizational performance. Firstly, it promotes efficiency by enabling rapid analysis of data derived from physical operations through IT systems, thereby facilitating more informed and timely decision-making processes. Secondly, it strengthens cybersecurity by ensuring that uniform security protocols are implemented across both digital and physical environments, thereby mitigating potential vulnerabilities. Lastly, this convergence serves as a catalyst for innovation, encouraging the development of new services and solutions that can drive competitive advantage and operational excellence.

Several strategies for enabling a successful convergence include, but are not limited to, the following:

- Establishing interdisciplinary teams that comprise individuals from both IT and OT sectors is essential for enhancing collaboration.
- Developing and encouraging transparent communication and mutual respect among team members is vital for fostering a productive work environment.
- The implementation of comprehensive security protocols that address both IT and OT vulnerabilities is crucial for safeguarding organizational assets.
- Continuous real-time monitoring for potential threats is necessary to ensure prompt detection and response to security incidents.

- Lastly, the utilization of sophisticated authentication and encryption techniques is imperative to protect sensitive data and maintain the integrity of systems.

It is our conviction that the convergence of physical and digital realms will occur in a manner that is both integrated and seamless. Historically, transformative technologies have a tendency to become so ingrained in our daily existence that they fade into the background, operating intuitively without drawing attention to themselves. Consider the evolution of electricity, the internal combustion engine, the telephone, television, and microprocessors that govern various electrical devices and LED lighting. While the pace of adoption may differ across technologies, those that achieve the highest levels of success ultimately become an intrinsic part of our daily lives, influencing not only individual consumers but also enterprises, governmental bodies, and most importantly, industrial operations.

Convergence extends well beyond merely merging technologies; it encompasses the integration of teams and processes as well. The introduction of OT introduces new stakeholders into the security landscape, necessitating that IT security teams adapt to the varied and immediate requirements of industrial settings. For instance, it is impractical to temporarily disable a smart grid for several hours to implement updates or modify configurations. Furthermore, OT systems may have been operational for significantly longer periods than their IT counterparts, which introduces additional security vulnerabilities that must be addressed and managed. Additionally, since OT systems were not originally designed for Internet connectivity, they require retrofitting with IoT devices and the implementation of appropriate security measures.

The convergence of IT and OT presents six primary security challenges that must be addressed, which are as follows:

1. Lack of collaboration and cooperation between IT and OT groups, often fighting for resources and funding, further creating or deepening the gap between the two groups;
2. Legacy systems, particularly OT, in which operating environments cannot change or update easily without completing a costly design review of current specifications;
3. Very different management styles of securing IT versus OT environments, with an ever-increasing need to bridge terminology gaps between IT and OT environments. This is especially true given that OT environments deal specifically with safety, reliability, and performance, as opposed to IT environments, which deal specifically with confidentiality, integrity, and availability.
4. Safety of an operation is critical, requiring constant review, modification, and implementation of newer specifications based

on found design basis threats, and plays an even greater role with the OT environments; whereas, with IT environments, such threats do not exist.

5. Critical demands in which OT systems cannot (and must not) suffer outages or downtime due to criticality of the operation(s) being performed; and,
6. Effects of disruption within OT environments that have a far devastating impact in a company's "bottom line" as opposed to IT systems. OT environments have different "business objectives," as they must satisfy safety, regulatory, and standards requirements, as opposed to IT, which may have only regulatory requirements.

The absence of collaboration between IT and OT teams has historically been a significant issue, resulting in potential security vulnerabilities that can complicate operations, leading to redundant efforts and escalating operational expenses, while creating openings for exploitation by malicious actors. To enhance security measures, it is imperative for these distinct teams to prioritize their efforts, engage in collaborative practices, and establish effective communication channels that may not have been feasible or required in previous years.

Legacy OT systems present a stark contrast to IT systems, which generally have a lifespan of no more than five years. In contrast, OT systems, particularly those utilized in manufacturing, can remain in operation for several decades. These legacy systems often lack adequate security measures and are frequently unable to be upgraded due to their proprietary designs or protocols. It is essential to conduct a thorough security assessment for every converged system, as those that do not meet current security standards may necessitate the acquisition of new or updated OT equipment to ensure compliance and protection against potential vulnerabilities.

Problems associated with accepted and approved engineering specifications, which encompass both safety and regulatory requirements, make it difficult for OT environments to constantly upgrade or update equipment and architectures as rapidly as IT environments. IT environments are continually patching their environments for several reasons, including security. OT environments, however, cannot be blanket-patched as the same as their IT counterparts, as some of these patches may adversely affect and impact critical operations, resulting in either operational failure, or worse, safety issues, such as an explosion or death of plant workers or local civilians.

Inadequate visibility presents a significant challenge. IT consistently depends on asset discovery and configuration processes to establish a comprehensive understanding of the managed environment. OT systems are required to facilitate the sharing of this environment, enabling discoverability as well as remote configuration and management capabilities. If an administrator lacks visibility into an OT environment, they are unable to effectively secure and manage that device. These deficiencies can result in potential security vulnerabilities.

Mission-critical requirements necessitate that OT production systems operate continuously (24×7), around the clock, throughout the entire year. These systems cannot be halted or deactivated for upgrades or updates without incurring substantial financial losses or exposing themselves to physical hazards. For instance, consider the implications of temporarily shutting down medical life support systems for software enhancements. As a result, organizations may overlook potential security vulnerabilities, prioritizing operational continuity over the necessary downtime required to address and mitigate these risks effectively.

The implications of disruption are significant and warrant careful consideration. While integration is generally regarded as beneficial, the consequences of disruption can be profoundly detrimental. For instance, when a factory's operational machinery experiences a sudden loss of communication due to a network failure, whether from equipment malfunction or an external denial-of-service attack, the repercussions can be severe. The convergence of IT and OT necessitates a thorough evaluation of resilience and the implementation of failsafe measures to mitigate such risks.

2.6 THE EVOLUTION OF RISK IN OT CYBERSECURITY

The phenomenon of convergence diminishes the standalone significance of industrial controllers. The specific models and performance characteristics that once served as key selling points for particular industrial controllers are likely to become less critical to consumers over time. Instead, customers will increasingly prioritize the comprehensive solutions offered by entire control platforms or systems, focusing on the issues these systems can address and their potential to enhance productivity and efficiency. The distinction between different types of controllers, whether they are programmable logic controllers (PLCs), PLCs integrated with PC-based technology, or distributed control system (DCS), will become less relevant. The advancement of industrial control systems will be more heavily influenced by software, information, and communication technologies.

This pivotal moment signifies a significant opportunity for both original equipment manufacturers of controllers and other automation providers seeking expansion. As industries converge, traditional market boundaries become increasingly indistinct, prompting companies to branch out from their foundational sectors. The landscape of industrial controls has evolved beyond a competitive environment solely among vendors of PLCs, industrial PCs, programmable automation controllers, motion controllers, embedded controls, and DCSs. It has transformed into a complex space where competition and collaboration frequently coexist. Technologies that were once distinct, including controllers, sensors, operator interfaces, motion control systems, software solutions, networking capabilities, and related services, now integrate resources and functions into a more combined manner. The convergence of control technologies presents fresh avenues for growth that transcend individual companies and impact broader economic frameworks.

2.7 THE SAFETY, RELIABILITY, AND PERFORMANCE MODEL

It should be noted that rather than focusing on only the data (via the "CIA Triad," which includes confidentiality, integrity, and availability; an alternative version switches availability with confidentiality, creating the "AIC Triad"), this new paradigm model focuses solely on the operation and its processes.

The "SRP Model"[4] shown in Figure 2.4 is recommended, whereby each factor has specific functions that many consider critical to control systems' operations. These include, but are not limited to, the following:

- Safety—pertains to several facets including:
  - Safety of plant staff and the general public (health deficits, injury, or loss of life);
  - Safety to the plant (or facility); and,
  - Maintaining a safely running operation.
- Reliability—pertains to several facets including:
  - Consistent results for the (overall) operation;
  - Equipment failure is minimized;

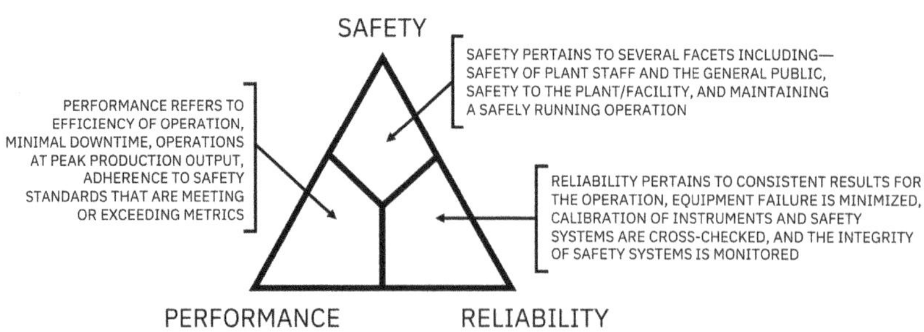

FIGURE 2.4 The SRP model.

  - Systems are cross-checked; and,
  - Integrity of safety systems is monitored (and reviewed).
- Performance—pertains to several facets including:
  - Efficiency of the (overall) operation;
  - Minimal downtown;
  - Operations perform at peak production output; and (most importantly),
  - Adherence to safety standards that meet (if not exceed) established metrics.

These three factors are essential to maintaining as optimal of performance to an (overall) operation as possible, without violating safety mechanisms implemented, while ensuring as efficient of a production rate as possible.

How does safety, reliability, and performance relate to cybersecurity?

A given system and its sub-systems (ad nauseum) have been designed and implemented to precise specifications. If just one aspect to the operation is either tampered with, or worse, compromised, the net result(s) would have devastating consequences. This is especially true with hazardous operations in which, if safety were compromised, the endgame would be an explosion, a radiological, or hazardous chemical release. Thus, the need for cybersecurity plays as equal, if not more so, to a plant's operation due to the fact that most plants/facilities are almost completely networked.

Combining both physical and OT provided innovative functionalities while preserving the sustaining extended lifespans associated with these environments. The integration of IT capabilities into physical systems gives rise to new behaviors, new threats, and (certainly) new vulnerabilities that would otherwise not have existed prior to their inclusion in such technology, as well as their adoption in production environments.

Introducing new threat vectors to already existing operational environments now carry significant risk considerations. Consequently, engineering now need to consider different or modified framework models, adjusting both digital and analytical approaches to tackle these emergent characteristics, which encompass interrelated aspects such as safety, reliability, OPSEC, and environmental impact. Unfortunately, these models are either out-of-date, or are still under deliberation to accurately describe and define these now hybridized environments. It is because of this reason why establishing a new baseline for approaching risk in OT environments has become even more critical now than ever before.

2.8 CONCLUSION

OT underpins the essential systems that keep modern society functioning, from energy and water to transportation, healthcare, and manufacturing.

This chapter has highlighted that OT is not only a collection of devices and processes, but also a complex ecosystem of interdependent systems where failures or compromises can cascade across multiple sectors. Unlike IT, which is primarily focused on protecting data, OT's core mission centers on the safety, reliability, and performance of physical operations—functions that directly impact human lives and community resilience.

We explored the distinctions between systems, processes, and functions, emphasizing that controls—both human and automated—exist to maintain continuity and prevent catastrophic failures. The discussion of interdependencies underscored how disruptions in one sector, such as telecommunications, can rapidly cascade into others, magnifying risks far beyond the initial point of failure.

The rise of IT/OT convergence has created new opportunities for efficiency, data-driven decision-making, and innovation; however, it has also introduced fresh vulnerabilities that necessitate new approaches to risk management and governance.

Finally, the Safety–Reliability–Performance model provides a practical perspective for understanding OT cybersecurity in its proper context: not as a separate technical discipline, but as an integrated safeguard for operational continuity. By focusing on operational safety, system reliability, and consistent performance outputs, organizations can better align their cybersecurity practices with their mission-critical objectives.

In conclusion, OT cybersecurity must be approached as a discipline rooted in the protection of operations rather than solely in information security. The challenge ahead lies in harmonizing IT and OT perspectives, strengthening resilience across interdependent infrastructures, and ensuring that technological advancement is matched with robust safeguards. This foundation sets the stage for deeper exploration of risk management, governance, and resilience strategies in the chapters that follow.

NOTES

1 Radvanovsky, Robert, & McDougall, Allan. *Critical Infrastructure, Homeland Security and Emergency Preparedness*, Fifth Edition, CRC Press, 2024.
2 https://www.thoughtco.com/maslows-hierarchy-of-needs-4582571.
3 Siahvashi, Ali & Moaveni, Bijan. (2010). Automatic Train Control based on the Multi-Agent Control of Cooperative Systems. *Journal of Mathematics and Computer Science*. 111, 247–257. https://doi.org/10.22436/jmcs.001.04.02.
4 The "SRP Model" was introduced by infracritical® circa 2018 and is meant to represent the three primary functions behind operational security, specifically pertaining to process control systems; URL: http://srpmodel.infracritical.com.

CHAPTER 3

Misinterpretation of Risk and Its Misuse

3.1 INTRODUCTION

This chapter explores the common misunderstandings of risk management in cybersecurity. Misinterpreting risk can lead to flawed decision-making and poor risk mitigation strategies. This chapter emphasizes the importance of properly perceiving and assessing risks, as well as understanding the psychological and organizational factors that influence these assessments. By examining various biases, cognitive errors, and industry examples, the chapter aims to highlight the consequences of mismanaging risk and provide guidance on developing more effective risk management strategies.

3.2 THE PSYCHOLOGY OF RISK

One of the most significant collective problems with risk is that both individuals and groups fail to correctly perceive, interpret, and respond to risk. They may also react to risk in ways that might seem irrational or inconsistent. Some real-world examples of these reactions are:

- An operational support team refuses to implement formal operating procedures for their activities because "they never make mistakes."
- An organization's leadership determines that it would rather shift risk from itself onto contractors in an effort to reduce its risk footprint.[1]
- Larger organizations focus their resources on addressing less important risk factors due to industry peer pressure.
- Smaller organizations focus their resources in accordance with guidance from sector agencies, rather than larger organizations which have different risk factors.

DOI: 10.4324/9781003610557-3

- An organization's leadership declines to invest in cybersecurity controls because they are unlikely to be the subject of an attack ("nothing will happen to us").
- An organization rolls out cost-saving improvements to its infrastructure such as the comingling of IT and OT equipment and data against the advice of a minority of experts highlighting a negative impact on safety, reliability, and performance.
- An organization immediately diverts all resources to address a vulnerability reported in a cybersecurity incident elsewhere, while failing to address intolerable risks that are more likely to cause an incident.

Some of the reasons for this behavior are as shown in Table 3.1.

3.3 ONE SIZE DOES NOT FIT ALL

To help organizations address their cybersecurity risk, government agencies, standards bodies, and other groups produce their version of a methodology. To date, most of the guidance, especially from government agencies, is too generic. It is essential that everyone understands the many reasons why a generic approach cannot work:

- Different industries face distinct risks. For example, a financial institution may prioritize cybersecurity and fraud prevention, while a manufacturing plant may focus on equipment failure and worker safety.
- Operational processes and environments vary widely across organizations. What works for a tech company may not be suitable for a healthcare provider.
- Large organizations with complex structures and processes require more comprehensive and detailed risk assessments compared to small businesses.
- Each organization has a different tolerance for risk, influenced by its culture, leadership, and strategic objectives. Risk assessments must align with this risk appetite.
- Different sectors are subject to various regulatory frameworks. Organizations must tailor their risk assessments to meet specific compliance standards, such as GDPR[8] for data privacy or ISO standards for quality management.[9]
- Geographic location can introduce unique risks, such as natural disasters, political instability, or local regulatory challenges.

TABLE 3.1 Psychological Reasons behind Risk Assessment

Reason	Effect	Example
Cognitive Bias People tend to overestimate the likelihood of events that are more memorable or have recently occurred. For example, after hearing about a plane crash, individuals might overestimate the risks of flying. This is called the *availability heuristic*.[2]	Mis-prioritization, due to knee-jerk reaction to a cybersecurity incident in the news, while neglecting other possible scenarios.	High-profile incidents such as the CyberAv3nger attacks on Unitronics PLCs[3] direct attention to this being a likely scenario whereas the most likely scenario remains a mistake from an authorized user.
Prospect Theory The way information is presented can also significantly affect risk assessment. For instance, people might respond differently to a treatment described as having a "90% survival rate" versus a "10% mortality rate." *Prospect theory* states that people experience losses more intensely than equivalent gains, making them more likely to avoid risks when faced with potential losses.[4]	Failure to sufficiently resource or focus on cybersecurity risks due to incorrect presentation or understanding of consequence.	Responses to ransomware demands tend to focus on the potential loss of their data (i.e., there is no guarantee that paying the ransom will result in the data being returned) as opposed to the guaranteed loss of the ransom money.
Emotional Factors Emotions like fear and anxiety can amplify perceived risks. Fear of losing money, for example, can lead to overly cautious investment strategies. On the other hand, people often believe they are less likely to experience negative events than others, leading to underestimation of personal risk. Individuals with personality traits such as sensation-seeking and impulsivity will be more likely to engage in high-risk activities.	Failure to sufficiently resource or focus on cybersecurity risks due to belief that the risk is lower for the organization than for others. Cybersecurity incidents because of a failure to follow procedures due to overconfidence in abilities.	The 2017 Equifax data breach was a direct result of a known vulnerability in the Apache Struts open-source framework they used,[5] for which a patch existed. Insufficient attention on addressing such issues can only occur when a company believes the risk is outweighed by the required remediation effort.

(*Continued*)

TABLE 3.1 (Continued)

Reason	Effect	Example
Heuristics and Overconfidence People often rely on heuristics or rules of thumb to simplify their assessment of risk. While useful, these shortcuts can lead to systematic biases and errors. In addition, people tend to be overconfident in their judgments and abilities, often underestimating risks and overestimating their knowledge or control over outcomes.	Cybersecurity incidents because people click on phishing email links as they have rules about taking immediate action when asked. Cybersecurity incidents because of a failure to follow procedures due to overconfidence in abilities.	Many companies believe that their employees will not make mistakes and so dismiss the need for written procedures and training.
Group Dynamics The desire for harmony and conformity can lead to poor risk assessment and decision-making, as dissenting opinions are suppressed. Peer behavior and media coverage can influence risk perceptions and actions, amplifying fears or downplaying real risks.	Poor decision-making in the implementation or enforcement of cybersecurity controls due to peer pressure or the need to avoid conflict.	Uber's 2016 data breach was covered up by the security team after pressure from executives. Uber paid the hackers to keep the breach quiet and disguised the payment as a bug bounty.[6]
Survivorship bias In this case there is a focus on events or entities that passed a selection process while ignoring others that did not.	The lack of analysis of all data results in incorrect conclusions.	Many companies fail to upgrade legacy equipment that is known to be insecure because they "haven't had an incident yet." This assessment fails to consider organizations that were affected but never reported an incident. This bias undoubtedly played a part in the 2017 WannaCry incident, which impacted over 250,000 computers running Windows XP Service Pack 2, an Operating System with many published vulnerabilities that were easy to exploit.[7]

- Having detailed information would detract from the overall objectives by providing generic strategies rather than detailed, how-to instructions.

Choosing a methodology or standard based on a risk assessment process, rather than a prescriptive checklist, is critical to ensure that all these aspects are considered. A tailored risk assessment ensures that the unique aspects of an organization, project, or scenario are adequately considered, leading to more effective risk management strategies. This customization enables the identification and mitigation of risks more accurately and efficiently, ultimately supporting better decision-making and enhancing the organization's resilience.

3.4 THE LAW OF DIMINISHING RETURNS

The phrase as low as reasonably practicable (ALARP, originating from health and safety legislation developed in the UK) is widely used in safety standards and legislation throughout the world. IEC 61508[10] defines the following for risks:

- Zero risk can never be reached; only probabilities can be reduced.
- Non-tolerable risks must be reduced (ALARP).

Optimal, cost-effective safety is achieved when it is addressed throughout the entire safety lifecycle.

Although some safety-critical industries do attempt to achieve zero risk (e.g., air traffic control, nuclear power plants, petrochemical refineries), the best that they can attain is tolerable risk.

The ALARP concept can be applied to managing cybersecurity risk. Figure 3.1 shows a visual representation of ALARP. Initially, minimal cost (or effort equated to cost) is expended to mitigate significant or intolerable risk. As risk is addressed, the cost to mitigate increases further. The ALARP point is reached when the cost of mitigating additional risk becomes disproportionate to the risk reduction.[11]

The failure to understand the ALARP concept is visible in cybersecurity incident surveys. Consider Figure 3.2, from the 2024 Control System Cyber Security Annual Report, published by (CS)2AI and KPMG.[12] The most common causes of a cybersecurity incident are the "negligent insider" and the "malicious insider." Together, these make up 77% of all incidents reported in the survey. This number is consistent with other surveys in IT and OT, and in many cases could be reduced by the application

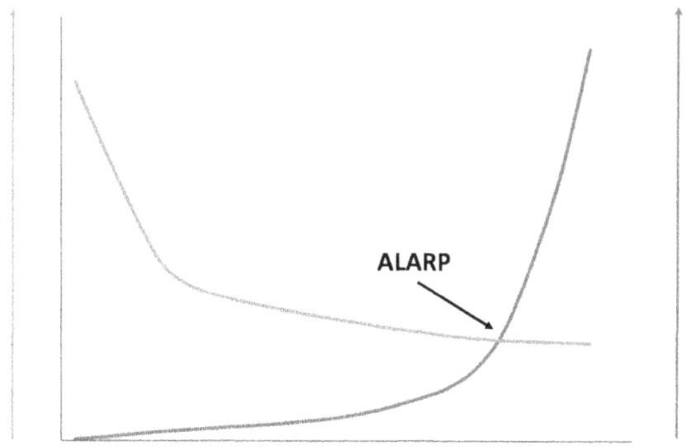

FIGURE 3.1 Visualizing ALARP.

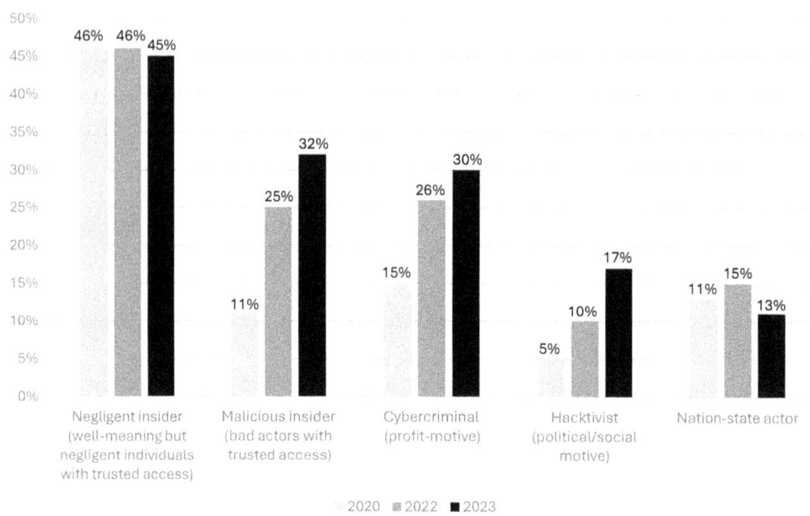

FIGURE 3.2 Threat actor(s) in cybersecurity compromises.

(Image redrawn; data and figures sourced from "The (CS)2AI-KPMG Control System Cybersecurity Annual Report", CS²AI.)[13]

and enforcement of relatively low-cost non-technical controls.[14] However, much of the investment in cybersecurity controls goes toward protecting against more complex threats, such as nation-states, requiring costly software, hardware, implementation, and maintenance.

3.5 IT RISK VERSUS OT RISK

The differences between IT and OT risk are generally well understood. For many years, this was explained using the CIA triad, highlighting that the relative priority for IT and OT was different: for IT the priorities are confidentiality ("C"), followed by integrity ("I"), and finally availability ("A") but for OT this is reversed, with availability as the priority, followed by integrity, then finally confidentiality.[15]

Despite this comparison, management of cybersecurity risk continues to be misunderstood, biased toward the IT definition. This presents several issues in organizations:

Although there are usually some similarities with the overall risk management approach in the organization (such as the use of "likelihood" and "consequence" to categorize each risk), the approach is not consistent. As a result, cybersecurity risks may not get the visibility they need.

IT consequences tend to be considered as failures of the IT equipment itself (e.g., loss of server, loss of network switch). In contrast, OT consequences manifest themselves in the physical world (e.g., loss of containment, damage to process machinery).

Prioritizing confidentiality over availability leads to a focus on the wrong controls. Protecting the perimeter to prevent exfiltration of data will not avoid a cybersecurity incident within the perimeter that causes a loss of production.

OT cybersecurity risks are unique, as they combine threats related to information security (destructive malware, DoS attacks) with the consequences related to safety (death or injury, harm to the environment, damage to equipment). Organizations must ensure that they incorporate industrial cybersecurity risk management into their safety protocols. This will help convince those with the ability to act—either leaders who can provide the resources, or individuals who can take their own mitigating actions—of the potential consequences of cybersecurity incidents in an industrial environment. Elevating industrial cybersecurity risks to the same level as safety risks makes them clearly visible to everyone in the company and forces senior management to treat them as they would a safety risk.

3.6 VULNERABILITY ASSESSMENT IS NOT RISK ASSESSMENT

A frequent issue in cybersecurity risk management is conflating the terms vulnerability assessment and risk assessment. While vulnerability assessments are critical components of an organization's security and risk management strategy, they are not risk assessments.

Cybersecurity risk comprises three factors:

- Threat;
- Vulnerability; and,
- Consequence

For a cybersecurity incident to occur, there first needs to be a threat. This can be a person, organization, circumstance, or event. There must also be a vulnerability. This could be a flaw in software or hardware, a configuration error, or a failure in a process or procedure. Finally, there must be a way to exploit or use the vulnerability, either intentionally or unintentionally. If a cybersecurity incident occurs, there are consequences for the organization. The relationship between these factors is shown in Figure 3.3.[16]

Focusing only on the vulnerability component alone means that organizations do not consider the threat or consequence. The impact of this is wide-ranging, particularly:

Focusing on the wrong controls due to a lack of consideration of threats. For example, an organization may need to focus on physical security to protect against malicious former insiders, but instead invests all its time and effort to protect against network attacks from nation-states.

Investing a disproportionate amount of time and effort in a certain control by considering vulnerability only. This is common in sectors with cybersecurity regulations because regulations tend to be based on yes/no responses to checklists, with little or no consideration of threats or consequences.

Failure to adequately mitigate a consequence due to the consideration of technical vulnerabilities only. In OT environments, consequences are manifested in the physical world. Mitigating a consequence, that is, responding to a cybersecurity incident, will require controls that cybersecurity specialists, such as mechanical failsafes like overspeed protection or shutdown valves, do not typically consider.

Risk assessments consider all three elements: threat, vulnerability, and consequence. To simplify the assessment process, threat and vulnerability are combined into likelihood, but this does not change the fact that to perform the risk assessment, the organization must consider threat, vulnerability, and consequence. Understanding all three ensures that the organization can properly prioritize its risk management activities.

FIGURE 3.3 The three elements of cybersecurity risk.

3.7 CYBER VERSUS OPERATIONS

As already noted, the consequences of a cybersecurity incident in an OT environment are very different from those in IT environments. This is not the only distinction between IT and OT when considering cybersecurity. Other considerations are equally crucial for cybersecurity to be managed appropriately in OT environments:

Agile methodologies popular in IT operations cannot be used in the same way in OT environments. Changes to OT environments necessitate a thorough risk assessment, testing, and procedure development to minimize the risk of incidents in the physical world. OT culture resists change as this impacts production and introduces unnecessary risk. OT-focused organizations emphasize safety culture as their number one priority.

Many of the cybersecurity tools and techniques that work well in IT environments cannot be applied in OT environments. Reasons include compatibility challenges due to the use of legacy equipment (e.g., older versions of Windows operating systems), lack of support for IT protocols used in cybersecurity tools (e.g., network discovery), use of non-IT compatible networks (e.g., Profibus, RS232, and RS485), and concerns over network traffic stability when using industrial protocols (e.g., Modbus).

3.8 DATA VERSUS PROCESS

As noted in Chapter 1, Edward Marszal and Jim McGlone's solution is to ensure that industrial cybersecurity risks are treated in the same way as safety risks: the security process hazard analysis (PHA) review, or SPR (pronounced spur). Their book[17] highlights the limitations of existing cybersecurity risk assessment methodologies and provides in-depth details of the SPR methodology.[18] SPR reuses the principles of safety risk assessment already in place.

The PHA methodology is used to assess hazards within industrial processes. In the United States, the Occupational Safety and Health Administration regulates high-risk facilities using process safety management, which, among other things, requires that a PHA be conducted every five years. There are several methods for performing a PHA. Of these, the hazard and operability study (HAZOP) is the most comprehensive, systematic, and commonly used method. A variation of the HAZOP, called CHAZOP (for control hazard and operability study), was developed to assess the safety impact of control system failures.

There have been attempts to align industrial cybersecurity risk assessment with these safety methods, with cyber PHA being the most common. CHAZOP may also incorporate cybersecurity risks. However, Marszal and McGlone note that cyber PHA and CHAZOP are more akin to failure modes and effects analysis (FMEA) than HAZOP. Whereas a HAZOP focuses on the hazards in the process, cyber PHA and CHAZOP focus on control system and network equipment failure. This is not ideal because of the following:

- The frequency of cyberattack is not random, like other equipment failures modeled in FMEA. Although it is possible to apply a frequency for the purposes of analysis, there is no statistical basis for it, unlike the random hardware and human failures in non-cybersecurity assessments. The output of such an analysis is therefore misleading. This could be addressed by rigorous collection of data, but that takes time, and this issue cannot wait.
- With the focus on control system and network equipment failure, the identification of safeguards is limited to the control system and the network, whereas the overall process analysis will identify other safeguards (such as mechanical protection).

Each scenario of the PHA is reviewed to determine whether it is hackable. This is a commonly used term in IT security. Still, in the SPR process, it means that "the scenario could be forced to occur by a malevolent actor who has taken control of the ICS [industrial control system]."[19] The cause or initiating event is reviewed first. The assumption is that computer-related causes can be hacked, but mechanical-related causes cannot.

If a cause can be hacked, the safeguards are then reviewed to determine if they can also be hacked. Again, the assumption is that all computer- or electronic-related safeguards can be hacked, but mechanical devices such as relief valves cannot.

Table 3.2 shows a simplified list of causes, consequences, and safeguards from a genericized PHA. Three causes are listed to highlight the hackable/non-hackable point.

TABLE 3.2 Simplified Causes, Consequences, and Safeguards from Genericized PHA

Cause	Consequence	Safeguard
Loss of pump suction	Pump damage	Low-flow alarm
Loss of lube oil cooling	Bearing damage	High-temperature alarm
Overpressure of vessel	Loss of containment, release of production fluids resulting in fire/explosion	Pressure safety valve

The loss of pump suction and loss of lube oil cooling would be hackable because the safeguards relate to computer-based elements, and the overpressure of a vessel would not, because its safeguard is mechanical.

From a cybersecurity perspective, the concern is warranted only when the cause and all the related safeguards can be hacked. If a cause, or any one of the safeguards for that cause, cannot be hacked, no further action is required from a cybersecurity perspective.

For each hackable scenario, there are two options:

- Assign security requirements based on the consequence category from the PHA and the risk tolerance of the process owner.
- Identify a *non-hackable* safeguard that can be introduced, that is, an inherently secure safeguard such as a pressure-relief device or check valve.

Note that some previously inherently secure safeguards, such as an overspeed trip, may now be digital and thus could be hackable.

3.9 NOT ALL CONTROLS ARE EQUAL

Many cybersecurity guidelines and vulnerability checklists pay no attention to control effectiveness. There is often no indication which controls will provide the most significant impact, which can be important to smaller organizations that need to target their investment. More important is the complacency that can occur once controls are in place. Understanding the effectiveness of cybersecurity controls is crucial for effective cybersecurity risk management.

Figure 3.4 shows the hierarchy of controls alongside a variety of standard cybersecurity controls. The hierarchy of controls makes clear that while multiple diverse controls are necessary, they are not equally effective. The same is true of cybersecurity. The defense in depth (add definition of defense in depth NISTIR 8183) approach is necessary, but the controls in the approach are not equally effective.[20]

Figure 3.4 shows that eliminating the hazard is the most effective method, while personal protective equipment (PPE, such as hard hats and goggles) is the least effective. Consider the scenario where workers are required to work with a chemical that is toxic if inhaled. The least effective control is to provide the workers with breathing PPE such as face masks or respirators. This is the least effective because it relies on people wearing the breathing PPE, which may be uncomfortable or inconvenient. The most effective control is to remove workers from exposure to the hazardous chemical, either by using a non-toxic alternative or by modifying the process so that workers are no longer at risk of exposure.

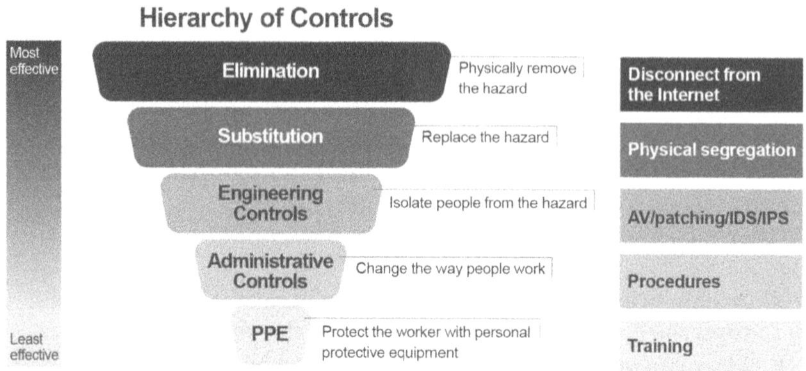

FIGURE 3.4 The hierarchy of controls and its relationship to cybersecurity.

In the case of cybersecurity, disconnecting from the Internet is like eliminating exposure to a hazardous chemical. On its own, disconnecting from the Internet eliminates certain risks (e.g., those related to unauthorized access from the Internet) but not others (e.g., those related to unauthorized physical access or introduction of malware through removable media). However, it is very effective at addressing those specific risks.

At the other extreme, cybersecurity training is essential, but it is the least effective type of control. This can be for a variety of reasons:

- **Content**—The material can be too generic to be of practical use to the trainees. The material can also quickly become out of date, as new threats and tactics arise, and new controls are introduced. The material may need to be varied based on job role to avoid it being too basic for some or too advanced for others.
- **Delivery Method**—Passive methods, such as presentations or videos, can result in poor long-term information retention. Repetitive, lengthy, or frequent training can cause fatigue that reduces the ability to absorb information. Active methods, such as group discussions and the use of technology, such as Virtual Reality, can enhance retention, as can shorter sessions that focus on specific topics.
- **Knowledge Assessment**—Training needs to be seen as more than simply satisfying a regulatory or compliance objective, and the knowledge assessment should reflect this. Ineffective training programs test simple fact recall at the end of training. Effective training programs track knowledge retention and effectiveness over time, using this information to adjust the programs as needed.

- **Oversight**—Perhaps the single most important criterion for determining the effectiveness of training is senior management support and enforcement. The importance of training needs to originate from the very top of the organization, and employees must believe it is critical to their role.

Overall, like many procedural- or people-based controls, training requires continuous effort to be effective. In contrast, elimination of a hazard (such as disconnection from the Internet) requires little or no effort (not withstanding that attention is paid to whether connections to the Internet are established).

The relative effectiveness of controls is crucial to understand, considering it may not be possible to deploy some safeguards on some systems. For example, it may not be possible to apply some engineering (more effective) controls, such as hardening, access control, and anti-malware, to systems or devices in an OT environment. For example, legacy operating systems may not support current anti-malware solutions, or embedded devices may have hard-coded or fixed features that cannot be disabled. In these cases, asset owners will need to use alternative, less effective safeguards for system protection, such as manual procedures to control access to devices.

3.10 EXAMPLE

Consider the following example that highlights the issues discussed in this chapter.

The term IT-OT convergence has many interpretations. One such interpretation involves the combination of infrastructure. Hyper-converged infrastructure is widely used in modern data centers to improve flexibility, scalability, and cost effectiveness. This approach consolidates computing power in virtual environments, transitioning from traditional hardware-based networks to software-defined networks that support centralized and remote management using unified toolsets.

Many of these concepts are bleeding over into modern OT environments. Some of these concepts can provide net benefits. For example, virtualizing control system servers and workstations can provide for better cybersecurity management. Patching and backups, for instance, can be done without taking entire systems out of service, and incident response can be more effective by supporting the restoration of virtual images if necessary.

One concept that is gaining prominence is the convergence of IT and OT networks. The arguments for implementing a converged IT/OT network are clear:

- Reduced capital cost of hardware by consolidating into one infrastructure.
- Reduced operating cost by enabling centralized network management across the entire infrastructure.

While the benefits are clear, the risks are less obvious. The challenge for organizations considering such a solution is to assess its pros and cons realistically. As already noted, the psychology of risk described earlier in this chapter can lead to incorrect conclusions, such as those shown in Table 3.3.

TABLE 3.3 Psychological Effects on Converged IT/OT Network Risk Assessment

Reason	Effect
Cognitive Bias	The reduced capital and operating costs are easy to calculate but the costs of remediating an incident arising from a converged network are not. This is especially true if such an incident has never occurred in the organization.
Prospect Theory	Controls may be applied disproportionately, focusing on highly publicized but rare incidents, such as state-sponsored attacks at the expense of more likely incidents, such as unintentional acts or malicious insiders.
Emotional Factors	There may be unjustified confidence in the effectiveness of controls based on personal beliefs, rather than objective facts. For example, while penetration testing can be used to validate the effectiveness of controls at a particular point in time, it does not guarantee effectiveness against new threats, tactics, or vulnerabilities.
Heuristics and Overconfidence	Assumptions of the relative effectiveness of different security controls may be incorrect. For example, how people rate the effectiveness of having separate physical networks versus programmable converged networks may depend on their own biases.
Group Dynamics	There will be a tendency in any organizational setting to go with the majority view to avoid conflict. Those who may intuitively know something is riskier may not be able to quantify that view in such a way to overcome the positive viewpoint of the majority (or even the loudest voice, even if not a majority).

Using an objective risk assessment method, it should be possible for an organization to determine an unbiased view of the risk of implementing a converged IT/OT network.

On July 19, 2024, CrowdStrike distributed a routine update to Falcon that caused roughly 8.5 million computers to crash and be unable to restart. It has been called the most significant outage in the history of information technology.[21] Leading computer security expert Mikko Hypponen called the outage "historic in scale."[22] Even though the error was discovered and fixed within hours, the remediation efforts took many more hours. The incident brought down businesses worldwide, and the financial damage has been estimated to exceed US$5 billion.[23]

The July 2024 CrowdStrike IT outage can help organizations place a cost on remediating incidents in hyper-converged networks.

CrowdStrike, a cybersecurity services and products company, produces an endpoint protection software product called Falcon. This product operates at the kernel level, the lowest level, of the Microsoft Windows operating system. As with other endpoint protection vendors, CrowdStrike issues regular updates to Falcon to address new threats.

Experts quoted in the various reports highlighted concerns that organizations are not well prepared to implement contingency plans involving single points of failure (in this case, the endpoint protection system). Although the consequences of the CrowdStrike incident were significant, such an outage in an OT environment could have been catastrophic, with a widespread loss of view or loss of control of critical infrastructure control systems.

The CrowdStrike incident provided an example of how differently OT and IT environments are managed. While it is common in IT environments to allow automated update of servers and workstations (indeed, it is impractical to do otherwise), doing so in an OT environment is contrary to all standards and best practices, as a potential outage could have significant safety or operational impacts. How then should a converged IT/OT environment operate? If the OT systems must operate over infrastructure that is updated according to IT rules, what safeguards are in place to protect the availability and integrity of the OT systems? How can the OT operating model be applied without impacting the IT environment risk?

Consider the conventional physically segregated OT network and the new hyper-converged IT/OT network solutions. The bowtie diagrams in Figures 3.5 and 3.6 show the typical preventative and mitigation safeguards for each approach.

On the face of it, the two solutions can be considered equivalent. Certainly, the proponents of the hyper-converged solution will argue that their solution is practically equal to the physically segregated solution.

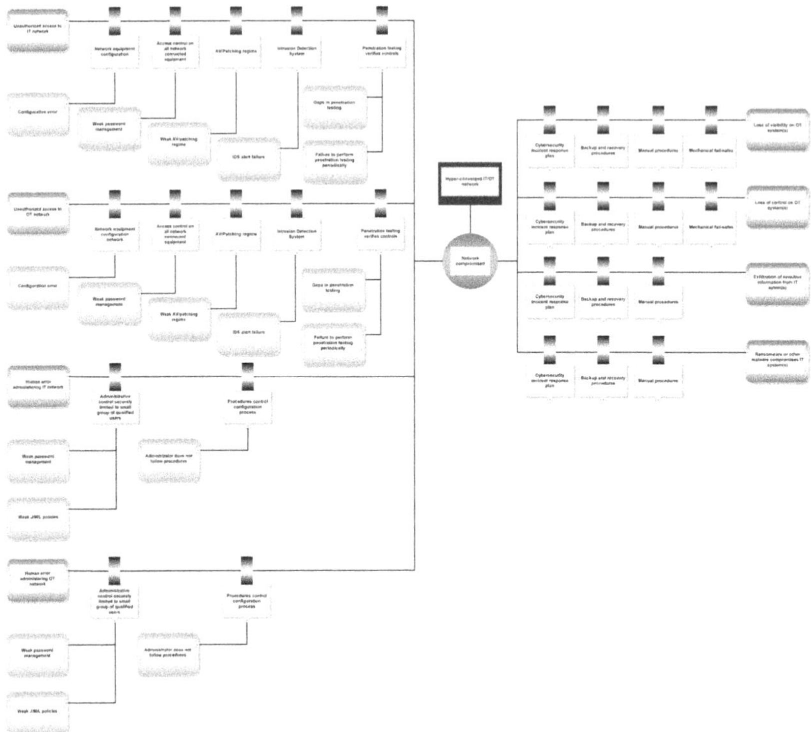

FIGURE 3.5 Bowtie diagram for physically segregated network.

However, the ISA/IEC 62443 series of standards does not consider logical and physical segregation to be equal:

> Logically segmenting networks based on their functionality provides some measure of protection, but may still lead to single points of failure if a network device is compromised. Physically segmenting networks provides another level of protection by removing the single-point-of-failure case, but it will lead to a more complex and costly network design. These trade-offs will need to be evaluated during the network design process.[24]

This is apparent from the bowtie diagram in Figure 3.5, which includes an additional safeguard related to the physical segregation.

The ISA/IEC 62443 series of standards defines four security levels (SL). These are intended to provide a "measure of confidence that the IACS is free from vulnerabilities and functions in the intended manner"[25] and are defined as follows:

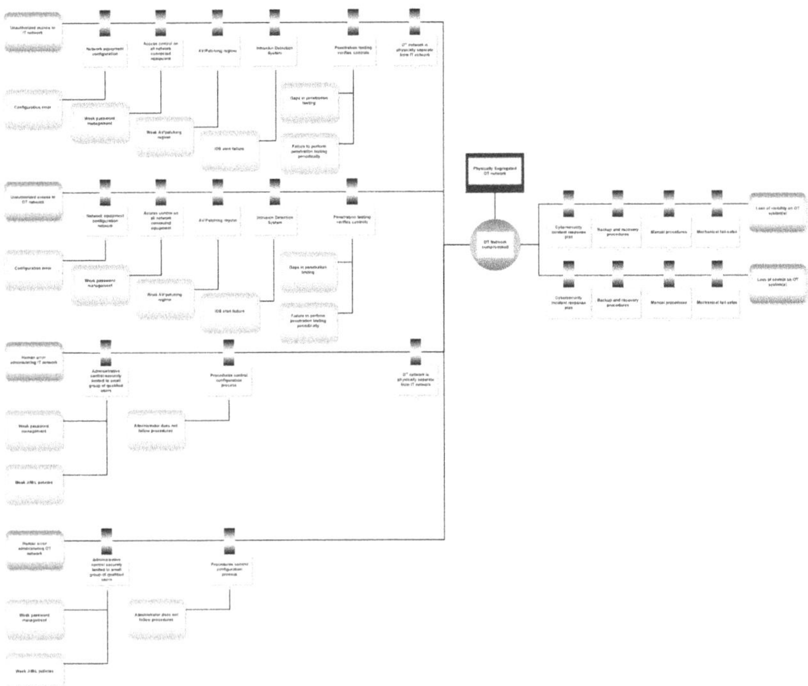

FIGURE 3.6 Bowtie diagram for hyper-converged network.

- **SL 1**—Prevent the unauthorized disclosure of information via eavesdropping or casual exposure.
- **SL 2**—Prevent the unauthorized disclosure of information to an entity actively searching for it using simple means with low resources, generic skills, and low motivation.
- **SL 3**—Prevent the unauthorized disclosure of information to an entity actively searching for it using sophisticated means with moderate resources, IACS-specific skills, and moderate motivation.
- **SL 4**—Prevent the unauthorized disclosure of information to an entity actively searching for it using sophisticated means with extended resources, IACS-specific skills, and high motivation.[26]

According to the standards, only SL 1 systems may use logical segregation; the others require physical segregation.

Even if not applying ISA/IEC 62443, the following points are apparent from a comparison of the bowtie diagrams:

In the physically segregated network arrangement, the physical segregation is, in effect, a non-hackable control. In the hyper-converged network arrangement, the controls rely on programmable electronic equipment to replicate physical segregation electronically (e.g., via VLANs) and are therefore vulnerable to hacking. The software or firmware may include defects, and the devices may be incorrectly configured.

Penetration testing will give some assurance of the effectiveness of the controls and configuration, but it is not prescriptive. The success or failure of penetration testing can arise from the tester or the approach. While a penetration test that succeeds in its objective proves that a vulnerability exists, a failure of a penetration test to achieve its purpose does not prove that a system is free of vulnerabilities.

Penetration testing only verifies a particular configuration at a specific point in time. New vulnerabilities (in software, firmware, or configuration) will arise in the programmable electronic equipment, new threats may appear, and new tactics may be developed. As a result, it will be necessary to regularly perform penetration testing to verify that the solution remains secure.

The hyper-converged arrangement increases the likelihood of compromise, as unauthorized access or human error in either the IT or OT network can result in consequences in the OT environment. In the physically segregated OT network, compromise or human error in the IT network does not result in a compromise in the OT environment.

There is significant reliance on procedural controls. Protecting against human error is highly dependent on procedural safeguards that, as noted earlier in this chapter, are less effective than eliminating the hazard or using technical controls.

Having highlighted the risks of the converged network, the organization can now assess the potential consequences and consider those against the estimated benefits. The specific decision will depend on each organization's risk appetite, but this risk appetite must be correctly informed.

3.11 CONCLUSION

In this chapter, the focus was on the misinterpretation and misuse of risk management, especially in cybersecurity. It discussed how cognitive biases, emotional factors, and group dynamics lead organizations to underestimate or overreact to risks, including real-world examples of these behaviors, such as companies ignoring significant risks due to overconfidence or focusing too much on less relevant threats.

The chapter also critiqued generic risk assessment methodologies, stressing the need for customized approaches that align with specific industries, processes, and organizational cultures. Concepts like ALARP and the difference between IT and OT (operational technology) risks were explored, showing how improper prioritization of risks can lead to costly or ineffective cybersecurity measures.

Finally, the chapter emphasized the critical distinction between vulnerability assessments and risk assessments, underscoring the importance of considering threats, vulnerabilities, and consequences together. It concluded with a case study highlighting the potential dangers of IT-OT convergence, arguing that while some convergence can offer benefits, it must be carefully managed to avoid catastrophic incidents in OT environments.

NOTES

1 The term "risk footprint" is risk that is determined by an organization's owners and investors for producing and promoting sound business stance that includes short-, medium-, and long-range mitigation strategies at various cost levels.
2 Cherry, K., "What Is the Availability Heuristic?", Very Well Mind, https://www.verywellmind.com/availability-heuristic-2794824, retrieved 20 October, 2024.
3 IRGC-Affiliated Cyber Actors Exploit PLCs in Multiple Sectors, Including US Water and Wastewater Systems Facilities, Cybersecurity Infrastructure and Security Agency, December 18, 2024, retrieved February 2, 2025, https://www.cisa.gov/news-events/cybersecurity-advisories/aa23-335a; http://riskbook.infracritical.com/book1/chapter3/ch3ref1.pdf.
4 Kahneman, D., & Tversky, A. (March 1979). Prospect Theory: An Analysis of Decision under Risk. *Econometrica*, 37, 2. https://www.jstor.org/stable/1914185, retrieved 20 October, 2024.
5 "Equifax Hacked Via Six Month Old Struts Vulnerability", Digital Guardian, September 14, 2017, retrieved February 2, 2025, https://www.digitalguardian.com/blog/equifax-hacked-six-month-old-struts-vulnerability.
6 Vijayan, J., "Uber's Ex-CISO Appeals Conviction Over 2016 Data Breach", Dark Reading, October 12, 2023, retrieved February 2, 2025, https://www.darkreading.com/cyberattacks-data-breaches/former-uber-ciso-appeals-conviction-over-2016-data-breach.
7 https://www.ibm.com/think/x-force/wannacry-worm-ransomware-changed-cybersecurity
8 The General Data Protection Regulation (GDPR) is a European Union law that protects the personal data of individuals and sets out requirements for how organizations can collect, store, and manage that data.

9 ISO 9001, produced by the International Organization for Standardization (ISO), is a globally recognized standard that helps organizations improve their quality management systems.
10 IEC 61508-1:2010, Functional Safety of Electrical/Electronic/Programmable Electronic Safety-Related Systems – Part 1: General Requirements (IEC [International Electrotechnical Commission]).
11 Mustard, S., *Industrial Cybersecurity: Case Studies and Best Practices*. International Society of Automation, (pp. 61–62). 2022.
12 "The (CS)2AI-KPMG Control System Cybersecurity Annual Report", CS^2AI, https://www.cs2ai.org/ot-cyber-reports-and-papers/2024-control-system-cyber-security-annual-report, retrieved 20 October, 2024.
13 https://www.cs2ai.org/ot-cyber-reports-and-papers/2024-control-system-cyber-security-annual-report, retrieved October 20, 2024.)
14 Mustard, S. *Industrial cybersecurity: Case studies and Best Practices*, International Society of Automation, (pp. 185–190), 2022.
15 Mustard, S. *Industrial Cybersecurity: Case Studies and Best Practices*. International Society of Automation, (p. 8), 2022.
16 Mustard, S. *A Guide to Cybersecurity for Water and Wastewater Utilities*. Water Environment Federation, (pp. 11–12), 2024.
17 Marszal, E., & McGlone, J. *Security PHA Review for Consequence-Based Cybersecurity*. International Society of Automation, 2019.
18 This should not be confused with the SRP Model, developed by infracritical®; URL: http://srpmodel.infracritical.com.
19 Marszal, E. and McGlone, J. *Security PHA Review for Consequence-Based Cybersecurity*, International Society of Automation, (p. 9). 2019.
20 Mustard, S. *Industrial Cybersecurity: Case Studies and Best Practices*. International Society of Automation (pp. 79–80), 2022.
21 "Slow recovery from IT outage begins as experts warn of future risks", The Guardian, July 19, 2024, https://www.theguardian.com/australia-news/article/2024/jul/19/microsoft-windows-pcs-outage-blue-screen-of-death, retrieved October 20, 2024.
22 Ross Sorkin, A. et al., "Counting the Costs of a Global IT Outage", New York Times, July 19, 2024, https://www.nytimes.com/2024/07/19/business/dealbook/tech-outage-crowdstrike-microsoft.html, retrieved October 20, 2024.
23 Gorelick, E. and Bloomberg, "CrowdStrike outage will cost Fortune 500 companies $5.4 billion in damages", https://fortune.com/2024/08/03/crowdstrike-outage-fortune-500-companies-5-4-billion-damages-uninsured-losses/, retrieved October 20, 2024.
24 ANSI/ISA-62443-3-3 (99.01.01)-2013, Security for Industrial Automation and Control Systems – Part 3-3: System Security

Requirements and Security Levels, p. 56. Research Triangle Park, NC: ISA [International Society of Automation].
25 ANSI/ISA-62443-3-3 (99.01.01)-2013, Security for Industrial Automation and Control Systems – Part 3-3: System Security Requirements and Security Levels, p. 56. Research Triangle Park, NC: ISA [International Society of Automation], p. 20.
26 ANSI/ISA-62443-3-3 (99.01.01)-2013, Security for Industrial Automation and Control Systems – Part 3-3: System Security Requirements and Security Levels, p. 56. Research Triangle Park, NC: ISA [International Society of Automation], p. 23.

CHAPTER 4

How to Measure Risk

4.1 INTRODUCTION

Operational risk is a prevalent concept within the financial sector, referring to the potential for loss arising from failures or disruptions that occur either within the organization or from external factors. This type of risk encompasses a wide array of potential issues, including but not limited to deficiencies in processes, human errors, system malfunctions, and fraudulent activities. Process risk represents a significant aspect of operational risk within an organization. It arises when there are failures or deviations from established procedures and practices, system failures, or human activities (intentional or otherwise) that the company typically employs. For instance, a petrochemical plant may encounter process risk if it inadequately deploys sufficient safety protocols, even though its process may have passed safety inspections or is adherent to safety regulations.

4.2 UNDERSTANDING OPERATIONAL CYBERSECURITY RISK

Every process carries inherent risks that can lead to unforeseen outcomes. By comprehensively understanding the origins of these risks and evaluating the reliability of their given process(es), organizations can effectively strategize to mitigate and ideally avert adverse results. This proactive approach to risk management fosters greater consistency in operational processes. Organizations employ various strategies to effectively navigate risks. Through risk and process analysis, they can identify potential pitfalls and devise appropriate responses. By pinpointing and evaluating elements that could threaten success or hinder strategic objectives, organizations can create processes specifically designed to address and manage these risks.

Typically, risk analysis concentrates primarily on two main factors: the probability of occurrence and the potential impact. Events deemed unlikely or minimally disruptive may not necessitate extensive process

DOI: 10.4324/9781003610557-4

enhancements or contingency measures. This methodology is akin to practices in the insurance and disaster recovery sectors. For instance, actuaries assess likelihood by examining variables such as frequency, predictability, and advance warning. In parallel, they evaluate the impact by considering factors such as duration, consequences, required redundancy, and potential financial losses.

Operational (or process) risk may be applied to both operational processes that are not cyber-related, as well as those that are cyber-related. The security of the overall operation is critically essential to maintaining its operational stance; however, the term "security" is a misnomer, as it encompasses several interpretations and deployments.

Security can refer to the guarantee of safeguarding an operation, small or in its entirety, while continuously maintaining as close to maximum performance and reliability levels without violating any safety protocols, laws, or regulations. This is crucial for industrial operations in which constant, repetitive, and (perhaps) dangerous tasks are performed regularly ad nauseam, utilizing a combination of human control, process control (through the use of procedures), and automation (machine control, some of which is cyber-controlled).

Security can also refer to controls implemented to protect information, access, and control over automated systems. This is cybersecurity. Unfortunately, too much emphasis has been placed on the information itself—at rest, in transit, and in storage—rather than on its processing. Too much emphasis over the past several decades has been devoted to protecting information rather than operations. For most corporations worldwide, information technology departments have assimilated the majority of the business's functions and operations of the overall corporation, often dictating how the business is to function. These departments dictate what is and is not essential to the corporation; thus, the corporation then makes business decisions based on what information technology departments deem as critical to the corporation, not their respective business units or divisions.

Essentially, corporations worldwide have forgotten what security should be implemented for their industrial environments, or they have interpreted security as the latter, more narrow definition above that relates to information, rather than security in the broadest sense. They have been taken over by those organizations that do not fully understand or comprehend the primary role and function of their industrial operations.

Simply put, their operation IS NOT about the information; their operation IS the operation.

Many corporations consider innovative strategies centered around information—its generation, formulation, transference, storage, and, as such, these corporations have become information-based organizations.

Why should executives, board of directors, and their shareholders (if a publicly traded company) be concerned about the minutiae of all tracking data (for example) of how much water pressure on Pipe 1306 at the corner of First Street and Corner Boulevard has been lost? Are they going to make an effective strategic decision based on something that's clearly an operational task? The answer would (and should) clearly be "no." Their roles and purpose for that publicly traded company are to ensure that the corporation is profitable, has suffered no serious or significant financial losses, and can project future quarterly and annual finances.

Why then would a water utility or a power company care about that much information?

That, therein, is the problem. Many cybersecurity programs for such companies focus on innovating information, rather than innovating processes. A water utility should focus on better methods of pumping more water through its piping system as quickly and safely as possible, whereas a power plant should focus on improving methods of generating more power using less fuel, also as quickly and safely as possible.

The problem is, unfortunately, the term "operational cybersecurity risk"[1] is often associated with the term "information cybersecurity risk,"[2] meaning the two are one and the same (as simply called "cybersecurity"). This is inaccurate.

Operational cybersecurity risk focuses (or should focus) on the operational process—how the industrial operation should continue its operation to produce a product or service safely, reliably, and efficiently. In contrast, information cybersecurity risk focuses on the information process for accessing, viewing, and controlling processes that could interfere with the industrial operation.

The operational process is the industrial operation; its focus is on producing something safely, reliably, and performing within tolerable specifications as designed. The business process is the financial operation; its focus is on generating financial revenue and wealth for the company. The two are divergent from each other.

The corporation is more concerned about external attacks to their information flowing into and out of their industrial operational environments, rather than focusing on potential insider threats, and more importantly, failed or substandard systems responsible for critical functions in an industrial operation. It is this mindset—and its culture—that has taken over and engulfed how industrial operations are performed. The corporation is more concerned with information than its operational function(s).

From an operations and engineering perspective, information is the least crucial factor for sustaining an industrial operation. In fact, it was never essential to begin with. It is about control—controlling a process, reliably and safely, and performing at its maximum capability. This is what operations and engineering staff want; this is what they wish to measure. The problem is—this is not what is focused on by the corporate staff. The message is misinterpreted or lost in translation. And once again, because information technology has (pretty much) taken over the majority of the corporation's functions, their focus continues to remain primarily on one and only one thing—information.

Are information technology departments (or divisions) solely responsible for this loss of focus? No, not entirely. Part of the problem focuses on generational shifts within operations and engineering staff—from older staff members who are nearing or have reached retirement, to those staff members who are clearly new to these environments that have existed for decades. Operations and engineering staff are (or were) capable of determining probable cause or post-regression analysis on failed (or near-failed) processes through manual efforts; the processes are ingrained within their years of service to the company. New generations rely on calculators and charts only. One generation created those calculations, formulas, and charts; they know the process(es) because they were the ones who built them. Another generation relies upon information given to them by the previous generation without fully knowing the process(es). And even still, not all previous generational staff members may fully or completely understand the process(es) of the operation.

This is a huge, if not potentially catastrophic, "time bomb" waiting to go off. Few really know what happens inside an industrial operation, and that number is dwindling even further.

In the movie *Idiocracy*, when it was determined that "Brawndo" was no longer necessary, automated information systems began laying employees off, and stock prices plummeted. The outlying issue was—no one really knew how "the system" worked. It was a "black box" that no one understood.[3]

The problem stems from a lack of knowledge of a corporation's own industrial operation. The company knows that it must generate whatever product or service it processes through its industrial operation; it knows that it wants a profitable return-on-investment; and it knows that it wants to avoid any fines or regulatory penalties. But, because its focus is more on information than operation, it has lost its focus entirely on its primary function—(again using our examples above) clean water treatment and distribution, and maximum power generated and transmitted to the electric grids.

Another relevant consequence of this loss of foundational knowledge is the ubiquity of cybersecurity risk methods that attempt to adequately assess the risk of a cybersecurity incident, when well-established and well-proven methods (such as design basis threat (DBT) and process hazard analysis (PHA)) already exist. This reinventing of the wheel highlights a lack of awareness of these key building blocks that can actually produce better results.

4.3 WHY MEASURE CYBERSECURITY RISK?

There is widespread agreement among experts, policymakers, businesses, and the public that cybersecurity is a significant and growing problem. This consensus is driven by the increasing frequency and severity of cyberattacks, the rising costs associated with breaches, and the expanding vulnerabilities in the digital landscape.

There can be little argument that cyberattacks are becoming more frequent, sophisticated, and impactful. For example, the 2023 Verizon Data Breach Investigations Report noted a sharp rise in ransomware attacks and data breaches across industries.[4]

High-profile incidents frequently make the headlines around the world. The Colonial Pipeline billing system ransomware attack, the SolarWinds supply chain attack, and the CrowdStrike Falcon incident all occurred in the last five years, and all underscored the vulnerable and fragile nature of critical infrastructure.

The cost of cyber incidents is also well known. As noted in Chapter 1, some studies estimate the average cost of remediation as $2.73M. The Cost of a Data Breach Report 2024 by IBM estimates the global average cost of a data breach at $4.88 million.[5] Irrespective of which number is used, the cost is significant.

Table 4.1 provides some other examples.[6]

TABLE 4.1 Examples of Cybersecurity Impacts

Organization	Primary Attack Vector	Operational Impact	Estimated Financial Loss
Basset Furniture (2024)	Logistics and supply chain IT encryption	Halted production due to order processing failure	$100M
MKS Instruments (2023)	Manufacturing Execution System	Semiconductor production delays	$250M
JBS Foods (2021)	IT network breach	Nationwide shutdown of meat processing plants	$11M ransom, $250M revenue loss
Toyota (2022)	Supplier ERP system ransomware	Halted production at 14 plants	$375M
Dole (2023)	ERP and inventory system encryption	Global food production disruptions	Undisclosed, estimated hundreds of millions

Beyond monetary costs, breaches harm organizational reputations, erode customer trust, and can result in legal and regulatory penalties. Surveys reveal growing public concern about cybersecurity. For example, a Pew Research Center study showed that many Americans are increasingly worried about data privacy and security threats.[7]

Organizations are aware and are acting. A 2023 Gartner survey found that cybersecurity risk remains a top priority for corporate boards, with many organizations increasing investments in cybersecurity technologies and staff.[8]

If this is the case, why is there a need to write about measuring risk? Chapter 3 highlighted the issues surrounding the misunderstanding and misinterpretation of risk, including how cognitive biases, emotional factors, and group dynamics lead organizations to underestimate or overreact to risks. The consequence of these issues is that organizations ignore significant risks due to overconfidence or focus too much on less relevant threats. Product vendors and consultants compound this problem by spreading fear, uncertainty, and doubt (commonly referred to as "FUD," pronounced as in "Elmer Fudd").[9,10]

Although the term "fear, uncertainty, and doubt" may have existed for well over a century, within the cyber and cybersecurity communities, there are several stories of origin, of which, the more prevalent one describes the acronym "FUD" established sometime in the 1970s by IBM Corporation in an effort to resolve stagnant sales of their mid- to large-range computing platforms. Organizations were sold expensive solutions to address problems that may never arise, while taking resources away from areas that may yield the most significant risk reduction. It was a method of ensuring constant sales of reliable equipment, while also providing additional services that customers generally would not or never need. Like many urban myths and legends, the origin of the term (and its acronym) is unreliable, as more than one origin appears to exist; in truth, no one really knows where the term (and its acronym) came from.

Organizations aiming to mitigate this issue should implement strategies that facilitate the objective assessment of risk. Adopting systematic approaches to evaluate potential threats and vulnerabilities can enhance their decision-making processes and allocate resources more effectively. This proactive stance not only aids in identifying and quantifying risks but also fosters a culture of accountability and transparency within the organization, ultimately leading to more informed and strategic risk management practices.

To address the challenges associated with risk management, organizations must adopt strategies that enable a more thorough and objective evaluation process of identifying and addressing any potential flaws in a business's functions. By employing systematic methodologies to assess various threats and vulnerabilities, these organizations can significantly improve their decision-making capabilities. This structured approach enables a more precise allocation of resources, ensuring that efforts are directed toward the most pressing issues at hand, thereby enhancing overall efficiency.

Fostering this culture prioritizes open communication and shared responsibility regarding risk management, further empowering employees to engage actively. This collective involvement is crucial for developing a comprehensive understanding of any or all risks faced, as well as promoting a unified response to mitigate them.

Ultimately, the implementation of these strategies leads to more informed and strategic practices. Organizations that prioritize systematic assessments are better equipped to navigate uncertainties and make decisions that align with their long-term objectives. This not only enhances their resilience in the face of potential threats but also positions them to capitalize on opportunities that may arise from a well-managed risk landscape.

By prioritizing systematic risk evaluation, these organizations enhance their capacity to withstand potential challenges and threats. This resilience is critical in an ever-evolving and rapidly changing business landscape, where the ability to anticipate and respond to risks can significantly influence an organization's stability and growth. Consequently, such organizations are better prepared to mitigate adverse impacts while simultaneously fostering an environment conducive to seizing emerging opportunities.

Furthermore, a well-structured risk management framework allows such organizations to navigate the complexities of their own operational landscape (and its pitfalls) with greater agility and speed. As they refine their risk management practices, they not only bolster their defenses against potential disruptions but also create a strategic advantage that enables them to leverage favorable conditions. This dual capability of risk mitigation and opportunity capitalization ultimately contributes to a more robust and sustainable organizational performance.

Assessing risk necessitates a comprehensive strategy that encompasses both cybersecurity and process-related risks. This integration of cybersecurity and process risk assessment is essential for a holistic understanding of potential threats. Traditionally, the focus of cybersecurity risks has been on the implications for information integrity and financial stability, as these risks are often associated with data breaches and financial losses, which can have far-reaching effects on an organization's reputation and operational viability. In contrast, process risks prioritize aspects such as the physical safety of personnel and residents, as well as the continuity of operations through the reliability of industrial equipment. By utilizing a hybridized model, organizations can effectively analyze the interactions between these two critical areas, thereby recognizing any common vulnerabilities that may emerge, as well as the interconnected repercussions that may arise from the integration of IT and OT systems.

A hybridized risk assessment model is particularly valuable in today's interconnected landscape, where IT and OT systems are increasingly integrated. This model enables a comprehensive examination of how vulnerabilities in one domain can propagate and exacerbate risks in another. For instance, a cybersecurity breach could lead to disruptions in operational processes, while failures in physical safety protocols could compromise data integrity and security. By recognizing and addressing these interdependencies, organizations can implement more effective risk mitigation strategies that enhance both cybersecurity and operational resilience, ultimately fostering a safer and more secure operational framework.

4.4 WHAT IS INTEGRATED RISK MANAGEMENT?

Risk management in organizations often distinguishes between cybersecurity risk and other types of risk. As already noted, the reality is that the consequences of cybersecurity risk are financial, legal, reputational, operational, safety, or environmental. There are no special cybersecurity consequences. This makes it critical to address risk in an integrated manner.

In the realm of organizational risk management, a clear differentiation is frequently made between cybersecurity and other categories of risk. As highlighted in the initial chapter, it is essential to recognize that any repercussions stemming from cybersecurity threats may often manifest in various forms, including financial losses, legal liabilities, damage to reputation, disruptions to operational processes, safety concerns, and environmental impacts. It is essential to recognize that cybersecurity has no unique consequences that are exclusive to it; instead, they intersect with broader organizational risks. Organizations can better prepare for and mitigate against these multifaceted impacts that may arise from these threats. Such an integrated approach not only enhances the organization's resilience but also ensures that all potential risks are evaluated and addressed cohesively, thereby fostering a more robust risk management strategy.

However, while the contemporary landscape of risk management primarily pertains to a business's day-to-day operations, the consequences of cybersecurity breaches can have far-reaching effects that extend well beyond an organization's operations, emphasizing the need for an integrated perspective that is of paramount importance. Organizations that embrace this holistic view are better equipped to navigate the complexities of most issues, ensuring that they are not only reactive to cybersecurity threats but also proactive in enhancing their overall risk posture.

This strategic alignment ultimately contributes to the long-term sustainability and integrity of the organization from a strategic perspective in an increasingly digital world.

Ultimately, cybersecurity risk must be treated as a larger part of the organization's risk management paradigm, as it is critical for organizations aiming to safeguard their assets while maintaining operational integrity, not to mention promoting their profitability and trust to investors and shareholders.

As stated earlier, acknowledging the interconnectedness of these various risk types, organizations can develop comprehensive strategies that not only address emerging cybersecurity threats but also enhance their overall defensive posture. It is because of this perspective that organizations will need to realize that it is vital for navigating the complexities of today's risk landscape, as any implications of a given cybersecurity incident can reverberate across multiple dimensions of an organization's function, both in its short-term and long-term sustainability. When considering the consequences of cybersecurity risks, organizations must understand the distinction between OT and IT. While the event arising from a cybersecurity incident will impact data integrity, data confidentiality, or system availability, the consequences for IT and OT environments vary. Both can involve financial loss, reputational damage, and regulatory non-compliance. However, impacts in OT environments can also result in severe consequences, such as equipment damage, environmental harm, or endangerment to human life. Understanding this distinction ensures the allocation of appropriate resources and the development of tailored strategies for each environment.

In the realm of cybersecurity, organizations must combine OT and IT when assessing the implications of potential risks. Cybersecurity incidents can compromise various aspects, including data integrity, confidentiality, and system availability. While both domains may experience financial setbacks, damage to reputation, and issues related to regulatory compliance, the stakes are particularly high in OT environments.

The ramifications of cybersecurity breaches in OT can extend beyond mere financial loss or reputational harm, leading to potentially catastrophic outcomes. For instance, incidents affecting OT systems may result in physical damage to critical equipment, pose threats to environmental safety, or even jeopardize human lives. Such severe consequences underscore the necessity for organizations to recognize the unique vulnerabilities and risks associated with OT, which are often not present in traditional IT frameworks; thus, the combined approach is lacking due to missing perceptions from both environments.

Organizations need to allocate their resources better while developing tailored strategies that address the specific needs of each environment, and strive simultaneously for a combined, more hybridized approach. This understanding is vital for implementing effective cybersecurity measures and countermeasures that not only protect data and systems but also safeguard physical assets and human safety. Ultimately, a nuanced approach to cybersecurity that considers the unique characteristics of both IT and OT will enhance an organization's resilience against potential threats. Failing to distinguish between IT and OT environments when considering cybersecurity risk impacts the risk response. The well-known CIA/AIC triad has been used to distinguish the relative priorities of IT and OT environments—confidentiality, integrity, and then availability for IT; and availability, integrity, and then confidentiality for OT. However, this is no longer sufficiently nuanced to describe the differences. For instance, many experts note that availability is crucial for both IT and OT.

The Colonial Pipeline incident is a perfect example. The unavailability of the billing system (due to ransomware infection) resulted in a six-day shutdown of the entire pipeline. The company decided that it could not continue supplying customers unless it could bill them.

Perhaps more crucial is that a focus on confidentiality in IT security has led to a belief that perimeter security should be the focus, often at the expense of other controls. The reality, as noted in Chapter 3, is that the most likely cause of a cybersecurity incident in IT or OT comes from an insider—either negligent (most likely) or malicious (next most likely). The CrowdStrike Falcon incident is a good example—a failure to adequately test an update that was rolled out to millions of users, causing widespread device and service unavailability. The controls needed to mitigate against this risk are not those required to protect a perimeter.

Understanding the relative likelihood and consequences of risks is therefore crucial for organizations. While consequences can be estimated, estimating likelihood is much more difficult. Moreover, the combination of probability and consequence is something most organizations struggle to estimate. For example, it is easy to envisage that the CrowdStrike Falcon incident could result in such a widespread impact (CrowdStrike could have asked "what would happen if we failed to perform regression testing on older channel file formats, and the resulting update was distributed to all customers simultaneously?"). Even if CrowdStrike envisaged this scenario, they did not estimate the possibility to be sufficiently likely to introduce any additional controls (in this case, further testing and oversight of changes). Like many similar companies, they perhaps assumed that their testing was sufficiently comprehensive and that "such a scenario would never happen."

The assessment of both the probability and potential impact of any threat is crucial for organizations aiming to navigate the complexities of their operational environments. While organizations can often quantify the consequences resulting from these threats, accurately predicting their likelihood presents a significant challenge. This difficulty is compounded by the fact that many organizations struggle to evaluate the interplay between probability and consequence, which is crucial for effective risk management—the pertinent example drawn from the CrowdStrike Falcon incident, where the potential for extensive repercussions was evident.

Even if CrowdStrike had contemplated this scenario, they may not have deemed the likelihood of such an event as high enough to warrant the implementation of additional preventive countermeasures. This oversight highlights a common pitfall among organizations, which often leads them to believe that their existing testing protocols are robust enough to mitigate against any risk or threat. This assumption can result in a false sense of security, ultimately leaving organizations vulnerable to unforeseen incidents. The failure to recognize the potential for risk, particularly in the context of technological updates and changes, can have far-reaching consequences that extend beyond immediate operational disruptions.

The case of CrowdStrike serves as a cautionary tale for organizations that may underestimate the importance of thorough risk assessment practices. It underscores the necessity for a more nuanced understanding of both the likelihood and consequences of potential risks, as well as the need for proactive measures in addressing them. By fostering a culture of vigilance and continuous improvement in risk management strategies, organizations can better prepare themselves to handle unexpected challenges. This approach not only enhances their resilience but also contributes to a more secure operational framework, ultimately safeguarding their interests and those of their stakeholders.

By implementing this method, organizations can significantly enhance their ability to navigate adversity while simultaneously maintaining a secure operational environment. This dual benefit is essential for maintaining the integrity of their objectives and safeguarding the interests of all parties involved, thereby promoting a culture of trust and reliability. The adoption of this framework serves to enhance both the resilience of the organization and the security of its operations' processes. In turn, this not only protects the organization's own interests but also those of its stakeholders, creating a comprehensive safety net that supports sustainable growth and long-term success.

Fortunately, for those in OT environments, even if CrowdStrike Falcon were deployed, the convention is to disable automated updates of any kind and test updates before applying them to operational systems. It could be days, weeks, or even months before such an update would be applied to an OT environment, and then only under strict management of change conditions, including a rollback plan in the event of an issue. This is an example of a difference between cybersecurity risk management in IT and OT environments, one that must be understood to maintain safe and reliable operations.

One last aspect that demands an integrated approach to risk management relates to the convergence of IT and OT systems. Although the availability and performance requirements of IT and OT systems may differ, their interdependencies are now unavoidable. Risk management must be performed holistically across the organization to ensure all scenarios and their consequences are considered. This holistic approach will help with resource allocation by combining efforts to ensure the optimized use of limited resources and mitigate high-priority risks.

4.5 IMPLEMENTING INTEGRATED RISK MANAGEMENT

In OT environments, proven risk models and frameworks already exist. Examples include:

- PHA
- Layer of protection analysis (LOPA)
- Control hazard and operability (CHAZOP) studies
- Failure mode and effects analysis and fault tree modeling
- Bowtie diagrams and barrier models

These methods identify shared vulnerabilities and consequences from an operational or process perspective. They can be used to inform cybersecurity risk assessment, or cybersecurity can be incorporated into these models and frameworks. This integrated approach can:

- **Identify Commonalities**—Map cybersecurity risks onto process risks using shared criteria, such as likelihood and consequence.
- **Highlight Interdependencies**—Such as a cyber-attack leading to equipment failure.
- **Develop Shared Controls**—Use hybrid safeguards, such as secure access controls, system redundancy, and operator training, to address process and cybersecurity risks.
- **Simulate Scenarios**—Conduct joint simulations to understand cascading effects. For example, assess how a malware attack could disable safety systems, leading to operational failure.
- **Visualize Interconnections**—Tools like bowtie diagrams help visualize how cyber threats impact physical processes and inform mitigation strategies. They also present risks, consequences, and controls in familiar ways for process and operational experts, helping them have a greater appreciation of their significance.

4.6 MEASURING CYBERSECURITY RISK

Measuring cybersecurity risk involves systematically evaluating the potential consequences of cyber threats and vulnerabilities on an organization. The process typically combines quantitative and qualitative methods to identify, assess, and prioritize risks based on likelihood and consequence. Table 4.2 lists the key components of a risk assessment and considerations for their estimation.

TABLE 4.2 Risk Components and Considerations

Component	Considerations
Scope	It is typically easy to identify the assets and systems, but without consideration of the associated operational processes it will be difficult to identify the potential consequences. Criticality of systems is based on many factors but their impact to operational aspects and physical processes is one of the most important to understand.
Data	Organizations may over-categorize some data and under-categorize other data. For example, while process variables or time series data in a control system may not be classified as confidential, the impact of manipulation or loss of this data could be as severe, if not more so, than the loss or manipulation of some confidential data.
Threats	Threat actors are well defined (e.g., hackers, insiders, nation-states) and methods (e.g., phishing, malware, social engineering) are tracked by government agencies and researchers. The challenge is for organizations to consider these threat actors and methods, irrespective of experience or personal bias. For example, many organizations will consider themselves immune to a threat from nation-states because they are "too small." Organizations should also use reports and surveys to inform them on the most likely threat actors and methods (e.g., negligent insider is most likely contributor to an incident).
Vulnerabilities	Government agencies, researchers, and product vendors provide excellent services reporting on technical vulnerabilities in hardware, software, and firmware. Many organizations fail to adequately consider weaknesses in processes and people, such as lack of documented procedures or lack of training despite these being the most likely controls to reduce incidents (e.g., negligent insider) and the lowest cost to implement.
Likelihood	Estimating the likelihood of a cybersecurity incident is the most difficult aspect of risk management, due to various factors including limited data, failure to detect incidents, and concerns over information sharing. Estimating likelihood is discussed later in this chapter.
Consequences	Organizations must evaluate the potential impact on the organization, considering financial, legal, reputational, operational, safety, or environmental categories. Organizations must consider the impact to the operation (e.g., billing), or the process (e.g., oil treatment), rather than the impact to the system itself (e.g., server or network outage.)
Context-specific factors	Organizations must consider industry-specific regulations and interdependencies, such as risks in supply chains or third-party services.

Risk management is a continuous process. All the above components may change over time:

- **Scope**—Changes may be made to systems, underlying operations, or processes.
- **Data**—New data streams may be introduced, or new devices introduced to collect or store data.
- **Threats**—New threat actors may be identified, or changes may occur that affect the influence of existing threat actors (e.g., global conflicts, pandemics), and new tactics will be discovered.
- **Vulnerabilities**—New flaws will be reported in products that require patching or the introduction of compensating controls.
- **Likelihood**—Changes in an organization (mergers and acquisitions, new locations, new markets) may result in threat actor interest.
- **Consequences**—Changes to processes may introduce new potential scenarios.
- **Context-Specific Factors**—New supply chain partners or offshoring/reshoring may change threats or vulnerabilities.

As a result, organizations must perform risk management continuously:

- Use various testing and simulation methods (e.g., penetration testing, red-teaming, and tabletop exercises) to validate risk assessments and analyze outcomes to refine likelihood and impact assessments.
- Integrate findings from incident reports and emerging threat intelligence.
- Regularly update risk assessments based on new threats, vulnerabilities, and organizational changes.

4.7 QUALITATIVE AND QUANTITATIVE RISK ANALYSIS

As outlined in Chapter 1, *qualitative risk assessments* are commonly used in many critical infrastructure sectors. They are considered valuable when taking the first steps of the risk analysis process, as they are used for prioritizing any identified risks for further evaluation. They provide some semblance of structure, used with a standard risk assessment method through brainstorming. These forms of assessments are highly effective in strategically identifying many risks and consequences associated with several critical infrastructure sectors and their respective industries. Companies have used results from these assessments to develop and implement both risk and operations management programs. While these types of evaluations may be effective at identifying hazards, they do not quantify the probabilities of any events; thus, assigning any risk rating would be considered subjective and often difficult to substantiate or attest.

A typical qualitative assessment is based on the valuation for each risk by using an assessor's professional judgment and experience. If available, any historic data from any operation (currently in production or similarly previous projects) that details specific risk datums is used as part of the risk assessment. The valuation is conducted by categorizing risks based on their probability of occurrence along with their cost and time impact, as noted in the following example (shown below):

- *Probability Range*—Any risk event with a probability of occurrence of 90% or above would be incorporated into the cost estimate, rather than the risk register. For example, one of the following options may be selected to define the probability of risk occurring:
  - Greater than 70% (but below 90)%.
  - 40% to 70%.
  - 20% to 40%.
  - 5% to 20%.
  - Zero to 5%.
- *Cost Impact*—This option defines the cost impact as a percentage of the baseline cost estimates. This may be applied to both current in-production operations or new projects; this example is projecting costs for a new project:
  - Greater than 70%.
  - 50% to 70%.
  - 25% to 50%.
  - 10% to 25%.
  - Less than 10%.
- *Time Impact*—This option defines the time impact for the production operation outage if the determined event were to occur:
  - Greater than 3 weeks.
  - 2 to 3 weeks.
  - 1 to 2 weeks.
  - Less than one week.
  - One to 3 days.

A sample impact matrix for cost and time is categorized based on the rating scale detailed in Tables 4.3 and 4.4. Impacts are identified as *very high, high, medium, low*, or *very low*.[11]

The formula used would provide a "Risk Value" that is based on probability and impact, both of which are subjectively determined from observed analysis using a weighted average from the impact component.

TABLE 4.3 Qualitative Assessment of Cost Impact Resulting from the Outage

Probability		Cost Consequence				
		> 70%	50–70%	25–50%	10–25%	>10%
	Scale	5	4	3	2	1
Greater than 70%	5	Very High	High	High	Medium	Low
40–70%	4	High	High	Medium	Medium	Low
20–40%	3	High	Medium	Medium	Low	Low
5–20%	2	Medium	Medium	Low	Low	Low
0–5%	1	Low	Low	Low	Low	Very Low

TABLE 4.4 Qualitative Assessment of Time Impact Resulting from the Outage

Probability		Time Consequence				
		> 3 wks	2–3 wks	1–2 wks	>1 week	1–3 days
	Scale	5	4	3	2	1
Greater than 70%	5	Very High	Very High	High	Medium	Low
40–70%	4	Very High	High	High	Medium	Low
20–40%	3	High	High	Medium	Low	Low
5–20%	2	High	Medium	Low	Low	Low
0–5%	1	Low	Low	Low	Low	Very Low

Quantitative risk assessments involve the assignment of factual, data-supported numerical values for assessing probabilities and their consequences. Often, these types of evaluations are used in conjunction with an initial qualitative assessment, focusing on the critical and high-risk areas that have been identified.

In contrast to qualitative methods, *quantitative risk assessments* account for the compounded effects between multiple scenarios (or events). This method involves identifying compounding effects by quantifying possible outcomes and the probability of their occurrence, enabling clearer risk-informed, risk-based decision-making in the face of uncertainty. As there are several methods for performing quantitative risk assessments, some of the more common approaches include conducting a quantitative assessment that can range from basic probability calculations to more complex and complicated models, such as multiple regression models and simulations (e.g., Monte Carlo simulations).

Quantitative assessments minimize human discretion in the collection and analysis process of data obtained, making them more objective, more consistent, more attestable, and less susceptible to any human biases. These analyses are also assessor-neutral; that is, they allow for similar like-for-like comparisons across a wide range of organizations (and their functions).

A significant limitation of quantitative assessments is their limited applicability, as calculated measurements may mask actual complexities in real-life scenarios. Thus, this may cause a skewed perspective, potentially misleading, especially when taken out of context or if the data is misinterpreted. Additionally, there remains the human factor, such that any resultant data must still be interpreted by a human, who will then ascertain which values are critically important, which ones are not, and how they are to be presented.

Quantitative risk analyses are performed against any risks that have been determined and prioritized through a qualitative risk analysis process as potentially (or substantially) impacting a project or a current in-production operation. Quantitative risk analysis is used to quantify these risks in terms of both cost and time impacts. Two types of quantitative risk analysis may be used:[12,13]

- *Formula-based analysis*, which uses a formula to calculate an averaged risk impact for each risk identified using minimum, maximum, and most likely cost and schedule impact categories.
- *Monte Carlo simulation*, which involves simulating anticipated or expected cost and schedule impacts for each risk identified to obtain a range of aggregated values combined with their probabilities.

4.8 FORMULA-BASED ANALYSIS

Utilizing a formula-based analysis is generally quantitative in nature, and under most circumstances, should produce the same results consistently. It uses predefined, already known, and generally accepted mathematical formulas (typically utilizing statistical formulas) to process objectively obtained data. This approach may be as simple as a calculation, such as averaging or determining percentages, or it can be a multi-staged series of calculations to predict future outcomes of potential or upcoming issues.

Some key aspects of this form of analysis include:

- *Predefined formulas*—This method relies on already-existing, generally accepted (and possibly proven) mathematical rules to produce the anticipated and expected results consistently, and with reasonably high reliability of its results.
- *Objective data*—Calculated formulas will use specific, consistent, reliable, and accurate data that is predominantly objective rather than subjective in nature, and that produces useful and meaningful results. The data used for the calculations is proven and confirmed, not arbitrary.
- *Applicability to multiple functions*—Many risk formulations can be applied and used for more than one function. For example, in finance, marketing, engineering, and other fields, a simple averaging method can be employed for the mean and average resultant.

However, there are challenges when using formula-based analysis, summarized in Table 4.5. The challenges arise from the very nature of the

TABLE 4.5 Challenges When Dealing with Formula-Based Analysis

Anticipated Challenge	Possible Solution
Uncertainty of future values of input variables is greater than uncertainty of model parameters.	Develop a scenario-based approach to address model development and calibration challenges, and ensure that model parameters would be applicable no matter the future conditions; the ideal model is to limit errors in conditional forecasts for particular scenarios.
Difficult to establish benchmarks against which performance of the models' predictive capabilities will be evaluated.	Hindsight (after the fact) is not a fair benchmark; research must be drawn on its methodological expertise to devise a systematic approach for comparing the performance of different predictors and calibration methods.
There is no holy grail—cannot observe future conditions before they occur.	Research may have identified a variety of ways for using models in a way to provide informed evaluation values for future conditions; however, this is not guaranteed, but speculated.

problem itself, which might entail determining some (or all) model parameter values for conditions that do not yet exist. They may not be observable, either directly or indirectly.

Analytical tools and simulation models are often used to support the evaluation, design, and planning of tactics used to enhance operational environments and policies aimed at improving OT and control systems. Models usually provide varying levels of detail, scope, granularity, temporal dynamics, and so forth, typically custom-tailored to the needs of a particular study or operation. These models would provide a practical, realistic depiction of the operations under review. Models usually entail mathematical relations and algorithmic processes that ingest specific variables as input and produce the desired output. These relations and processes are often referred to as *parameters*, whose values are estimated for the operations under review. The determination of the values of parameters that govern various aspects of the model is referred to as *calibration*. Calibration methods vary in rigor and complexity depending on the nature of the models and the available data. It inherently requires observation of existing system conditions, as the analyst seeks to estimate model parameter values that match the available observational data as closely as possible.[14]

4.9 MONTE CARLO SIMULATION

Monte Carlo simulation is a mathematical methodology that utilizes repeated random sampling to understand and predict the behavior of complex systems, events, or incidents with inherent uncertainty. Specification involves defining which variables are to be simulated, the calculated distribution of each of these variables (based on the samples collected), and the number of iterations performed. By repeating this process for many iterations, a statistical frequency distribution is created, which then approximates the actual probability distribution for a given result. The random sampling process, averaged over many iterations, is effectively the same as integrating what may be a very difficult or impossible equation.

Typically, five steps are performed, which include (but are not limited to) the following:

- *Define the system(s) (and their model).* As with any system to be analyzed, the first step must identify the system(s) being observed, which includes all relevant input variables, and, if possible, probability distributions. Input variables for the calculation(s) can include:
  - Risk register.[15]

  - Historical records (especially where similar risks were encountered).
    - Actual costs.
    - Time impact.
    - Operations impact.
  - Subject matter experts.
    - Delphi techniques.[16]
    - Interviews of staff, craft workers, retirees, and others who are familiar with the site's operations.
  - Technical records, such as safety reports, previous risk assessments, quality assessments, environmental assessments, etc.

    As data is gathered, sorted, and finalized, it must be reviewed for any bias or misperceived observations. Using such data will skew the net result(s) by "contaminating"[17] the data. Consideration should also note the success of the identified risk methodology and how any potential failure of its handling may be reflected negatively in the impact identified through the method.
- *Produce randomly sampled data*—With each uncertain input variable, the simulation repeatedly draws random values from its defined probability distribution.
- *Calculate sampled data*—The randomly sampled data is then used to perform calculations that will simulate either an entire operation or specific portions of it within the model. Please note that the greater the randomness of "sampled data," the more significant the opportunity for calculated errors. In such circumstances, statistical errors are not reliable, and if there are too many, the entire sampling may need to be discarded.
- *Repeat*[18]—The entire process is repeated iteratively until it is satisfied that a sufficient number of calculations have been performed.
- *Analyze the results*—By collecting outcomes from these calculations, a distribution frequency can be generated from the outputs. The distribution will then provide possible impact scenarios based on threshold settings and configurations, along with the likelihood of the impact scenarios, and the overall scored uncertainty, which is determined through the combination of all calculated factors.

The Monte Carlo simulation allows risk managers capabilities through modeling methodologies where accurately calculating precise probability distribution(s) of outcome(s) is difficult or impossible. Instead, it relies upon random samples and repeated iterations to approximate a distribution of potential outcomes.

4.10 LIKELIHOOD MEASUREMENT

Consider the risk matrix shown in Figure 1.3. The severity rating is classified into different consequence types (health and safety, environmental, financial, reputation, public disruption, and regulatory) and categorized with terms ranging from Low to Severe. The likelihood is categorized in terms of the frequency of occurrence, from Improbable (less than ten years) to Frequent (once a month). The common criticisms of this method from the cybersecurity community are as follows:

- There is insufficient data on cybersecurity incidents to estimate the likelihood accurately.
- Although it may be possible to estimate a financial loss, there is some skepticism that a cybersecurity incident could directly lead to consequences such as injury, death, or damage to the environment.

There is also a genuine concern about such matrices, as they can produce confusing or contradictory results if poorly defined. For instance, in the risk matrix in Figure 1.3, a financial consequence of less than $10,000 is considered low, whereas a loss of more than $1,000,000 is seen as severe. However, if the low-consequence event occurred frequently (once a month), it could cost the organization more than the severe-rated consequence.

Douglas Hubbard and Richard Seiersen offer methods to provide qualified estimates in their book *How to Measure Anything in Cybersecurity Risk*. They suggest two proven statistical methods, Monte Carlo simulation and Bayes' theorem.

In Monte Carlo simulation, a large number (hundreds of thousands or even millions) of scenarios are run to predict the likelihood of a particular event. Using Hubbard and Seiersen's method, it is possible to use Monte Carlo simulation to calculate an estimated range, for instance, the financial impact of a cybersecurity incident, together with a *confidence interval*. This confidence interval, expressed as a percentage, represents the level of certainty that the economic impact will be within the estimated range.[19]

This approach not only provides a quantitative assessment but also enhances the understanding of any uncertainties involved in such events, as this interval serves as an indicator based on the degree of certainty regarding any financial consequences falling within the predicted range. For instance, if the confidence interval is set at 95%, it implies that there is a 95% likelihood that the actual financial impact of the cybersecurity incident will lie within the calculated bounds. This statistical insight is crucial for organizations as it aids in risk management and decision-making processes.

The application of the Monte Carlo simulation in this context not only facilitates a more nuanced understanding of potential financial impacts but also allows organizations to prepare more effectively for adverse events. Through their quantifications, risks associated with any cybersecurity incident, the business can allocate resources more judiciously and develop strategies that are informed by empirical data. Ultimately, this method enhances the overall resilience of organizations in the face of evolving cybersecurity threats, enabling them to navigate uncertainties with greater confidence.

Monte Carlo simulation is already widely used in organizations for other purposes, such as major projects analyzing cost and schedule and to produce risk-based confidence estimates, such as P10, P50, or P90, where *P* stands for *percentile*. Government entities (e.g., UK Ministry of Defense, U.S. Securities and Exchange Commission) all use such ranges in their work.

Using the same ranges to quantify cybersecurity risk should provide a familiar basis for probability.

In addition to providing a qualitative estimate of the impact of a cybersecurity incident, the method provides a way to evaluate the effectiveness of cybersecurity controls. Hubbard and Seiersen call this the *return on control*, calculated using the following formula:[20]

$$Return\ on\ Control = \frac{Reduction\ in\ Expected\ Losses}{Cost\ of\ Control} - 1$$

In the EU Network and Information Systems directive, this return on control is called "appropriate and proportionate."[21] This is another way of saying as low as reasonably practical.

In statistical analysis, one of the primary challenges lies in the fact that the precision of any given estimate is inherently linked to the size of the sample from which it is derived. When sample sizes are small, the potential for error increases, making it difficult to draw reliable conclusions. Concordantly, it is impractical (or impossible) to collect a sample size sufficiently large enough to be accurate. Frequentist statistics, which involves the collection of sample data and estimating mean and standard deviation, works well when the data is normally distributed but is less reliable otherwise. The application of the Bayesian theorem allows for a more nuanced approach to inference, especially when traditional statistical methods may falter due to insufficient data.

By incorporating prior knowledge from previous cases or incidents into the analysis, the Bayesian theorem provides a framework that can yield more robust estimates even when the sample size isn't optimal. This is particularly useful in fields where data collection is expensive or logistically challenging, as it might enable researchers to make better or more informed decisions based on whatever data or information is available.

One of the reasons why cybersecurity is so challenging is the lack of data; more specifically, reliably suitable data. In this case, the Bayesian method can be the best approach, provided there is some data that can be used to refine the estimate. One source of this data can be post-regression analysis. A comprehensive incident response and recovery process must incorporate the collection and analysis of such data to be able to better predict future incidents. By failing to perform this step, organizations are constantly left with very wide confidence intervals that do not help them better plan for future incidents.

Figure 4.1 shows a simplified example. The expectation based on frequentist statistics is the normal bell curve. Using the mean and standard deviation of this curve would indicate a remote probability of an event occurring. This could provide false reassurance.

The strength of the Bayesian theorem lies in its ability to update probabilities as new evidence emerges, thereby refining estimates over time. This dynamic process contrasts sharply with classical statistical methods, which often rely on fixed sample sizes and may not adapt well to new information. Consequently, the Bayesian theorem not only addresses the limitations posed by small sample sizes in cybersecurity but also enhances the overall reliability of statistical inference in uncertain environments, possibly even through better "guesstimates." The term "guesstimate" infers that, even with sufficient information provided, there are or may be lacking pieces to the overall puzzle that would allow for sound decisions. Thus, under extreme or dire circumstances, snap decisions may be made based on a hunch.

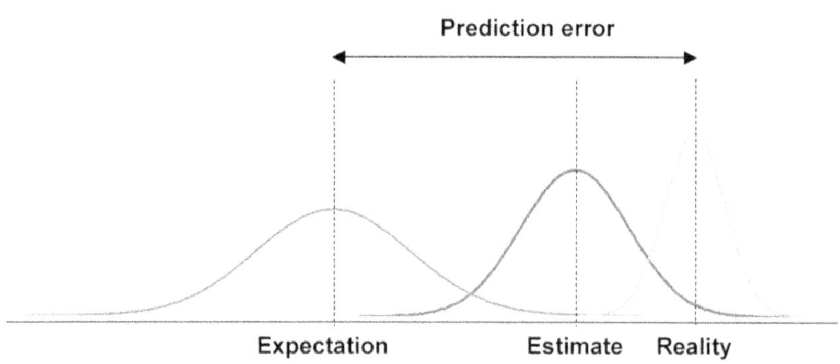

FIGURE 4.1 Frequentist statistics are poor at estimating unlikely events.

Bayes' theorem is explained in more detail by Hubbard and Seiersen.[22] In summary, Bayes' theorem enables the re-estimation of the probability of an event occurring based on a posterior (or prior) estimate and new evidence. The formula is:

$$P(A \mid B) = \frac{P(A)P(B \mid A)}{P(B)}$$

Using Bayes' theorem provides a robust framework for refining estimates, allowing for a more precise approximation of the values. Thus, it is possible to narrow the range of the estimate shown in Figure 4.1 from the wide (expectation) to something approaching reality. This process involves updating prior beliefs with new evidence, thereby enhancing the reliability of the estimates and reducing any possible uncertainties.

The result is still, like in Monte Carlo simulation, a confidence level (e.g., a 90% probability that something will occur), but with more re-estimation, the confidence level improves. However, it should be noted that the key distinction lies in the iterative nature facilitated through the Bayesian theorem.

The integration of this theorem into the estimation process can not only improve the accuracy of any prediction but also provide a more systematic approach to managing uncertainty that may arise. Through continuous updates and with estimates based on any new information, practitioners can achieve a higher degree of confidence in their forecasts, thereby making more informed decisions in various applications. This iterative refinement underscores the importance of evidence-based reasoning in statistical analysis and decision-making.

4.11 CONSEQUENCE MEASUREMENT

Consequence measurement in the context of risk refers to the systematic approach employed to address and mitigate the impacts of adverse events or incidents that may arise from identified risks. This process encompasses a range of strategies and actions aimed at minimizing negative effects on individuals, organizations, and their environments. By focusing on the aftermath of risk events, consequence measurement seeks to ensure that appropriate measures are in place to respond effectively, thereby safeguarding resources and maintaining operational continuity.

The framework of consequence measurement involves several key components, including assessment, planning, response, and recovery. Initially, it requires a thorough evaluation of potential consequences associated with various risk scenarios, which informs the development of contingency plans tailored to specific situations. These plans outline the necessary steps to be taken in the event of an incident, including communication protocols, resource allocation, and coordination among stakeholders. The effectiveness of consequence measurement is contingent upon the preparedness of an organization to implement these plans swiftly and efficiently when faced with an actual risk event.

Therefore, it is not a static process; it is a continuous process that necessitates constant monitoring and improvement. Organizations must regularly review and update their risk assessments and response strategies to adapt to changing circumstances and emerging threats. This dynamic approach ensures that lessons learned from past incidents are integrated into future planning, thereby enhancing resilience and reducing vulnerability. Effective consequence measurement plays a crucial role in fostering a proactive risk culture, where organizations are better equipped to handle uncertainties and protect their interests in an increasingly complex risk landscape.

Another illustrative case of consequence measurement can be observed in the realm of environmental disasters, such as oil spills. When an oil spill occurs, the immediate response involves containment and cleanup efforts to limit environmental damage. However, consequence measurement extends beyond these initial actions. It encompasses the assessment of ecological impacts, the restoration of affected habitats, and the implementation of policies to prevent future spills. This multifaceted approach ensures that the long-term consequences of the disaster are addressed, fostering resilience in both the environment and the communities that depend on it.

Within the corporate environment, consequence measurement is crucial in the event of a data breach. For instance, when a company experiences a cyberattack that compromises sensitive customer information, the immediate response may involve securing systems and notifying affected individuals. However, effective consequence measurement requires a comprehensive strategy that includes forensic investigations to understand the breach, legal compliance to mitigate liability, and the development of enhanced cybersecurity measures to prevent future incidents. By addressing both the immediate and long-term consequences of the breach, organizations can restore trust in their overall risk management framework.

In contrast, industrial environments, such as power plants, face their own unique set of challenges regarding consequence measurement. The operational complexities and safety-critical nature of these facilities require a different framework for managing consequences, particularly in the event of a security incident or operational failure. Here, the focus extends beyond data protection to encompass physical safety, environmental impact, and regulatory compliance, highlighting the need for comprehensive risk management strategies that integrate both cybersecurity and operational integrity.

The comparison between corporate and industrial consequence measurement reveals distinct priorities and methodologies tailored to their respective contexts. While corporations may prioritize data integrity and customer trust, industrial settings must emphasize safety protocols and environmental stewardship. This divergence necessitates a nuanced understanding of the specific risks and consequences associated with each sector, ultimately guiding the development of targeted management strategies that address the unique challenges posed by data breaches and operational disruptions in their respective environments.

4.12 RISE MEASUREMENT

Most conventional cybersecurity risk methodologies use likelihood and consequence to create an overall risk measurement, employing a matrix such as the one shown in Figure 1.3. This methodology is analogous to that used in estimating safety risk. This may not be sufficiently nuanced for presenting cybersecurity risk. While vast quantities of data exist to allow estimation of safety incident likelihood, the same is not true for cybersecurity. This, together with all the biases described in Chapter 3, means that a simple likelihood/consequence perspective may not be sufficient to understand the risk.

Hillstrong proposes one way to improve this understanding. They define a calculation called RISE that incorporates the following four measures:

- Risk exposure (R) and Impact (I) are the likelihood and consequence as measured in conventional methodologies.
- Speed of recovery (S) and Effort to mitigate (E) are additional measures that provide additional insight into the cybersecurity risk. Like risk exposure and impact, the methodology assigns a value (e.g., 1–5, 1–10, etc., the same range used for likelihood and consequence) to these, indicating the increasing time to recover or effort required to mitigate, respectively.

Speed of recovery is an estimate of the time required to restore affected systems. An effort to mitigate is a measure of the level of difficulty in implementing controls.

The resulting RISE score is the product of these measures. Hillstrong also assigns weighting to each measure, which allows organizations to adjust the significance of measures to suit their particular situation.

TABLE 4.6 RISE Scoring for JBS Foods 2021 Incident

Factor	Score (1–10)	Weighted Contribution
Risk Exposure (R)	9 (JBS was a high-profile target)	9 × 0.3 = 2.7
Impact on Production (I)	10 (Halted all U.S. meat processing operations)	10 × 0.3 = 3.0
Speed of Recovery (S)	5 (Took 4 days, so moderate)	5 × 0.2 = 1.0
Effort to Mitigate (E)	8 (Complex network dependencies made recovery difficult)	8 × 0.2 = 1.6
Total RISE Score	**8.3/10**	**High Risk**

Using this method, Hillstrong estimates the RISE score for the JBS Foods ransomware attack of 2021. In this case, they use a score of 1–10 for each measure, and weightings of 0.3, 0.3, 0.2, and 0.2 for risk exposure, impact on production, speed of recovery, and effort to mitigate, respectively. The result is a total RISE score of 8.3 out of 10, for example, extremely high. This is shown in Table 4.6.[23]

Although the combined risk exposure and impact on production would have indicated a high risk, neither factor is entirely within their control. Being a high-profile target cannot be changed, and the impact on production if an incident occurs cannot be entirely removed. Adding the speed of recovery and effort to mitigate helps communicate to leadership two factors that are within their control. By introducing better mitigation controls to reduce the time to recover, or better prevention controls to reduce the likelihood of an incident would reduce the total RISE score.

For example, implementing RISE scoring methodologies in the context of nuclear power plants is essential for enhancing safety protocols and operational efficiency. This approach involves the systematic assessment of potential risks associated with various operational scenarios, enabling the quantification of measures that can be monitored over time. By applying this scoring system, stakeholders can identify critical vulnerabilities within the plant's infrastructure and operational procedures, thereby facilitating informed decision-making regarding necessary improvements and resource allocation. In the nuclear energy sector, the application of RISE scoring serves as a proactive measure to mitigate potential hazards. This scoring system evaluates the likelihood and impact of various factors, including equipment failure, human error, and external threats. Using a clear framework for assessing these risks, nuclear generation facilities can prioritize their safety measures and implement targeted strategies to address the most pressing concerns, ultimately leading to a more resilient operational environment.

4.13 THE IMPORTANCE OF UNDERSTANDING PROCESS RISK

Process risk is regarded as a critical aspect of operational security due to its inherent focus on the vulnerabilities and potential failures within organizational processes that can lead to significant operational disruptions. Unlike traditional IT cybersecurity, which primarily addresses threats to information systems and data integrity, process risk encompasses a broader spectrum of risks associated with the execution of business operations. This includes evaluating workflows, human factors, and the interaction of various systems and technologies that contribute to an organization's overall operational effectiveness. By identifying and mitigating process risks, organizations can enhance their resilience against disruptions that may arise from both internal and external sources.

The distinction between process risk and traditional IT cybersecurity lies in their respective scopes and methodologies. Traditional IT cybersecurity is predominantly concerned with protecting digital assets from cyber threats such as malware, hacking, and data breaches. It employs a range of technical measures, including firewalls, encryption, and intrusion detection systems, to safeguard information systems. In contrast, process risk management takes a more holistic approach, examining not only the technological components but also the organizational culture, employee behavior, and procedural adherence that can impact operational security. This comprehensive perspective allows for the identification of risks that may not be immediately apparent through a purely IT-focused lens.

As such, implications of process risk extend well beyond the realm of information technology, influencing overall business continuity and strategic decision-making. Organizations that prioritize process risk management are better equipped to anticipate and respond to potential disruptions, thereby safeguarding their operational integrity and stability. This proactive stance fosters a culture of continuous improvement, where processes are regularly assessed and refined to effectively mitigate risks. In contrast, traditional IT cybersecurity often reacts to threats as they arise, which may leave organizations vulnerable to unforeseen operational challenges. Thus, understanding and addressing process risk is essential for achieving a robust operational security framework that supports long-term organizational success.

The assessment of any inferences associated with process risk and operational security within industrial settings is a testy and critical area of study. This involves a comprehensive evaluation of how various risks can impact operational efficiency and safety. By systematically measuring these consequences, organizations can identify vulnerabilities in their processes and implement strategies to mitigate potential threats. This approach not only enhances the resilience of industrial operations but also ensures compliance with regulatory standards and promotes a culture of safety. In the context of industrial environments, measuring consequences related to process risk encompasses a range of factors, including the likelihood of incidents, the severity of potential outcomes, and the effectiveness of existing security measures. This multifaceted analysis requires the integration of quantitative and qualitative methodologies to provide a holistic view of operational security.

Advanced risk assessment tools and techniques enable organizations to prioritize their risk management efforts and allocate resources more effectively, thereby minimizing disruptions and safeguarding their assets. Furthermore, the ongoing monitoring and evaluation of process risks and operational security are essential for maintaining a robust industrial framework. As technologies and operational practices evolve, so too do the associated risks. Therefore, continuous improvement in consequence measurement practices is necessary to adapt to changing conditions and emerging threats. This dynamic approach not only protects the integrity of industrial operations but also fosters innovation and competitiveness in an increasingly complex global market.

One prominent example can be found in the chemical manufacturing sector, where the potential for hazardous material leaks necessitates rigorous consequence assessments. By evaluating the impact of such incidents, companies can implement appropriate safety measures, such as enhanced containment systems and emergency response protocols, thereby minimizing the risk to both personnel and the surrounding community. This proactive approach not only safeguards human life but also protects the environment from potential contamination.

Another significant application of consequence measurement is evident in the oil and gas industry, particularly in offshore drilling operations. Here, the consequences of operational failures, such as blowouts or equipment malfunctions, can be catastrophic, leading to environmental disasters and substantial financial losses.

Systematically analyzing the potential outcomes of various risk scenarios enables organizations to develop robust risk management strategies that incorporate regular maintenance schedules, advanced monitoring technologies, and comprehensive training programs for personnel. This thorough assessment of consequences enables companies to mitigate risks effectively and maintain operational integrity.

For the manufacturing sector, especially in the context of automated production lines, this illustrates the importance of consequence measurement in operational security. In this environment, the failure of machinery or cyber-attacks can disrupt production processes, leading to significant economic repercussions. By quantifying the potential consequences of such disruptions, manufacturers can prioritize investments in cybersecurity measures and equipment upgrades to mitigate these risks. This strategic focus on consequence measurement not only enhances the resilience of production systems but also fosters a culture of safety and security within the organization, ultimately contributing to long-term sustainability and success.

4.14 THE CHALLENGES OF OVERSIMPLIFICATION

Organizational and behavioral factors impact the effectiveness of risk measurement.

One factor is that organizations often prefer linear models over hyperbolic ones due to their simplicity and ease of interpretation. Linear models facilitate clearer communication and decision-making processes for executive corporate management, allowing them to grasp complex data more readily. However, the reality of operational dynamics is that most phenomena do not conform to a straight line. When organizations attempt to apply linear data models, particularly in contexts where cybersecurity intersects with safety, they are in peril to misrepresentation of the complexities of a given assessment.

This oversimplification can lead to significant inaccuracies in evaluating potential threats.

The RISE scoring system exemplifies a weighted data model that acknowledges the multifaceted nature of performing assessments. While it is not without its limitations, the RISE system offers a framework for understanding various outcomes based on these weighted factors. This approach enables organizations to consider a range of potential scenarios, rather than relying solely on a limited perspective through linear modeling with a minimal dataset.

By incorporating multiple variables and their respective weights, the RISE scoring system aims to provide a more nuanced understanding of risk, particularly within the intricate domains of cybersecurity and safety. The reliance on these linear models for business decision-making can obscure the complexities inherent in real-world situations. As organizations navigate the challenges posed by cybersecurity threats, it is crucial to adopt more sophisticated modeling techniques that reflect the dynamic nature of these cyber threats. The RISE scoring system, while not flawless, represents a step toward embracing a more comprehensive approach. Through recognition that there are limitations to most linear models, through the integration of this weighted data, businesses can enhance their ability to make informed decisions in an increasingly complex landscape.

4.15 SOCIALIZATION OF GROUP DYNAMICS IN RISK-BASED DECISIONS

Another factor affecting risk measurement is behavioral. A pertinent example can be drawn from the field of public health, particularly in the management of infectious disease outbreaks. When a new virus emerges, health authorities must implement a series of measures to mitigate the impact on the population. This includes not only immediate responses (also referred to as "immediate mitigation controls"), such as quarantine and vaccination campaigns, but also long-term strategies (also referred to as "preventative mitigation controls") like enhancing healthcare infrastructure and improving surveillance systems. By managing the consequences of the outbreak, authorities can minimize morbidity and mortality rates while also preparing for future incidents.

The awareness of an event occurring and any subsequent actions taken in response to that event represent a fundamental distinction in human behavior and decision-making processes. Recognizing that something has transpired is merely the first step in a continuum of engagement with that reality. This awareness can lead to a range of emotional and cognitive responses, but it is the transition from recognition to action that delineates a proactive approach from a passive one. The ability to distinguish between merely acknowledging an occurrence and actively addressing it is crucial in various contexts, including personal development, social responsibility, and organizational effectiveness.

When individuals or groups become aware of a situation, they're faced with the choice of either remaining passive observers or becoming active participants in the resolution of the issue at hand. Various factors, including personal values, social norms, and the perceived urgency of the situation, influence this choice. This distinction between knowing and doing is not only a matter of individual agency but also reflects broader societal dynamics, where collective action can lead to significant change.

The interplay between individual agency and social structure is a subject of considerable academic debate. Scholars often explore the extent to which social systems impose constraints on an individual's personal actions and choices. While some argue that social structures significantly limit individual agency by dictating the available options and shaping the context in which decisions are made, others contend that individuals possess the capacity to navigate and sometimes transcend these limitations. This ongoing discourse highlights the complexity of human behavior and the multifaceted nature of social influence.

Relationships between individual agency and business decision-making processes are underscored by the need for a supportive organizational culture that encourages autonomy and critical thinking. Leaders must recognize the importance of empowering their teams to make informed decisions, as this fosters a sense of ownership and responsibility.

Cultivating an environment where individuals are valued can enhance an organization's overall effectiveness in consequence management. This synergy between individual decision-making and organizational strategy ultimately leads to more informed, agile, and resilient business practices, enabling companies to thrive in an increasingly complex and competitive landscape.

In the context of cybersecurity, decisions that are made play a significant role in shaping the responses to threats, as employees at all levels are often the first line of defense against cyber incidents. Their ability to recognize suspicious activities, report anomalies, and adhere to security protocols can significantly impact the effectiveness of an organization's cybersecurity framework. However, when groupthink prevails, there is a tendency to conform to prevailing opinions or practices, which can stifle innovation and critical thinking. This dynamic can lead to complacency, where individuals may fail to question established procedures or challenge the status quo, thereby increasing vulnerability to cyberattacks.

Through balancing the strengths of individuals' initiatives with the collaborative insights of group dynamics, organizations can develop a more robust cybersecurity strategy that not only anticipates potential threats but also adapts to the evolving landscape of cyber risks. This can be achieved through training programs that empower employees to take ownership of their cybersecurity responsibilities while also promoting a culture of open communication and constructive feedback.

This, too, is an area where the RISE method can be helpful. Identifying the factors that measure risk is the first step. Recognizing that risk exposure (R) and impact on production (I) are outside of anyone's control, but that speed of recovery (S) and effort to mitigate (E) can be used to empower teams to focus on the things they can do, and observe the impact in an improved RISE score.

4.16 ANTICIPATED RISKS TO CYBER SYSTEMS OF CRITICAL INFRASTRUCTURES

The landscape of cyber threats is evolving (very) rapidly, particularly concerning critical infrastructures, which are essential for the functioning and well-being of our society. Over the next two decades, experts anticipate a significant increase in the frequency and sophistication of cyberattacks targeting these vital systems.[24]

These attacks may manifest in various forms, including ransomware incidents that could cripple essential services, advanced persistent threats that infiltrate networks to steal sensitive data, and distributed denial-of-service attacks aimed at overwhelming systems to disrupt operations. The potential for state-sponsored cyber warfare is also a growing concern, as nations may leverage cyber capabilities to undermine the stability of their adversaries. As technology continues to advance, the interconnectivity of critical infrastructures will likely create new vulnerabilities that cybercriminals can exploit. The integration of Internet of Things devices into critical systems, such as power grids, water supply networks, and transportation systems, presents a double-edged sword. While these technologies can enhance efficiency and monitoring, they also expand the attack surface for malicious actors. Consequently, the next two decades may witness a surge in attacks that leverage these vulnerabilities, leading to significant disruptions in essential services and potentially catastrophic consequences for public safety and (perhaps even) national security. In response to these anticipated threats, it is imperative for governments and organizations to adopt a proactive approach to cybersecurity. This includes investing in advanced security technologies, fostering increased or enhanced and revised collaboration between public and private sectors, while developing comprehensive incident response strategies. And lastly, there is a pressing need for ongoing training and awareness programs to equip personnel with the skills necessary to identify and mitigate cyber threats by defined prioritizing cybersecurity measures and fostering a culture of resilience. Stakeholders can better prepare for the challenges posed by the evolving cyber threat landscape over the next 20 years.

Not to focus too much on threats and vulnerabilities as opposed to measuring it, cyber threat actors have increasingly demonstrated their ability to identify and exploit vulnerabilities in human-machine interfaces (HMIs) that are accessible via the Internet. A notable incident which occurred sometime in 2024, pro-Russia hacktivists targeted HMIs within water and wastewater management systems.[25,26]

Their actions led to the manipulation of critical equipment, including water pumps and blowers, which were forced to operate beyond their designed parameters. This breach not only highlighted the ease with which such systems can be compromised but also underscored the pressing need for enhanced cybersecurity measures in critical infrastructure.

In the aforementioned incident, the hacktivists employed a range of tactics to achieve their objectives. They maximized operational set points, modified various system settings, disabled alarm systems, and altered administrative passwords, effectively locking out the legitimate operators of the water utility. This multifaceted approach not only disrupted the normal functioning of the water systems but also poses significant risks to public safety and operational integrity. The ability to manipulate these systems with relative ease raises serious concerns about the robustness of existing cybersecurity protocols in place to protect essential services. The consequences of such cyber intrusions were profound, forcing the affected water systems to abandon automated processes and revert to manual operations.

This shift not only increased the workload for utility operators but also heightened the risk of human error in managing critical resources.

The operational disruptions experienced by these facilities serve as a stark reminder of the vulnerabilities inherent in modern infrastructure, emphasizing the urgent need for comprehensive cybersecurity strategies that can effectively safeguard against such malicious activities.

As the landscape of cyber threats continues to evolve, it is imperative that organizations prioritize the fortification of their systems to mitigate whatever risks were posed by the increasingly sophisticated adversaries.

This proactive approach is crucially necessary in order to effectively address the threats presented by adversaries as they're becoming increasingly sophisticated in their tactics and techniques. By focusing on enhancing their security measures, organizations can better prepare themselves to face the challenges posed by these evolving threats. Additionally, the emphasis and implementation of sound recovery and diligent mitigation strategies definitely play a vital role in reducing overall risk—essentially, the sooner to recover, the sooner to restoring operations and generating revenue. Organizations that invest in robust incident response strategies and recovery plans are better equipped to handle potential breaches or attacks. This not only minimizes the impact of such incidents but also fosters a culture of resilience, enabling organizations to bounce back more quickly and maintain operational continuity in the face of adversity. The combination of continuously fortifying systems while prioritizing rapid recovery efforts creates a comprehensive defense strategy against cyber threats. Through the adoption of a proactive program, organizations can significantly diminish their "vulnerability footprint" to attacks while simultaneously enhancing their ability to respond effectively when incidents occur. This duality of focus on prevention and recovery is essential for navigating the complexities of the modern cyber landscape and ensuring long-term security and stability.

A "vulnerability footprint" is the method by which an organization proactively, continuously, and regularly deploys updated countermeasures (such as patching, periodic reviews of systems' integrity against new vulnerabilities, etc.) for the ever-rapidly-changing landscapes, while at the same time reducing and then maintaining as small of risk to the organizations' overall operation as possible. This never-ending cyclical process of constant improvement, though potentially costly, is now necessary for organizations to profitably exist today; essentially, it now has become the part of doing business.

4.17 MERGING PROCESS RISK AND CYBERSECURITY

Although originally developed and utilized by engineers specifically for identifying unintentionally designed flaws in a given design specification, generally, the term "design basis threat" refers to a set of potential challenges and risks that a facility or system must be prepared to address in its design and operational protocols. This concept is particularly relevant in the context of critical infrastructure and national security, where understanding the nature of threats is essential for ensuring the safety and resilience of systems. This term encompasses a range of scenarios, including various forms of attacks, natural disasters, and other disruptive events that could compromise the integrity and functionality of a facility. It has been used almost exclusively by the nuclear generation industry; however, based upon its premise to predictively ascertain threats before they happen within their engineered design, it could (possibly) be applied to any industrial and manufacturing-based operation for every critical infrastructure using OT.

However, due to the rapidly emerging uses of cyber-based systems (and their threats) in industrial- and manufacturing-based environments, by defining and applying cybersecurity-based threats in conjunction with this methodology, organizations must now conduct thorough risk assessments in identifying and evaluating the most plausible (the term "plausible" is based on who is observing the threat) and impactful threats they may face. This process involves analyzing historical data, current intelligence, and emerging trends in security threats to create a comprehensive profile of potential adversaries and their capabilities. Through careful analytics defining these potential threats, organizations can implement appropriate security measures, engineering controls, and operational strategies that align with the identified risks, thereby enhancing their overall preparedness and response capabilities.

Today, as far as risk management and cybersecurity pertain to DBTs, it serves as a foundational element in the development of a hybridized security framework (and its protocols) through the combined engineered design and construction efforts of physical barriers, surveillance systems, emergency response plans, and cyber system implementations, ensuring that they are tailored to effectively mitigate the identified risks. By integrating this concept into planning processes, organizations can foster a proactive security culture that prioritizes resilience and adaptability in the face of evolving threats. Though many organizations may not see using such predictive (forecasted) analysis within their industrial operations, some industries, such as nuclear generation, air traffic control, and petrochemical refining, practically dictate the necessitation for using such processes.

One area of contention is if there is a differentiation of DBTs, external and internal. The distinction between external and internal DBTs is significant in the context of cybersecurity and system integrity. External threats typically originate from outside the organization, encompassing a range of malicious activities such as hacking, phishing, and other forms of cyberattacks that exploit vulnerabilities in a system's architecture. In contrast, internal threats arise from within the organization, often involving employees or contractors who may intentionally or unintentionally compromise system security (often associative with the term "insider-based threat"). Understanding these differences is crucial for developing effective security protocols and risk management strategies, as each type of threat requires tailored approaches to mitigate potential risks.

For example, a non-malicious, unintentional threat, introduced by an OT hardware manufacturer, might be the continued support of discontinued and end-of-line products. The implications of these threats extend to the management of firmware patches and updates, particularly for discontinued control systems that no longer receive active support from manufacturers. When a system is no longer supported, it becomes increasingly vulnerable to both external and internal threats, as any discovered vulnerabilities will not be addressed through official updates. This lack of support necessitates a proactive approach from organizations, which may involve implementing their own security measures or seeking third-party solutions to safeguard against potential exploits. The absence of the manufacturers' support can complicate the process of applying firmware patches, as organizations must navigate the challenges of ensuring compatibility and effectiveness without official guidance. Additionally, some industries, such as nuclear electric generation, are bogged down by layers of regulatory requirements (and paperwork) that must be addressed before even considering replacement, often taking years to replace just one piece of a collective whole of a given system (or its sub-system). Furthermore, the impact of these DBTs on firmware management is compounded by the evolving landscape of cybersecurity. As new vulnerabilities are discovered and attack vectors become more sophisticated, organizations must remain vigilant in their efforts to protect outdated systems. This may involve conducting regular security assessments, investing in additional training for personnel, and developing contingency plans to address potential breaches. Ultimately, the interplay between external and internal threats and the management of firmware updates underscores the necessity for organizations to adopt a comprehensive and adaptive security posture, particularly when dealing with legacy systems that lack ongoing manufacturer support. For some industries, such as (once again) the nuclear electric generation industry, oftentimes, manufacturers will extend warranties, working hand-in-hand with their customers, to resolve the matter involving replacement of discontinued items with newly supported items. Nonetheless, discontinued and end-of-line products do pose a serious risk to several critical infrastructures industries, as simply swapping out one electronic device for another is not as simple as swapping computer servers.

The exploration of DBT models is essential for understanding the various frameworks that guide security assessments and risk management in different environments. These models serve as foundational tools for organizations to identify potential threats and vulnerabilities, allowing them to develop appropriate countermeasures. A comprehensive analysis of existing threat models reveals a variety of approaches, each tailored to address specific security concerns and operational contexts.

One prominent model is the "Strawman Threat" Model, which provides a simplified framework for identifying potential threats by outlining hypothetical scenarios that could impact an organization. This model encourages stakeholders to engage in discussions about security risks, fostering a collaborative environment for threat identification. Initially an IT-based model, the Strawman Threat Model represents a sophisticated framework aimed at addressing the visualization and analytical requirements of simulation code teams engaged in multi-physics computations on exa-scale computing platforms. Its architecture is informed by essential needs articulated by a variety of simulation coding teams, which emphasize the importance of efficient utilization of shared resources, the capability for batch processing, the ability to harness contemporary computing architectures, and a user-friendly interface that facilitates both software integration and operational use during simulation activities—much of which can be applied to OT-based environments.[27]

Another significant model is the "Attack Tree" Model, which visually represents the various ways an adversary could exploit vulnerabilities to achieve a specific goal.[28] This model allows for a systematic analysis through a visual representation of potential attack vectors, assists organizations prioritize their security efforts based on the likelihood and impact of different threats, allowing security professionals to analyze the best possible paths an adversary might take to exploit any vulnerabilities discovered. This is applied through two approaches to its analysis: inductive and deductive. An example is shown in Figure 4.2, showing a simplified view of various ways a SCADA system could be compromised.

In the realm of system analysis, the delineation of failure, particularly in its complete form, is relatively straightforward. This clarity stands in stark contrast to the complexities involved in defining "success." The multifaceted nature of success encompasses a variety of dimensions that are not easily quantifiable or reducible to simple metrics. As a result, the analytical framework surrounding success is often less precise, making it more challenging to establish clear criteria for what constitutes a successful outcome. This inherent ambiguity underscores the difficulties faced when attempting to measure success in a systematic manner.

Given these complexities, the exploration of failure space in analytical contexts proves to be significantly more advantageous than that of success space. The ability to clearly identify and categorize failure events allows for a more structured approach to understanding system performance and reliability. By focusing on the parameters and conditions that lead to failure, analysts can derive valuable insights that

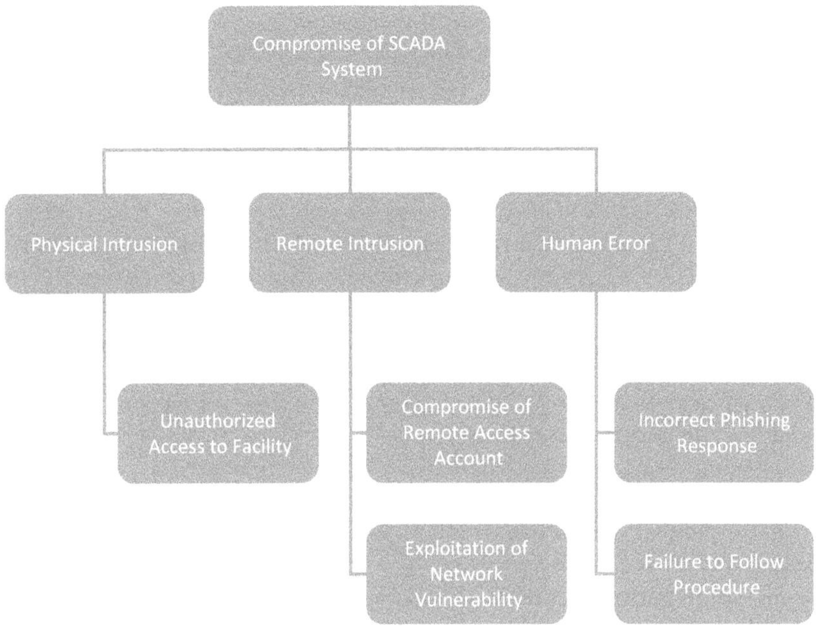

FIGURE 4.2 Example attack tree.

inform improvements and optimizations within a system. Consequently, the emphasis on failure analysis not only enhances the understanding of potential pitfalls but also contributes to the overall enhancement of system design and functionality.

The "Kill Chain" model, developed by Lockheed Martin,[29] offers a structured approach to understanding the stages of a cyberattack, from initial reconnaissance to the final objective. By breaking down the attack process into distinct phases, this model enables organizations to identify critical points where defensive measures can be implemented to disrupt the attacker's progress. Each of these models contributes to a more nuanced understanding of security threats, allowing organizations to tailor their defenses to the specific risks they face.

The framework can be utilized to enhance security measures by providing a structured approach to threat detection and response. For instance, during the reconnaissance phase, attackers may gather information about the ICS architecture, network configurations, and operational protocols. By understanding this phase, organizations can deploy monitoring tools to detect unusual scanning activities or unauthorized access attempts. Furthermore, as the attack progresses through its stages such as delivery, exploitation, and installation, critical infrastructure operators can establish robust incident response protocols that are more custom-tailored to the unique characteristics of their systems, ensuring that they can quickly identify and neutralize threats before they escalate.

The application of the framework to OT not only aids in the identification of potential attack vectors (an "attack vector" is a method by which a potential attacker attempts to break into or subversively enter an otherwise restricted area) but also fosters a proactive security posture.[30] By integrating the principles of the kill chain into their cybersecurity strategies, organizations can enhance their resilience against cyber threats, ensuring the integrity and availability of critical infrastructure. This approach emphasizes the importance of continuous monitoring, regular security assessments, and employee training, all of which are essential components in safeguarding industrial control systems from the evolving landscape of cyber threats.

Additionally, some industries have implemented hybridized approaches by combining multiple cybersecurity frameworks together. Many organizations feel that combining multiple analytic models may help cover any gaps that one may have over another. One such example is the combination of the "Kill Chain" with the "Attack Tree" model. The integration of the cyber kill chain and attack tree analysis frameworks presents a multifaceted approach to enhancing cybersecurity measures. The cyber kill chain, which delineates the stages of a cyberattack from reconnaissance to execution, provides a structured methodology for understanding and mitigating threats. By employing this hybridized framework, organizations can identify vulnerabilities at each phase of an attack, allowing for proactive measures to be implemented. This systematic breakdown not only aids in the detection of potential intrusions but also facilitates a more comprehensive understanding of the attack vectors that adversaries may exploit.

In conjunction with the cyber kill chain, attack tree analysis serves as a powerful tool for identifying and analyzing the root causes of system failures. Unlike the kill chain which is a contiguous never-ending cycle, the attack tree employs a one-time top-down approach to dissect complex systems, enabling security professionals to visualize the interdependencies and potential points of failure within their cybersecurity infrastructure. When combined with the cyber kill chain, the attack tree enhances the ability to assess individual or targeted likelihoods of specific attack scenarios and their potential impact on organizational assets. This synergy allows for a more thorough risk assessment, ensuring that both preventative and responsive strategies are informed by a detailed understanding of system vulnerabilities. Moreover, the collaborative use of these frameworks fosters a culture of continuous improvement in cybersecurity practices. By regularly analyzing incidents through the lens of both the cyber kill chain and attack tree analysis, organizations can refine their security protocols and incident response strategies. This iterative process not only strengthens the overall security posture but also cultivates a more resilient organizational environment capable of adapting to the evolving threat landscape. Ultimately, the combined application of these frameworks equips organizations with the necessary insights to anticipate, mitigate, and respond to cyber threats effectively.

4.18 SOLVE THE PAST, FACE THE FUTURE

As there is the need for determining risk in both current and future states, there is an even greater need for learning from past events or incidents. Though there are several forms of past historical reasoning models, performing post-regression analysis is by far probably the best model to use for determining risk measurements from past events or incidents.

Post-regression measurements can be long and complex, but with safety thrown into the equation, it can provide a much more meaningful analytic model for cybersecurity, specifically within operational environments in which safety plays such a crucial and critical part to a critical infrastructure organization.

Simply put, if we can't learn from our past mistakes, how can we effectively predict our (potential) future?

Due to the lengthy and complex issues, not to mention the complex fundamentals involved for calculating net cybersecurity risk results, this book includes an entire chapter specifically on this one topic.

4.19 CONCLUSION

Measuring cybersecurity risk in OT and IT environments is complex and nuanced. This chapter has emphasized that risk is not simply about tallying threats or vulnerabilities, but about understanding how likelihood and consequence intersect with operational, financial, safety, and reputational impacts. It has been shown that reducing risk measurement to simplistic models—such as linear matrices—can obscure reality, whereas more advanced methods, like Monte Carlo simulation, Bayesian inference, and frameworks like RISE, provide richer, evidence-driven insights into uncertainty.

A central lesson is that organizations must broaden their perspective. Too often, cybersecurity is treated narrowly as an information problem, when in truth it is inseparable from process risk and operational performance. By integrating traditional engineering methods—such as PHA, LOPA, CHAZOP, and bowtie models—with cybersecurity analysis, organizations gain the ability to see common vulnerabilities, interdependencies, and cascading consequences across domains. This integrated risk management approach provides not only more accurate assessments but also practical, shared controls that bridge IT, OT, and business priorities.

Equally important is the recognition that human and cultural factors—such as group dynamics, cognitive bias, or loss of operational knowledge—shape how risk is perceived and acted upon. Technical models are only as strong as the decision-making cultures in which they are embedded. Organizations that foster vigilance, empower staff to focus on controllable factors like recovery speed and mitigation effort, and learn systematically from past events will be better positioned to adapt to evolving threats.

Ultimately, measuring risk is not a one-time calculation but a continuous cycle of assessment, testing, refinement, and improvement. By combining process safety rigor with modern cybersecurity analytics and by treating risk in an integrated, enterprise-wide context, organizations can move beyond reactive firefighting. They can instead establish a proactive, adaptive posture—where risks are not only measured, but meaningfully managed in ways that safeguard operations, protect people and the environment, and ensure long-term resilience.

NOTES

1 The term "operational cybersecurity risk" refers to measuring possible risk scenarios involving financial loss, safety loss (often leading to financial loss), disruption and/or destruction of operational environments (and its assets), specific digital systems resulting from improper or insufficient configurations, and/or failed operational processes resulting from either a single (or some combination thereof) involving people (aka insider threat), systems (or any of its sub-systems, and/or individual component of those systems), and/or external events or incidents (such as an adversarial attack or successful breach).

2 The term "information cybersecurity risk" refers to similar aspects of "operational cybersecurity risk," except it pertains solely to information, regardless of whether it is enterprise corporate-wide, division-wide, or site-wide, or if it involves information sent to/from an operational environment; any form of information is considered part of this risk-based definition.

3 https://www.imdb.com/title/tt0387808/

4 https://www.verizon.com/business/resources/reports/2024-dbir-data-breach-investigations-report.pdf, retrieved December 1, 2024.

5 https://www.ibm.com/reports/data-breach, retrieved December 1, 2024.
6 Roger Hill, Rethinking OT External Threat Risk: Addressing the Real Impact of Ransomware on Manufacturing Operations, Hillstrong Security Group, February 7, 2025, https://hillstrongsecurity.com/white-paper/rethinking-ot-external-threat-risk-addressing-the-real-impact-of-ransomware-on-manufacturing-operations/.
7 https://www.pewresearch.org/short-reads/2023/10/18/key-findings-about-americans-and-data-privacy/, retrieved December 1, 2024.
8 https://www.gartner.com/en/newsroom/press-releases/04-12-2023-gartner-identifies-the-top-cybersecurity-trends-for-2023, retrieved December 1, 2024.
9 https://www.wired.com/1999/04/fud-counter-fud/
10 https://medium.com/@wssounddesign/the-story-of-fud-f4287d9cd93b
11 Risk Assessment for Public–Private Partnerships: A Primer, January 2014, p.16; URL: https://www.fhwa.dot.gov/ipd/pdfs/p3/p3_primer_risk_assessment_021014.pdf (alt URL: http://riskbook.infracritical.com/book1/chapter4/ch4ref1.pdf).
12 Risk Assessment for Public–Private Partnerships: A Primer, January 2014, p.16; URL: https://www.fhwa.dot.gov/ipd/pdfs/p3/p3_primer_risk_assessment_021014.pdf (alt URL: http://riskbook.infracritical.com/book1/chapter4/ch4ref1.pdf).
13 It should be noted that there are more than simply two quantitative analytical models, specifically for cybersecurity, that exist; however, there are no all-encompassing, generalized models that exist for OT/ICS-based cybersecurity.
14 https://ops.fhwa.dot.gov/publications/fhwahop20057/ch1.htm (alt URL: http://riskbook.infracritical.com/book1/chapter4/ch4ref2.pdf).
15 A "risk register" is one or more recorded prior risk assessments, with its weighed matrices, that helps track, analyze, and plan for any potential setbacks which may crop up during the simulated analyses. This source of information helps ground the sampled data with actual data, thus reducing any increased chances for error.
16 A Delphi technique is a form of structure communication process often used for forecasting, decision-making, and development of policies which rely upon subject matter experts who have reached a consensus through one or more iterative processes through questionnaires and controlled discussions.
17 The term "data contamination" (alternatively "data pollution") often refers to the mixing of biased and unbiased data within the same calculation. Using biased data will affect the outcome(s), which will provide inconsistent and skewed results for decision-makers.

Examples of biased versus unbiased data would be basing data from prior events or incidents that were subjectively observed to personal opinion, as opposed to objectively observed through attestable and validated data.

18 Tammy Bailey, "Algorithm Design", Slide #26, p.5, May 17, 2004, URL: https://web.archive.org/web/20041117080553/; https://www.cs.duke.edu/courses/summer04/cps001/lectures/Lecture3.pdf (alt URL: http://riskbook.infracritical.com/book1/chapter4/ch4ref3.pdf).

19 Douglas W. Hubbard and Richard Seiersen, *How to Measure Anything in Cybersecurity Risk*, Hoboken, NJ: John Wiley & Sons, 2016, p. 38.

20 Hubbard and Seiersen, *How to Measure Anything in Cybersecurity Risk*, p. 52.

21 European Union Agency for Cybersecurity (ENISA), "ENISA's Position on the NIS Directive," January 2016, accessed June 21, 2021, https://www.enisa.europa.eu/publications/enisa-position-papers-and-opinions/enisas-position-on-the-nis-directive (alt URL: http://riskbook.infracritical.com/book1/chapter4/ch4ref4.pdf).

22 Hubbard and Seiersen, *How to Measure Anything in Cybersecurity Risk*, pp. 161–165.

23 Roger Hill, Rethinking OT External Threat Risk: Addressing the Real Impact of Ransomware on Manufacturing Operations, Hillstrong Security Group, February 7, 2025, https://hillstrongsecurity.com/white-paper/rethinking-ot-external-threat-risk-addressing-the-real-impact-of-ransomware-on-manufacturing-operations/.

24 https://www.dni.gov/files/CTIIC/documents/products/Recent_Cyber_Attacks_on_US_Infrastructure_Underscore_Vulnerability_of_Critical_US_Systems-June2024.pdf (alt URL: http://riskbook.infracritical.com/book1/chapter4/ch4ref5.pdf).

25 Internet-Exposed HMIs Pose Cybersecurity Risks to Water and Wastewater Systems, U.S. Cyber and Infrastructure Security Agency, December 13, 2004; URL: https://www.cisa.gov/sites/default/files/2024-12/joint-factsheet-epa-cisa-internet-exposed-human-machine-interfaces-508c.pdf (alt URL: http://riskbook.infracritical.com/book1/chapter4/ch4ref6.pdf).

26 House Homeland Releases 'Cyber Threat Snapshot' Highlighting Rising Threats to US Networks, Critical Infrastructure", The House Committee on Homeland Security, November 12, 2024; URL: https://homeland.house.gov/2024/11/12/new-house-homeland-releases-cyber-threat-snapshot-highlighting-rising-threats-to-us-networks-critical-infrastructure/ (alt URL: http://riskbook.infracritical.com/book1/chapter4/ch4ref7.pdf).

27 https://www.osti.gov/servlets/purl/1358306 (alt URL: http://riskbook.infracritical.com/book1/chapter4/ch4ref8a.pdf); https://software.llnl.gov/strawman/Overview.html#requirements (alt URL: http://riskbook.infracritical.com/book1/chapter4/ch4ref8b.pdf).

28 https://www.ncsc.gov.uk/collection/risk-management/using-attack-trees-to-understand-cyber-security-risk (alt URL: http://riskbook.infracritical.com/book1/chapter4/ch4ref9.pdf).

29 "Fault Tree Handbook", U.S. Nuclear Regulatory Commission, NUREG-0492, January 1981; URL: https://www.nrc.gov/docs/ML1007/ML100780465.pdf (alt URL: http://riskbook.infracritical.com/book1/chapter4/ch4ref10b.pdf)

30 Recommended Cybersecurity Practices for Industrial Control Systems, 3rd Annual National Cybersecurity Summit, U.S. Cybersecurity and Infrastructure Security Agency, no date: URL: https://www.cisa.gov/sites/default/files/publications/Cybersecurity_Best_Practices_for_Industrial_Control_Systems_508.pdf; alt URL: http://riskbook.infracritical.com/book1/chapter4/ch4ref11b.pdf

CHAPTER 5

Risk Assessment Frameworks

5.1 INTRODUCTION

In today's current landscape of OT, it is important to identify risk models that are currently available to cybersecurity professionals to bolster cyber systems (and their initiatives). Many of these models serve as frameworks for assessing vulnerabilities and threats, thus enabling organizations to implement better, more effective security strategies that are tailored to their specific operational environments and needs. As such, through better awareness and training, organizations can now apply these models as useful, measurable tools for safeguarding their critical infrastructure posture(s) against a plethora of cyber threats. The increasing reliance on digital systems and their interconnected networks has made them attractive targets for malicious actors seeking to disrupt these operations, steal sensitive information, or cause physical damage. These threats can manifest in various forms, including ransomware attacks, data breaches, and denial-of-service attacks, all of which can have devastating consequences. As such, it is imperative for critical infrastructure providers to implement robust cybersecurity measures, conduct regular risk assessments, and foster a culture of security awareness to safeguard against these evolving threats.

Conducting risk assessments is a crucial aspect of evaluating risk in the OT environments of numerous organizations, which provide valuable insights into the organization's risk posture by offering a thorough understanding of potential weaknesses within their systems and sub-systems, as well as the various threats that may take advantage of these vulnerabilities. Quickly identifying and evaluating these risks, organizations can prioritize their security efforts, allocate resources more effectively, and thus, develop strategies that can be specifically custom-tailored to mitigate the unique challenges posed within their operational contexts. This proactive approach not only enhances the overall security posture but also ensures compliance with industry regulations and standards—more on that topic shortly.

 DOI: 10.4324/9781003610557-5

Many of the existing models function through structured frameworks that facilitate the evaluation of vulnerabilities and threats. Utilizing these frameworks means that organizations can systematically analyze their security landscape, identify possible areas of concern, and focus on specific systems (sub-systems and their environments) that may require immediate attention.

It is essential for an organization to adopt a meticulous and structured strategy when addressing its operational environments, prioritizing issues from the most critical to the least critical. This approach must be grounded in a commitment to safety, which should always take precedence. As such, it is crucially vital that these safety measures are not merely viewed as optional considerations; but, instead, they should be firmly established as mandatory requirements that guide all operational decisions, especially where safety is primarily focused. To effectively implement this structured approach, organizations must cultivate a culture that values thorough planning and prioritization. Recognizing safety as a fundamental requirement rather than as a secondary consideration can create a more secure and productive operational environment. This commitment to a detailed and systematic methodology will not only enhance safety but also improve overall organizational performance and resilience in the face of challenges. Regulations exist for minimal adherence to industry definitions and their standards (if any). But for fostering such programs, even if they pertain primarily to cyber-based vulnerabilities and threats, there is no choice to ever bypass or ever disregard considering performing such assessments regularly; based on how the organization is established, will determine the frequency and length of an assessments' duration; whether it is performed annually, or quarterly, this makes no difference other than based on level of importance(s) of a given operation. This is where engineering design specifications meet operational requirements.

Furthermore, the implementation of, along with the constant revision of, these tailored security strategies help foster a culture of continuous improvement within organizations. By regularly revisiting and updating their vulnerability and threat assessments, organizations can adapt to the ever-evolving landscape of cyber threats through their technological advancements (if any). This ongoing process ensures that security measures remain relevant and effective, ultimately leading not only to more resilient operations, but potentially forethought threat resistance. In this way, the integration of these assessments into any given risk management framework is not just merely considered a best practice, but a critically vital necessity for safeguarding organizational assets and ensuring a safe and as close to efficient operational continuity as possible.

It is essential to re-iterate that safety is the top priority—without exception. The foundation of any successful operation lies in the unwavering commitment to safety. Only when there is a meticulous and ongoing equilibrium between safety, reliability, and performance can we achieve a seamless and effective operational synergy, maintaining perfect harmony in a delicate and beautiful "operational dance." The term "operational dance" refers to a structured and coordinated series of movements or actions that are executed within a specific operational context. This concept often applies to a plethora of various fields, where the term encapsulates the intricate interplay of roles, responsibilities, and strategies that individuals or teams engage in to achieve a common objective. The essence of this synergy lies in its emphasis on synchronization and adaptability, allowing participants to respond effectively to dynamic environments while maintaining a clear focus on their goals. In a business setting, it can be seen in the way departments collaborate in streamlining their processes and productivity. As each team member plays a distinctive role, their expertise contributes collectively to create a cohesive workflow that maximizes production output. This collaborative effort requires not only individual skill(s) but also a deep understanding of how each role interacts with others, much like dancers in a choreographed performance. The ability to adjust to unforeseen challenges and shifts in the operational landscape is crucial, as it ensures that the collective effort remains aligned with the overarching mission. It should be noted that it extends beyond its mere execution; it encompasses the strategic planning and foresight necessary to anticipate potential obstacles and opportunities. Just as dancers must practice and refine their movements to achieve harmony, organizations must continuously evaluate and adapt their operational strategies to remain competitive. This dynamic approach fosters a culture of innovation and resilience, enabling teams to navigate complexities with agility and purpose, ultimately leading to successful outcomes in their respective fields.

5.2 VULNERABILITY AND THREAT ASSESSMENTS VERSUS RISK ASSESSMENTS

It should be noted that there is clearly a distinction between vulnerability and threat assessments versus risk assessments, as they do not reveal sufficient information to provide a clear picture of their impact in their environments. Significant limitations in accurately measuring risk within the realm of OT cybersecurity pose a dangerous challenge, especially when it pertains to safety. Vulnerability assessments primarily generally focus on identifying one or more weaknesses within systems, sub-systems, applications, and networks and often overlook the broader context in which these vulnerabilities may exist. This narrow approach can lead to an incomplete picture and fundamental understanding of the actual risk landscape, as it fails to account for any potential impact(s) of external threats to specific operational environments of their supporting OT systems, which often include unique hardware and software configurations such as automated control systems (and their supporting parts and components, such as sensory equipment).

However, despite any shortfalls encountered through these assessments, threat assessments can still provide a "taste"—a form of litmus test,[1] if you will—aimed at providing an evaluation of potential adversaries and their capabilities; yet they, too, fall short in providing a comprehensive risk measurement. Therefore, these assessments will typically emphasize any given likelihood of various threat actors that, when given the possible chance and capability, can exploit these identified vulnerabilities without adequately considering the operational consequences of such exploits. In OT environments, where the stakes are often significantly higher due to their critical nature of the systems involved, this oversight from these assessments, no matter how through they may be, may result in a skewed perception of any risk(s), and as such, does not fully incorporate any possible or potential ramifications of a successful attack on physical processes and safety, with the latter being the critical key success factor.

Consequently, relying solely on vulnerability and threat assessments alone will more often than not lead organizations to adopt a reactive, rather than proactive, stance toward cybersecurity in OT. This can be found with industries that are significantly and heavily regulated, such as the electric industry, the petrochemical industry, and several modals of the transportation industry—and, in this case, the airline industry—can't have airplanes falling out of the sky now, can we? To many, this is a serious and significant liability when attempting to show and demonstrate the existence of risk, especially when regulatory requirements often impose counter-productive, as well as counter-imposed compliance requirements that would negate solutions to proactively remediate any vulnerabilities and threats in an organization's OT environment. For this reason, a more holistic approach is necessary, such as one that integrates these assessments with a thorough understanding of their operational context, including any interdependencies between systems and their potential impacts of disruptions, and aligns them smartly against regulatory requirements. By doing so, organizations can develop a more nuanced risk profile that not only identifies their vulnerabilities and threats but can also prioritize possible pre-mitigative strategies based on actual risks posed to critical operations. Unfortunately, this sometimes complicates the application of risk remediation efforts due to regulatory requirements and often requires compromises by "meeting in the middle" between regulations and safety industry standards.

5.3 CYBERSECURITY RISK FRAMEWORKS

OT cybersecurity is an increasingly critical area of focus as industries become more interconnected and reliant on digital systems. The integration of IT and OT has created new vulnerabilities, necessitating robust risk management frameworks tailored specifically for the unique challenges faced by operational environments. These frameworks serve as structured approaches to identify, assess, and mitigate cybersecurity risks associated with OT systems, which often control essential processes in sectors such as manufacturing, energy, and transportation. By implementing these frameworks, organizations can enhance their resilience against cyber threats while ensuring the safety and reliability of their operations.

Several prominent risk framework models have emerged to address the specific needs of OT cybersecurity. One notable example is the National Institute of Standards and Technology (NIST) Cybersecurity Framework (CSF), which provides a flexible structure that organizations can adapt to their specific operational contexts. This framework emphasizes the importance of identifying critical assets, assessing vulnerabilities, and implementing protective measures, all while fostering a culture of continuous improvement. Another example is the ISA/IEC 62443 series, which focuses on the security of industrial automation and control systems (IACS). This framework outlines a comprehensive set of guidelines and best practices that help organizations establish a secure environment for their OT systems, addressing both technical and organizational aspects of cybersecurity. In addition to these established frameworks, organizations are increasingly looking toward industry-specific models that cater to their unique operational requirements. For instance, the Oil and Gas Cybersecurity Framework developed by the American Petroleum Institute provides tailored guidance for the energy sector, addressing the specific risks and regulatory considerations faced by companies in this field. Similarly, the Smart Manufacturing Cybersecurity Framework offers a roadmap for manufacturers to secure their digital supply chains and production processes. By leveraging these diverse frameworks, organizations can better navigate the complexities of OT cybersecurity, ultimately leading to improved operational integrity and reduced risk exposure.

5.3.1 NIST Cybersecurity Framework

The first model commonly referenced is the NIST CSF, which provides a comprehensive approach for managing cybersecurity risks through a set of standards, guidelines, and best practices. For the sake of clarity, the term "best practice" in this context means matching an organization's approach to addressing and remediating issues against what other organizations perform within the same industry.

Developed by the NIST, this framework provides a structured approach that organizations can adopt to enhance their cybersecurity posture. It encompasses a range of activities, including identifying vulnerabilities, protecting critical assets, detecting potential threats, responding to incidents, and recovering from potential security breaches. Through this framework, organizations can establish a robust cybersecurity strategy that aligns with their specific operational needs that we refer to as the "risk footprint." The "risk footprint" serves as a suitable measurement tool for organizations to prioritize their risk management strategies; it would allow the mapping of risks across different departments and functions, ranking them accordingly by highlighting areas that may require more stringent controls or greater proactive measures. Taking this holistic-viewed approach not only aids in the allocation of their resources, but may also enhance decision-making processes by providing a framework for understanding the interconnectedness to such risks. It is essential for fostering a culture of awareness within an organization; in this book, the awareness is through safety. It encourages stakeholders to engage in more meaningful dialogue about management practices concerning risk by remaining vigilant and continuously identifying and keeping abreast of any emerging threats. Thus, defining and establishing a clear and detailed strategy will enable organizations to better prepare for any uncertainties, ensuring resilience and adaptability in an ever-evolving digital landscape.

Depending on how the organization defines risk within their operational environment—and this will vary from organization to organization within the same industry—this concept may identify and evaluate risk factors (as outlined previously), which include operational, financial, reputational, and compliance-based risks. Organizations can gain a better understanding of their exposure to potential adverse conditions through analyzing elements that can impact such events and, therefore, their overall objectives and sustainability.

The alignment of the NIST CSF with the execution of internal risk assessments in automated environments is a critical area of focus for organizations seeking to enhance their cybersecurity posture. The framework provides a structured approach that helps organizations identify, assess, and manage cybersecurity risks effectively. In such operational environments, where systems and processes are increasingly interconnected and reliant on digital technology, the framework's guidelines can be instrumental in ensuring that risk assessments are comprehensive and tailored to the unique challenges posed through the use of automation systems. But, this does not preclude some confusion with those from several critical infrastructure industries between NIST Special Publication (SP) 800-53 and NIST CSF.

The distinction between NIST SP 800-53 and the NIST CSF lies primarily in their purpose and application within the realm of cybersecurity. NIST SP 800-53 is a comprehensive catalog of security and privacy controls designed to protect federal information systems and organizations; it provides a detailed set of guidelines that organizations can implement to manage risk and ensure compliance against federal regulations. This publication is particularly focused on the specific controls necessary for safeguarding sensitive information and maintaining the integrity of (primarily) information systems.

In contrast, the NIST CSF is a much more flexible and higher-leveled framework that offers a strategic approach to managing cybersecurity risks across various sectors and is not limited to federal entities. It is structured around six core functions: Govern, Identify, Protect, Detect, Respond, and Recover. This framework is designed to be adaptable, allowing organizations of all sizes and industries to tailor their cybersecurity practices according to their unique risk profiles and operational needs. The NIST CSF emphasizes a more risk-based management approach, enabling organizations to prioritize their cybersecurity efforts based on their specific circumstances.

In contrast to each other, both frameworks serve useful purposes, and depending on their application, will determine which one is utilized. Table 5.1 provides a comparison of the two frameworks.

Due to its adaptability, it should be noted that several key infrastructure sectors, such as energy, have adopted and incorporated NIST's CSF as part of their regulatory requirements mappings.[11]

TABLE 5.1 Comparison of NIST CSF and NIST SP 800-53

	NIST Cybersecurity Framework (CSF)[2,3]	**NIST Special Publication 800-53[4]**
Purpose	Strategic-level framework for managing cybersecurity risks	Detailed-level catalog of security and privacy controls for federal organizations, contractors, and some private organizations
Applicability	Voluntary for critical infrastructure organizations	Mandatory for federal organizations, contractors, and some private organizations
Key Functions/ Components	Govern, Identify, Protect, Detect, Respond, Recover	20 control families

(Continued)

TABLE 5.1 (Continued)

	NIST Cybersecurity Framework (CSF)[2,3]	NIST Special Publication 800-53[4]
Flexibility	Flexible, non-prescriptive, and adaptable	Non-flexible, prescriptive, and not as adaptable
Level of Detail	Strategic-level guidelines and recommended controls	Detailed-level mandates with specific security and privacy controls
Focus	Strategic risk management	Detailed security controls
Compliance	Not mandatory	Mandatory for federal organizations, contractors, and some private organizations
Use Case	Suggestive controls for improving cybersecurity posture	Mandated detailed controls regardless of cybersecurity posture
Integration	May be integrated and included with other frameworks (e.g., CIS[5], COBIT[6])	Can be used with other frameworks, but must adhere to SP 800-53 first and foremost
Updates	Periodically updated to reflect new threats and practices; latest is Revision 2[7]	Regularly updated; latest is Revision 5[8]
Privacy Controls	Inclusive to current framework	Comprehensive privacy controls (as of Rev 5)[9]
Supply Chain Management	General, non-specific guidance is included, but can incorporate more if needed	Specific controls and enhancements in Rev 5[10]
Global Recognition	Primarily based for U.S. use	Designed for U.S. use, but adopted globally in some sectors (particularly energy)
OT-Tailored	Yes, can be tailored for OT application	No, not by design

5.3.2 Comparison to Other Frameworks

Many frameworks exist for assessing risk as part of a cybersecurity assessment, and each has its own advantages and disadvantages. It is not the purpose of this book to endorse any particular framework. No one framework is ideal for all scenarios.

Key frameworks that may be used in an OT risk assessment include (but are not limited to) the following:

- Factor Analysis of Information Risk (FAIR)—this is a quantitative risk assessment methodology that enables organizations to measure cybersecurity risk in financial terms. Developed by The Open Group, FAIR breaks down risk into components such as threat event frequency, vulnerability, and loss magnitude, enabling detailed analysis and modeling.
- Operationally Critical Threat, Asset, and Vulnerability Evaluation (OCTAVE)—Developed by CERT/SEI, OCTAVE is a self-directed, scenario-based risk assessment methodology that emphasizes organizational knowledge and operational context. It enables organizations to evaluate risks based on their business mission, critical assets, and threat environment.
- ISO/IEC 27005—This is part of the ISO/IEC 27000 family and provides detailed guidance on establishing, maintaining, and improving risk management processes in the context of information security. It is closely aligned with ISO/IEC 27001 and supports the implementation of an Information Security Management System (ISMS).
- STRIDE—Developed by Microsoft, STRIDE is a threat modeling framework that categorizes threats into six types: Spoofing, Tampering, Repudiation, Information disclosure, Denial of service, and Elevation of privilege. It's used primarily in the design and analysis of software and systems to identify and mitigate vulnerabilities.

5.3.2.1 FAIR

The FAIR framework is a quantitative model for understanding, analyzing, and measuring information risk in financial terms. Developed by The Open Group, FAIR provides organizations with a structured approach to evaluate the probable frequency and magnitude of future loss. Unlike qualitative methods that often rely on subjective labels like "high," "medium," or "low" risk, FAIR breaks down risk into measurable components such as threat event frequency, vulnerability, and loss magnitude.

At its core, FAIR uses a taxonomy of risk that includes:

- Asset at risk
- Threat agent and event
- Vulnerability
- Loss event frequency
- Probable loss magnitude

This allows organizations to calculate risk in terms of expected monetary loss, helping prioritize risk mitigation strategies based on business impact. FAIR is often used alongside frameworks like NIST CSF or ISO 27005 to enhance decision-making with financial insights. It's particularly valuable for justifying cybersecurity investments to business stakeholders and aligning risk with enterprise risk management (ERM) practices.

5.3.2.2 OCTAVE

OCTAVE is a self-directed, qualitative risk assessment methodology developed by the CERT Division at Carnegie Mellon University. It helps organizations identify, evaluate, and manage information security risks based on organizational priorities and operational needs.

OCTAVE emphasizes stakeholder involvement and organizational context. The process involves:

- Identifying critical assets and their security requirements
- Evaluating threats and vulnerabilities affecting those assets
- Developing mitigation plans based on risk tolerance and business impact

The most commonly used version, OCTAVE Allegro, streamlines the original method for faster implementation and better scalability. OCTAVE is especially well suited for organizations that require a flexible, business-oriented risk assessment without heavy technical or regulatory constraints. It complements frameworks like NIST CSF by enriching the "Identify" function with deeper stakeholder engagement and internal process insight.

5.3.2.3 ISO/IEC 27005

ISO/IEC 27005 is an international standard that provides guidelines for information security risk management. It supports the implementation of ISO/IEC 27001 by offering a structured approach to assess and treat risks associated with the confidentiality, integrity, and availability of information.

The risk management process under ISO/IEC 27005 includes:

- Context establishment
- Risk identification
- Risk analysis and evaluation
- Risk treatment
- Risk acceptance and communication

ISO/IEC 27005 promotes continuous improvement and aligns well with broader ERM strategies. It is widely used in regulated industries and by organizations pursuing ISO/IEC 27001 certification. While it is not prescriptive about tools or techniques, it encourages integration with existing risk management and ISMS.

5.3.2.4 STRIDE

STRIDE is a threat modeling framework developed by Microsoft to help security professionals identify and categorize threats during system and application design. It serves as a mnemonic for six common threat types:

- **Spoofing** identity
- **Tampering** with data
- **Repudiation** of actions
- **Information Disclosure** (data leaks)
- **Denial of Service** (availability attacks)
- **Elevation of Privilege** (unauthorized access)

STRIDE is often used in conjunction with data flow diagrams to trace how data moves through a system and where vulnerabilities may exist. It is especially valuable for developers, architects, and engineers seeking to build secure systems from the ground up. Although STRIDE does not provide a full risk assessment methodology, it complements other frameworks like NIST CSF by strengthening the "Identify" and "Protect" functions.

5.3.3 Consequence-Based Frameworks

A shift toward a consequence-based model could offer a more effective strategy, as it emphasizes the potential impacts of security breaches rather than merely focusing on compliance metrics. This transition could enhance the resilience of OT systems against evolving threats.

Incorporating consequence-based modeling into existing frameworks, whether NIST CSF and/or ISA/IEC 62443 are included or not, might involve integrating engineering principles that both include as well as prioritize design basis threat scenarios, as discussed in a previous chapter. Focusing on potential consequences through the identification of various threat scenarios, organizations can better understand potential vulnerabilities within their operational environments, and ultimately, develop more robust defenses. This approach encourages a proactive mindset, prompting organizations to anticipate and mitigate risks based on the severity of potential outcomes rather than solely on regulatory requirements. Such a shift would not only improve compliance but also foster a culture of security that is more adaptable to the dynamic nature of cyber threats.

There are several consequence-based cybersecurity risk frameworks. The first one is "Cyber PHA" or "Cyber HAZOP."

It serves as a safety-centric methodology designed to perform cybersecurity risk assessments specifically for industrial control systems and safety instrumented systems. This approach is systematic and consequence-driven, drawing upon established industry standards such as ISA 62443-3-2, ISA TR84.00.09, ISO/IEC 27005:2018, ISO 31000:2009, and NIST SP 800-39. By adhering to these standards, the framework ensures a comprehensive evaluation of potential risks, emphasizing the importance of safety in the context of cybersecurity.

The methodology has been aptly named "Cyber PHA" or "Cyber HAZOP," reflecting its close relationship with traditional process hazard analysis (PHA) and hazard and operability study (HAZOP) techniques widely utilized in process safety management. These studies are particularly relevant in sectors that manage highly hazardous industrial processes, such as oil and gas and chemical manufacturing. By aligning with these established practices, Cyber PHA and Cyber HAZOP facilitate a familiar framework for professionals in these industries, allowing for a seamless integration of cybersecurity considerations into existing safety protocols.

The Cyber PHA and Cyber HAZOP methodologies effectively bridge the gap between process safety and cybersecurity, necessitating collaboration among instrumentation, operations, and engineering disciplines. Modeled after the traditional PHA and HAZOP processes,[12] these methodologies enable the identification and analysis of cyber hazards in a manner akin to other process risks. Importantly, they can be implemented as a follow-up activity to conventional HAZOP studies, making them applicable to both existing brownfield sites and newly developed greenfield projects.[13] This adaptability ensures that the integration of cybersecurity assessments does not disrupt established safety processes, thereby enhancing overall operational resilience.

The Cyber PHA/HAZOP technique is predominantly employed in a workshop setting, which is facilitated by an experienced leader and a scribe well-versed in the Cyber PHA/HAZOP methodology. This environment is enriched by the presence of various subject matter experts who possess in-depth knowledge of the industrial processes, IACS, as well as the associated IT systems. The workshop team is typically composed of representatives from diverse fields, including operations, engineering, information technology, and health and safety. The inclusion of a multidisciplinary team is crucial for the effective development of realistic threat scenarios, thorough impact assessments, and achieving a consensus on the credibility of identified threats, known vulnerabilities, and existing countermeasures.

In preparation for the workshop, the facilitator and scribe take on the responsibility of collecting and organizing all necessary information, such as system architecture diagrams, vulnerability assessments, and insights from previous PHA/HAZOP analyses. They may also provide training to the workshop participants on the methodology, ensuring that everyone is adequately prepared to contribute. This foundational work is essential for fostering an environment where informed discussions can take place, allowing the team to effectively navigate the complexities of cyber risk assessment.

During the workshop, a worksheet is utilized to document the findings of the cyber PHA/HAZOP assessment. Various tools, including spreadsheet templates, databases, and specialized commercial software, have been developed to support this cyber assessment method. Typically, the organization's risk matrix is integrated into the worksheet, enabling the team to evaluate the severity and likelihood of identified risks and to determine the corresponding risk scores. The facilitator plays a pivotal role in guiding the team through the assessment process, ensuring that all contributions are considered, consensus is reached, and the workshop progresses efficiently. The assessment continues until all zones and conduits have been thoroughly evaluated, after which the results are compiled and presented to the workshop team and relevant stakeholders for further action.

In the future, several U.S. federal government initiatives are under way, one of which is through the Idaho National Laboratory (INL) Cyber-Informed Engineering (CIE) Framework as well as their application utilizing Consequence-driven Cyber-informed Engineering. Both show promise to establishing future standards that are consequence-based.[14]

CIE is a strategic framework that integrates cybersecurity into the engineering design of critical infrastructure systems. Developed in part by INL and supported by the U.S. Department of Energy, CIE aims to embed cyber resilience principles into the earliest stages of system design.

CIE emphasizes reducing the consequences of cyber-physical attacks through:

- Secure system design
- Attack surface minimization
- Cyber-physical consequence modeling
- Cross-disciplinary collaboration between engineers and cybersecurity professionals

Rather than relying solely on operational controls, CIE encourages organizations to "engineer out" vulnerabilities before systems are built or deployed. This is particularly crucial in sectors like energy, water, and manufacturing, where cyber incidents can have physical consequences. CIE complements frameworks like NIST CSF and ISA/IEC 62443 by shifting the focus upstream in the system lifecycle, aligning safety, security, and engineering goals.

5.4 CONCLUSION

This chapter differentiates between vulnerability/threat assessments and comprehensive risk assessments. While vulnerability assessments focus on weaknesses and threat assessments evaluate potential adversaries, neither fully addresses the potential consequences or risk impacts in OT environments. Therefore, a risk assessment must integrate these elements with an understanding of operational context and system interdependencies to enable proactive and consequence-focused decision-making.

A detailed review of cybersecurity risk frameworks begins with the NIST CSF. This flexible, strategic framework enables organizations to assess and manage cybersecurity risks using core functions: Govern, Identify, Protect, Detect, Respond, and Recover. It is contrasted with the more prescriptive NIST SP 800-53, which outlines specific control families required for federal entities.

Consequence-based methodologies like Cyber PHA/HAZOP are introduced as practical tools for OT cybersecurity risk analysis, borrowing principles from traditional process safety frameworks. These methods emphasize collaboration among multidisciplinary teams to model, assess, and mitigate risks specific to physical operations.

The chapter also examined several other widely used frameworks. No single framework can address cybersecurity risk management for an organization or scenario. Each organization must choose its frameworks to suit its particular context.

There is a critical need to embed risk assessment into the organization's culture and strategy. It encourages continuous improvement, operational integration, and aligning engineering design with cybersecurity and safety goals. Frameworks should not be applied in isolation but tailored to organizational priorities and combined with practices that ensure resilience, regulatory alignment, and long-term operational continuity.

NOTES

1 The term "litmus test" in this context refers to performing a sampled validation of whatever results have been discovered as part of the partial assessment. As the term itself asserts testing for acidity of alkalinity, in much the same way this term is used for the "tasted" assessment performed.

2 https://www.nist.gov/cyberframework (alt URL: http://riskbook.infracritical.com/book1/chapter5/ch5ref1.pdf).
3 https://csrc.nist.gov/pubs/cswp/29/the-nist-cybersecurity-framework-csf-20/final (alt URL: http://riskbook.infracritical.com/book1/chapter5/ch5ref2.pdf).
4 https://csrc.nist.gov/pubs/sp/800/53/r5/upd1/final (alt URL: http://riskbook.infracritical.com/book1/chapter5/ch5ref3.pdf).
5 https://www.cisecurity.org/controls.
6 https://www.isaca.org/resources/cobit.
7 https://csrc.nist.gov/pubs/cswp/29/the-nist-cybersecurity-framework-csf-20/final (alt URL: http://riskbook.infracritical.com/book1/chapter5/ch5ref2.pdf).
8 https://csrc.nist.gov/pubs/sp/800/53/r5/upd1/final (alt URL: http://riskbook.infracritical.com/book1/chapter5/ch5ref3.pdf).
9 https://csrc.nist.gov/pubs/sp/800/53/r5/upd1/final (alt URL: http://riskbook.infracritical.com/book1/chapter5/ch5ref3.pdf).
10 https://csrc.nist.gov/pubs/sp/800/53/r5/upd1/final (alt URL: http://riskbook.infracritical.com/book1/chapter5/ch5ref3.pdf).
11 https://www.nerc.com/pa/RAPA/ra/Reliability%20Assessments%20DL/August-2021_NERC_CIP_CSF_Paper.pdf (alt URL: http://riskbook.infracritical.com/book1/chapter5/ch5ref4.pdf).
12 Refer to Chapter 6 for a description of the PHA/HAZOP process.
13 A brownfield site is a property, the expansion, redevelopment, or reuse of which may be complicated by the presence or potential presence of a hazardous substance, pollutant, or contaminant.; URL: https://19january2017snapshot.epa.gov/brownfields/brownfield-overview-and-definition_.html (alt URL: http://riskbook.infracritical.com/book1/chapter5/ch5ref6.pdf); URL: https://19january2017snapshot.epa.gov/sites/production/files/2015-10/documents/09brochure.pdf (alt URL: http://riskbook.infracritical.com/book1/chapter5/ch5ref7.pdf).
14 https://web.archive.org/web/20230611174333/https://inl.gov/wp-content/uploads/2021/05/CIE-and-CCE_20210503.pdf (alt URL: http://riskbook.infracritical.com/book1/chapter5/ch5ref5a.pdf); https://web.archive.org/web/20230611174725/https://inl.gov/wp-content/uploads/2021/01/CCE_FactSheets_Tier1vsTier2_1.18.21.pdf (alt URL: http://riskbook.infracritical.com/book1/chapter5/ch5ref5b.pdf); https://www.osti.gov/servlets/purl/2480936 (alt URL: http://riskbook.infracritical.com/book1/chapter5/ch5ref5c.pdf); https://factsheets.inl.gov/FactSheets/Consequence-driven%20Cyber-informed%20Engineering.pdf (alt URL: http://riskbook.infracritical.com/book1/chapter5/ch5ref5d.pdf).

CHAPTER 6

Risk Assessment Process

6.1 INTRODUCTION

Performing a risk assessment is more than simply clicking checkboxes to ensure that a task has been completed or a condition has been met; it's about thoroughness, completion, patience, and adaptability. The concept behind risk cannot be overlooked as it exists everywhere; and, despite society's aim to completely remove risk entirely, there will always be some semblance of it out there in the wild, perhaps not in a manner or place once previously encountered or expected. It may have "mutated" into another form due to either modified, new, or removed factors that were part of the original design. As strange as it may sound, removing a contributing factor when performing a risk assessment may actually increase overall risk, rather than reducing it, as its lack of existence now places greater emphasis on the other contributing risk factors, which now will have an altered "risk footprint" to address.

Dozens of risk management models exist, many containing cybersecurity only partially, but are by no means the primary reasoning behind the model; instead, they include cybersecurity in a secondary, some even tertiary capacity, as these models focus more on specific business models, not necessarily complete industries. Additionally, those models that do include cybersecurity often have incomplete or inaccurate areas that pertain to IT more than operational technology (OT), or are missing the very essence behind the concept of operations instead of information.

This book aims to convey a sample of processes that *could* be used, but not in a standalone capacity. As such, we intend to clarify to readers that, in more than one case, cybersecurity risk assessment models should be used collectively and in multiples. Simply put, no one size fits all. That is, using only one model to perform an assessment will not conclude with a complete evaluation—it will remain incomplete, often excluding factors such as safety, reliability, and performance of operational functions. Again, the emphasis has been, and continues to be, all about the information entering and exiting an operational environment of an industrial-grade facility, such as, for example, a generation facility, an oil refinery, or a water treatment facility.

DOI: 10.4324/9781003610557-6

As already noted with frameworks, it is not the purpose of this book to recommend a single method for risk assessment. These are a few models that can be useful when performing a risk assessment. Organizations must choose their method(s) to suit their particular circumstances.

6.2 HAZOP AND PHA ANALYSES

HAZOP (HAZard and OPerability study) is a structured and systematic risk assessment technique used to identify potential hazards and operational issues in industrial processes, engineering systems, and critical infrastructure. It is widely applied in industries such as oil and gas, chemical processing, pharmaceuticals, and power generation to improve safety and efficiency.

The Process Hazard Analysis (or "PHA") methodology is used to assess hazards within industrial processes. In the United States, the Occupational Safety and Health Administration regulates high-risk facilities using Process Safety Management, which, among other things, requires that a PHA be conducted every five years. There are several methods for performing a PHA. Of these, the HAZOP is the most comprehensive, systematic, and commonly used method. A variation of the HAZOP, called CHAZOP (for "Control HAZard and OPerability" study), was developed to assess the safety impact of control system failures.

The primary objective of HAZOP is to identify hazards that could lead to accidents (such as fires, explosions, or chemical leaks) and propose mitigation measures to enhance process safety and reliability.

The first step is to define the scope, that is, identify the process, system, or operation to be analyzed. The scope is divided into nodes, including pipelines, vessels, valves, and process units. Each node is analyzed separately to ensure thorough evaluation.

In the analysis, the team uses predefined guide words to explore potential deviations from regular operation. Table 6.1 shows typical guide words.

During the second step, the team identifies possible causes, which include (but are not limited to) the following: (1) equipment failure, (2) human error, and (3) external factors.

The team then analyzes consequences, which include (but are not limited to) the following: (1) safety risks, (2) environmental impact, and (3) production downtime for each deviation.

Finally, the team recommends safeguards and corrective actions. This is all documented, and an action plan has been developed.

HAZOP promotes cross-functional collaboration as engineers, operators, and safety teams collaborate.

Edward Marszal and Jim McGlone developed a solution that incorporates cybersecurity into HAZOP. The Security PHA Review (or "SPR,"

TABLE 6.1 Typical Guide Words in HAZOP

Guide Word	Meaning	Example Deviation	Possible Hazard
NO/NOT	Complete absence of intended process	No flow in a pipe	Pump failure, blockage
MORE	Higher quantity or rate than expected	Excess pressure in a vessel	Risk of explosion
LESS	Lower quantity or rate than expected	Reduced cooling water flow	Overheating of equipment
AS WELL AS	Unintended additional material	Contaminant in a chemical feed	Product quality issues
PART OF	Missing component or step	Incomplete chemical reaction	Unstable product formation
REVERSE	Process operating in the opposite direction	Backflow in a pipeline	Contamination or pressure buildup

pronounced "spur") is described in their book *Security PHA Review for Consequence-Based Cybersecurity*.[1]

Utilizing these frameworks to incorporate cybersecurity will likely add one or more levels of complexity in today's increasingly digital industrial environments. Cyber threats can significantly impact the safety and operability of processes, necessitating both HAZOP and PHA to address any possible vulnerabilities in the control systems' environments. This will likely involve an extensive analysis of internal and external threats, as well as the development of strategies to mitigate these risks. Any added complexity is further compounded by the need for continuous monitoring and adaptation, since cyber threats are constantly evolving. This rapid and continually shifting landscape will require organizations to continue being vigilant and proactive, promoting a culture of security awareness with employees and stakeholders. As these environments are no longer isolated from external threats, internal threats pose as significant, if no more important, threats to any given operation. For instance, a HAZOP study may identify how a cyber intrusion may conclude that there may be deviations in process parameters. In contrast, a PHA study might evaluate broader implications of an intrusion to the overall system safety and compliance requirements with regulatory and/or industrial standards.

Cybersecurity integration efforts with any industrial framework also necessitate collaboration with various departments and their disciplines.

It is no longer sufficient for IT personnel to operate in isolation; instead, a holistic approach that might include input from legal, compliance, and operational groups may be necessary. Additionally, these operations can no longer offload the majority of their cyber-related roles and tasks to only IT—it must be a joint effort. This is crucial in reducing risk to as low a level as possible.

SPR reuses the principles of safety risk assessment already in place. As the authors note:

> The process industries have already established methods for risk assessment that have been successfully in use for decades. The optimal solution for assessment of cybersecurity risks is not to start from scratch with new studies but to extend the existing studies to incorporate new objectives and requirements.[2]

Figure 6.1 shows a simplified overview of the SPR process. The beauty of the process is that the SPR is either part of an overall HAZOP study or uses the output of a HAZOP study. This elevates cybersecurity in the overall process, where it can be appropriately addressed. The company's safety organization must understand that cybersecurity risks can contribute to process hazards, and they should not be treated as unrelated issues to be managed by others in the company. This is easier said than done: plant-based OT personnel may not have the time or resources to address these issues. IT personnel may not have the domain knowledge to properly appreciate the issues.

Each scenario of the HAZOP is reviewed to determine whether it is hackable. This is a commonly used term in IT security. Still, in the SPR process, it means that "the scenario could be forced to occur by a malevolent actor who has taken control of the ICS [industrial control system]." The cause or initiating event is reviewed first. The assumption is that computer-related causes can be hacked, but mechanical-related causes cannot.

If a cause can be hacked, the safeguards are then reviewed to determine if they can also be hacked. Again, the assumption is that all computer- or electronic-related safeguards can be hacked, but mechanical devices such as relief valves cannot.

When a specific device or piece of software is found to be vulnerable to attack, it necessitates a thorough examination of any safeguards to assess their susceptibility to (perhaps) other breaches. This process continues operating under the premise that any safeguard linked to any electronic system is potentially vulnerable to attack. The rationale behind this assumption stems from the growing sophistication of cyber threats and their inherent vulnerabilities present in almost all digital infrastructures. Consequently, a thorough evaluation of these electronic safeguards

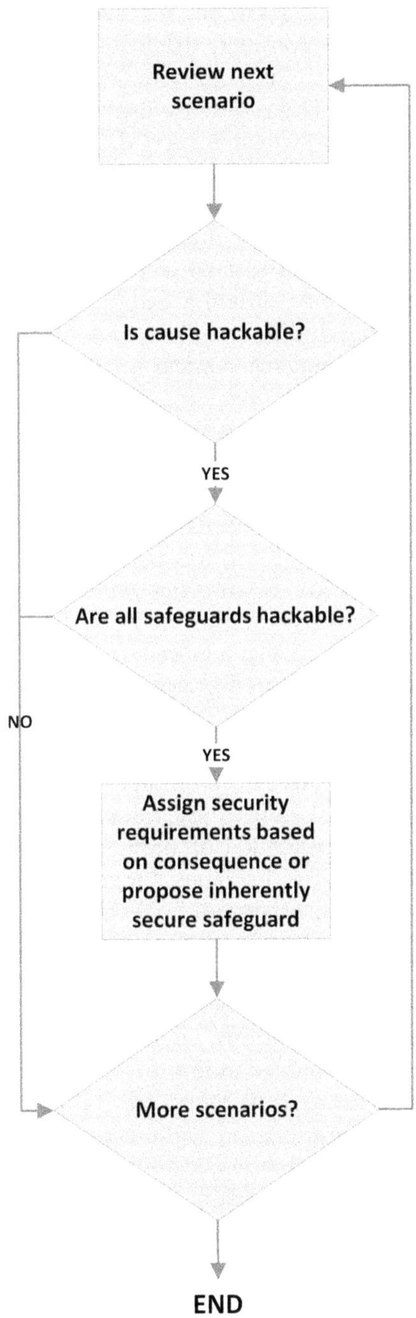

FIGURE 6.1 Overview of the SPR process.

is essential to identify any weaknesses that could be exploited by actors with malicious intent. In contrast, mechanical devices, such as relief valves, switches, relays, etc., are considered to be generally more secure against attack attempts. These devices operate on physical principles rather than electronic ones, which ensures that they are significantly less susceptible to attack types that can compromise such safeguards. While mechanical systems can still fail due to wear and tear or other physical factors, the risk of attack against them is significantly lower than that of their electronic counterparts. This distinction highlights the greater importance of understanding different categories of safeguards, as well as their respective vulnerabilities.

Assessing electronic and mechanical safeguards is crucial in creating a comprehensive security strategy. Management should consider that electronic systems are inherently more vulnerable to attack; thus, organizations should prioritize their efforts to fortify these areas. Consequently, acknowledging the security posture of mechanical devices will enable a balanced approach to risk management, ensuring that all potential vulnerabilities are effectively addressed. This dual focus will not only enhance the overall security posture but will foster a better proactive stance against emerging threats in this increasingly digital environment.

HAZOP may be effectively adapted for enhancing cybersecurity within operational environments by systematically identifying potential hazards and additional operability issues. This may help organizations identify and pinpoint vulnerabilities in their OT systems that could be exploited by potential threats. This approach involves a thorough review of processes and systems already in use, allowing opportunities to focus on deviations from their intended or designed operations, which may lead to any potential security breaches. Organizations need to create a structured framework for assessing any risks that have been identified, as well as those associated with those threats, thus ensuring that safety and security are prioritized.

Integrating cybersecurity practices with HAZOP may require a collaborative effort among operations, engineering, IT, and OT teams, as well as a comprehensive understanding of the unique challenges posed by combining these domains. Integration may be achieved by incorporating cybersecurity considerations throughout the HAZOP study process, allowing team members to analyze not only the physical and operational aspects of the technology but also any potential cyber-related risks associated with each component. Organizations can develop more holistic views of their risk landscape, enabling them to apply specifically targeted security measures that address both operational and cyber vulnerabilities. This delicate synergy between HAZOP and cybersecurity practices may establish a stronger foundation for a culture of safety and security, which could lead to more resilient operational environments. Many of these principles are founded predominantly on traditional aspects of safety and operational design in those operational environments, through rigorous and careful planning and design work that went into their initial conception and eventual operation.

6.3 FAULT TREE ANALYSIS

Fault tree analysis is commonly used in the specification of system availability, and so is well-suited for use in cybersecurity risk assessment. In fault tree analysis, each scenario (e.g., loss of view) is considered, the causes identified and shown in graphical form, such as the simplified example shown in Figure 6.2. This analytical technique provides a systematic approach of examining potential failures within a given system, identifying various pathways that could lead to potentially undesirable outcomes. Through this approach of decomposition of those complex systems into their fundamental components, the fault tree analysis provides a clear visual representation of how different failures may interact and give way to system vulnerabilities. This structured approach is extremely valuable in the context of cybersecurity, such that its understanding of

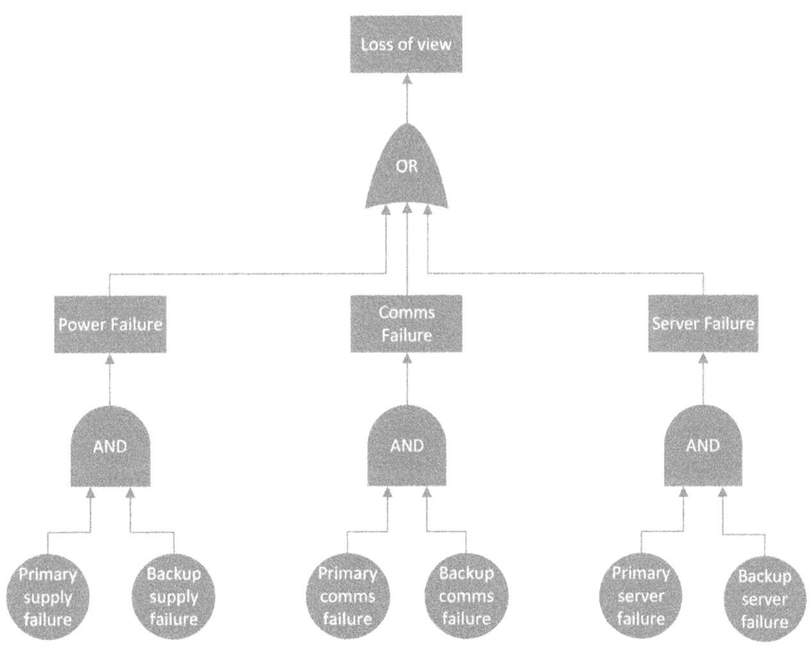

FIGURE 6.2 Example fault tree.

any interplay between various threats as well as system weaknesses is crucial for developing more robust defenses.

The application of fault tree analysis facilitates a comprehensive understanding of risk factors that could compromise system integrity. When used for system availability assessment, if the probabilities of the individual events (e.g., primary supply failure) are known, it is possible to calculate the overall likelihood of the scenario (e.g., loss of view). This can then be used to define availability figures for each scenario. Organizations can prioritize their security measures and countermeasures based on the likelihood and impact of discovered threats. This proactive stance enables the identification of critical vulnerabilities and supports the development of targeted strategies to mitigate risks. As cyber threats continue to evolve, an organization's ability to anticipate and analyze potential failure points becomes increasingly essential for maintaining system resilience and ensuring operational continuity.

As already discussed in this book, determining the probability of individual cybersecurity events is difficult, and any resulting likelihood is dependent on the quality of this data. However, without this probabilistic measure of a cybersecurity incident, the fault tree method can provide significant benefits to those assessing risk. Even in the absence of probabilistic determination of potential cybersecurity incidents, this approach systematically and analytically identifies potential failures through their causes, allowing assessors to visualize which pathways could lead to a possible security breach. Breaking down these complex systems into more manageable components, the fault tree analytical method may enable a more thorough examination of any vulnerabilities, thus enhancing the understanding of any potential risks associated with cybersecurity. This methodology provides a structured approach to prioritizing risks based on their potential impact and likelihood of occurrence. Thus, any prioritization determined that is based on examined analytical results will be crucial for organizations to focus on and allocate resources effectively through implementation of better and more appropriate mitigation strategies.

Representing various scenarios visually can help communicate the sequence of events and the approach to remedying the situation. This can lead to a better-quality incident response plan, in terms of:

- Scenario identification, especially the initiating causes and the various contributions to those scenarios. This can identify the need for additional resilience in design (e.g., hot standby devices) and backup resources (e.g., backup power source, diverse communications media). Identifying case-specific scenarios is crucial, particularly in comprehending initiating factors and their elements which may contribute to processes involving a thorough analysis identifying any potential risks and vulnerabilities that may impact operations. Building resilience into any design is crucial and a key outcome resulting from any given scenario identification. For instance, if implementation of (always ready) hot-standby devices may provide immediate redundancy, thus ensuring critical functions will continue to remain operational even in the event of a failure. Additionally, consideration of using backup resources, such as alternative power sources, diverse communication channels, etc. is vital. Using such measures not only provides a safety cushion to operations, they may safeguard against single points of failure while also enhancing overall robustness of the operational environment, enabling organizations to maintain continuity in their operations under adverse conditions.

- Response procedures, including overall objectives, communications plans, and step-by-step processes. These procedures encompass a comprehensive framework designed to guide organizations by effectively managing various situations. These procedures could outline overarching objectives that the organization might want to take to achieve during a response, ensuring all actions are aligned with their strategic goals. A well-structured communication plan is integral to any good response procedure. This plan should detail how information is to be disseminated among team members, stakeholders, as well as the public, ensuring that everyone involved is informed accordingly. Effective communication is extremely vital for minimizing any confusion by enhancing collaboration, particularly when multiple parties are engaged with the response effort. Lastly, step-by-step processes outlined in these procedures may serve as a practical guide for executing necessary actions during, and after, an incident. These processes should include detailed outlines breaking down complex tasks into manageable steps, allowing team members to follow a much more clearer path toward a resolution.
- Backup requirements, identifying specific backups that are needed to meet recovery objectives set by the business. This process may involve a thorough assessment of specific data and systems that may need to be backed up, taking into account any unique or "quirky" needs of the business. Organizations may then prioritize possible backup strategies to align against their recovery goals, ensuring that, in the event of a potential incident, only the most crucial assets are safeguarded and the operation may be restored promptly.
- Spares and equipment requirements, especially the location of these spares and equipment. If a spare part takes 24 hours to

arrive, the fault tree can highlight which scenarios would result in a loss of service for this duration. Organizations may systematically review potential failure points of their supply chain management and procurement process, as well as their consequences on service delivery. This method not only highlights any scenarios which may lead to extended downtime but may also assist in prioritizing which spare parts should be stocked in advance. If a particular piece of equipment is known to frequently fail and requires a specific spare part, ensuring that this part is readily available may mitigate the risk of a prolonged service loss. Consequently, this strategic approach to implementing this method of spare parts management may enhance overall operational resilience. Many organizations with such or similar critical operations may already know and plan accordingly for such sorts of contingencies; however, many may not take into account cybersecurity-related incidents and may not have planned accordingly, or may have stocked up on the wrong parts or equipment. This, too, is absolutely critical for restoring crucial points of an operation.

- Requirements for maintenance providers, as with backup and spares requirements, the fault tree will clearly show where dependencies on maintenance providers and thus where service level agreements (SLAs) will need to be defined. Understanding these dependencies is essential for effective resource allocation and management. The fault tree analysis serves as a visual representation that highlights potential points of failure and the corresponding maintenance needs. This clarity allows organizations to proactively define SLAs that not only address immediate maintenance requirements, but also anticipate future needs based on the identified dependencies or discrepancies discovered. Consequently, this strategic approach fosters a more resilient operational framework.

Furthermore, the fault tree method can be used to model modifications to the system design (e.g., the addition of a backup communications option) to evaluate incident scenarios with and without the modification.

6.4 BOWTIE ANALYSIS

A bowtie diagram is a risk assessment tool that visually represents the relationship between hazards, potential incidents, preventive barriers, and mitigation measures. It is widely used in safety and industrial risk management to systematically analyze threats and control measures.

Figure 6.3 shows a simple bowtie diagram related to safety risk. The diagram is shaped like a bowtie, with:

- The risk (e.g., loss of primary containment).
- The *top event*, or the critical incident that occurs if the hazard is not controlled (e.g., overfill/overpressure of free water knockout vessel). Continuing the example of the use of the water knockout vessel, when it experiences an overfill condition, the excess liquid can lead to a breadth of operational challenges, including the potential for spills or leaks. Such occurrences may have detrimental effects on surrounding environments such that they may necessitate costly cleanup efforts. Additionally, overpressure conditions can result in structural damage to the vessel itself, increasing the likelihood of ruptures or potential explosions. These scenarios can underscore the importance of implementing robust hazard control measures for mitigating any risks associated with the operation of such equipment.
- One or more threats, or possible causes leading to the incident. In this case only one is shown (flow valve fails open). In the context of the aforementioned example, a specific threat is identified: the failure of a flow valve to remain closed, this malfunction can result in an uncontrolled influx of liquid, exacerbating the risk of overfilling and subsequent overpressurization of the vessel. Understanding these threats is essential for developing effective risk mitigation strategies.
- One or more *preventive* (or *preventative*) barriers between threats and the top event. These barriers are the controls in place to prevent the incident from occurring (e.g., pressure indicating controller opens pressure valve). For instance, a pressure indication controller that activates a pressure relief valve may effectively manage the pressure levels within the vessel, thus preventing overpressure situations.
- One or more *mitigating* barriers between the top event and the resulting consequences. These barriers are the controls that reduce the impact of the incident (e.g., emergency shut down). Mitigating barriers, such as an emergency shutdown system, can significantly reduce the consequences of the event, safeguarding both personnel and equipment from severe damage.
- Consequences. These are the potential outcomes if the incident happens (e.g., fire/explosion).

The name "bowtie" comes from the fact that there can be multiple threats and multiple consequences and so the diagram looks like the neck garment with the risk as the knot in the middle.

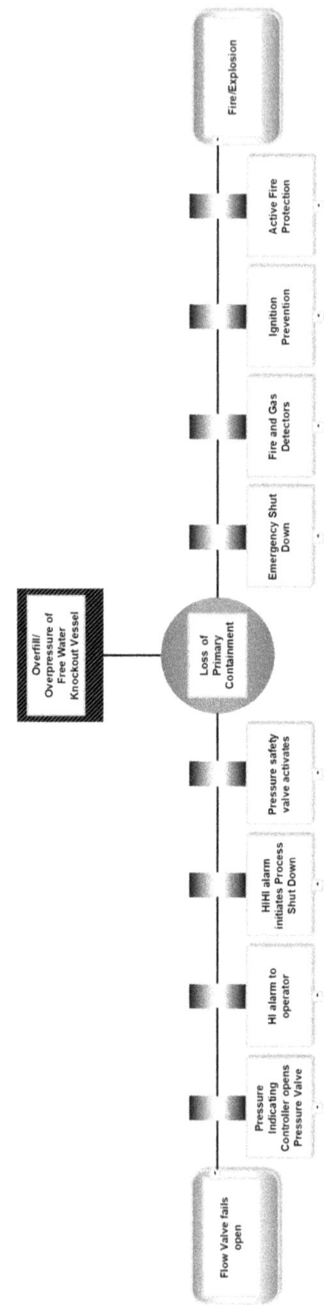

FIGURE 6.3 Example of single pathway safety bowtie diagram.

Figure 6.4 shows a simple cybersecurity bowtie. In this case, the initiating cause (malware deployed on system) leads to a generic hazard (cybersecurity threat), event (cybersecurity incident), and ultimately a consequence (loss of control), which is system, rather than process, focused. As a result, the preventive and mitigating actions are focused on the system rather than the process.

The bowtie framework is a risk management tool that effectively integrates with OT cybersecurity by delivering a structured approach to identifying, assessing, and mitigating risks. This framework visualizes the relationship between potential threats and their consequences, allowing organizations to create a comprehensive risk profile. In the context of OT cybersecurity, the bowtie model assists the delineation of various pathways in which cyber threats may exploit vulnerabilities in industrial control systems, thereby affecting critical infrastructure. Through mapping out these pathways, organizations might understand the interplay better between preventive measures and response strategies, thus ensuring that both aspects are adequately addressed.

In the bowtie framework, the left side of the analytical model represents threats and preventive controls which may be implemented for mitigating risks. For OT environments, this may include measures such as network segmentation, access controls, and the use of standard security assessments. Using standard security assessments for OT environments is acceptable as they identify the more common threats and vulnerabilities associated with IT-based threats and vulnerabilities, such as malware attacks or insider threats; thus, organizations may focus, and then customize, their cybersecurity strategic defenses specifically for their OT environments. Strategies, such as network segmentation, play a crucial role by dividing the overall network into distinct segments, thereby limiting any potential impact of a security breach; or, if there is a security breach, would allow minimization by blocking off, then isolating and containing the breach. This approach not only helps in containing any threats, but also facilitates a much more effective monitoring and management strategy of network traffic. Additionally, use of access controls also plays a critical role for ensuring only authorized personnel can interact with sensitive systems, again, thereby reducing any likelihood of insider threats or accidental exposure to any potential vulnerabilities; essentially, exposure is minimized and contained. Consistent and regular security assessments are equally important, as they permit organizations to identify any weaknesses within the purview of their defenses and then adapt accordingly.

The right side of the analytical model illustrates any potential consequences resulting from a potentially successful cyber incident and its corresponding recovery measures which may be enacted. The dual focus on prevention and response is particularly crucial, especially in OT settings,

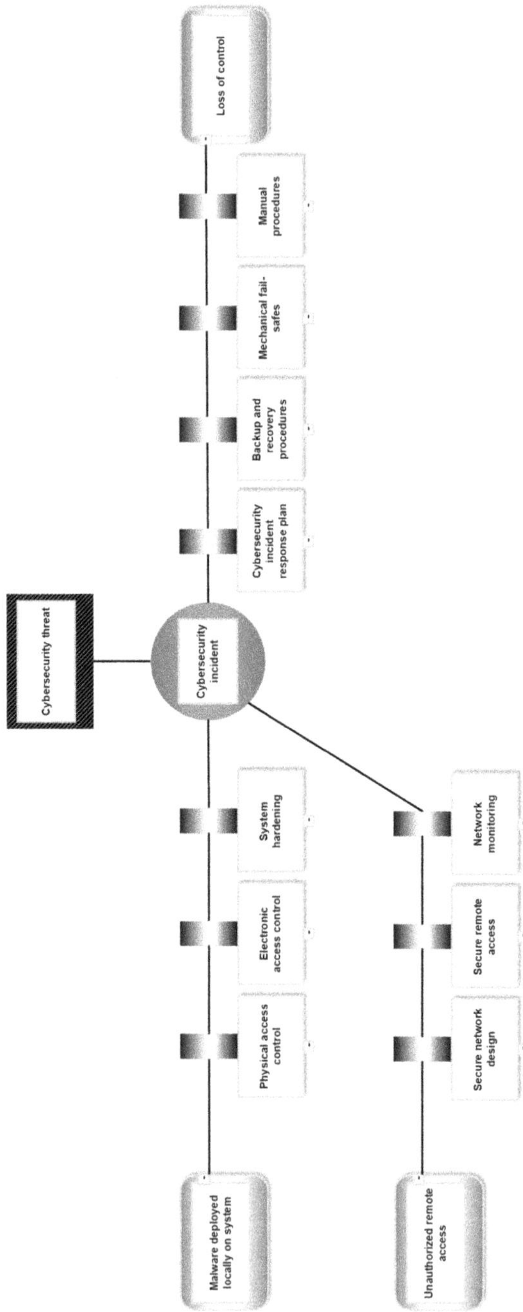

FIGURE 6.4 Example cybersecurity bowtie diagram.

where any downtime or breaches may lead to significant operational disruptions (or outages) as well as increased safety hazards. This aspect of the model emphasizes the importance of not only anticipating and preventing cyber threats but also preparing for the aftermath of such incidents.

In a nutshell, the bowtie framework facilitates communication and collaboration between various stakeholders identified in OT cybersecurity, providing a clear visual representation of the risks and controls, and enabling cross-functional teams—which includes IT, operations, and management—to engage in informed discussions about risk tolerance and resource allocation. This collaborative approach not only enhances the overall security posture of the organization but also fosters a culture of shared accountability of cybersecurity responsibilities. Ultimately, integrating the bowtie framework into OT cybersecurity practices may empower organizations to proactively manage their risks while also ensuring resilience of their infrastructure against potential future cyber threats.

6.5 LOPA

Used for many decades, LOPA (known as "Layers of Protection Analysis") provides a quantitative analytical risk assessment methodology (albeit it somewhat) may be considered more so of a thought process—or better yet, analytic perspective—used in several key-critical infrastructure sectors (and respective industries) where extremely hazardous environments exist, and safety (above all else) plays not only an integral part of the environment(s), but is essential to the continued operations, industrial assets, and the personnel who support it. It utilizes a suite of simplified, conservative rules and tasks that define any risks of those environments in terms of frequency, severity, and their potential consequential outcome(s). As it is defined as a simplified risk methodology, many industries have defined and adopted their own variations to this mindset, assigning agreed-upon universally accepted values which reflect areas of risk, ranking them based on severity and outcome levels, from minor to catastrophic.

One of the primary objectives behind the development of LOPA is its straightforward application within and throughout an industrial setting. Simply put, the whole premise is to make a given risk assessment more objective—and less subjective. This quantifies not only its outcome(s) but also provides a measurable metric, one that can be used as a key performance indicator ("KPI") for both current and future analysis. This may include post-regression analytic methods, which may consist of past (or former) risk assessments that may be utilized as part of a current environment under evaluation, or provide potential future outcomes based on predictive analytical methods. Either way, the use of this analytical method, substantiated with factual, accurate data, can provide something attestable, and can demonstrate—hopefully accurately—trends and patterns that could potentially affect and impact operational environments.

LOPA is often created using resultant data from an identification or process discovery analysis, such as PHA or HAZOP (as discussed earlier within this book), and then incorporated using this analytical method. As both PHA and HAZOP offer a structured form of process discovery analysis, identifying potential hazards is considered, although possibly subjective, and is then supported and confirmed with quantifiable data generated from the LOPA.

Most risk auditors who work within such hazardous industrial environments will agree that their version of LOPA is the best method of analyzing risk over many other methods.

However, this does not mean that cybersecurity is exempt from using LOPA as part of its evaluative study of an industrialized operational environment. If at all, cybersecurity risk assessments are—or should be—an integral part of a LOPA study—not the other way around. Within a hazardous environment, conditions can easily—and quickly change—with little or no notice—requiring immediate remediation. Cybersecurity is, and should be, a part of an overarching suite of processes, making up an integral part of an all-hazards[3] approach to risk to an operational environment. It is not, nor should it ever be, the "center of the universe."[4]

If, however, cybersecurity is the end-all/be-all and an industrialized operational environment is defined around the controls and requirements of cybersecurity doctrine rather than the other way around, this introduces a plethora of error, risk, and severe consequential factors into the overall operation. In other words, whatever is measured will be based solely on cyber doctrine and not on operations doctrine. With more digitization of industrialized operational environments becoming not only increasingly automated, but networked, an insurmountable amount of risk is now being introduced into those environments—something that may not have existed since that specific industry began decades (perhaps centuries) ago.

Figure 6.5 shows the nine layers of LOPA.

However, within the cybersecurity community, LOPA is already used. Referred to as "defense-in-depth" (or "DID"), this methodology is a measurement of risk in terms of both safety and security measures and countermeasures. Several key critical infrastructure sectors (and their industries) rely on, if not dictate, the use of DID; one of those industries is the nuclear electric generation industry. The concept of DID is a deterministic[6] principle by which there are several layers, which, ultimately, protect the core process or operation within that environment. For nuclear, the core process is the nuclear reactor; everything is focused on the reactor due to extremely long-lasting impacts resulting from the improper

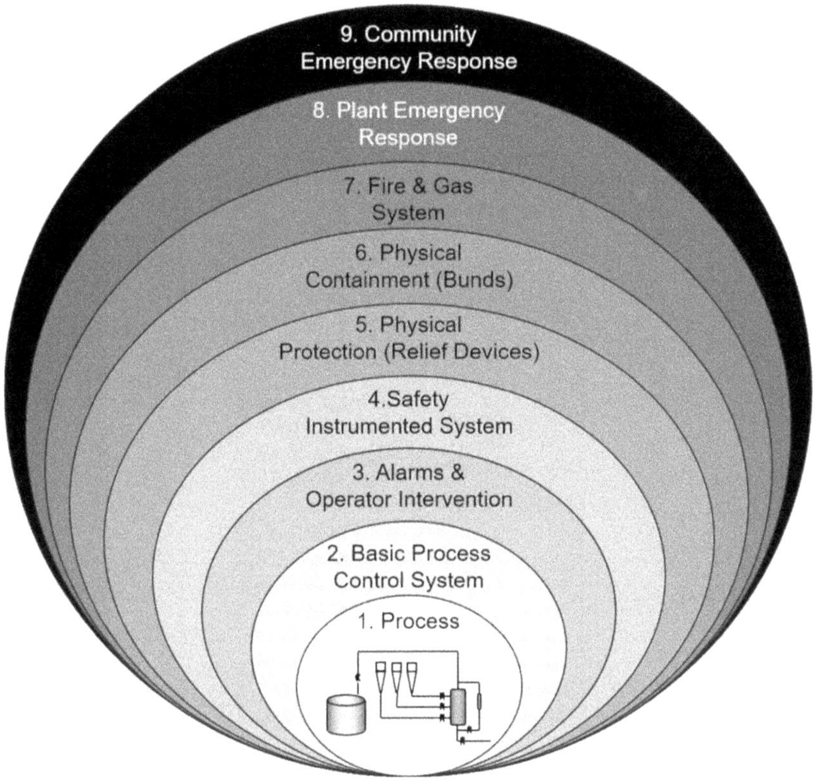

FIGURE 6.5 LOPA visualized example.[5]

handling and exposure to the highly radioactive environment(s). As such, safety is not only critical important, it is dictated.

There are distinctively two different types of DID: (1) safety and (2) cyber systems.[7]

Historically, safety DID for nuclear power plants (NPPs) has considered deterministic evaluation of NPP designs. DID treatment is considered a barrier approach where physical barriers are placed between radioactive material and the environment. Through design evolutions and maturation, NPP designs began to include active systems to respond to various design basis events (DBE).[8,9] The incorporation of active systems changed the risk assessment landscape. Prior to the development of modern PRA, NPP risk assessments were similar to "what if?"[10] analyses that focused on evaluation of events that would challenge physical barriers. The incorporation of active systems and development of PRA created a new paradigm for DID evaluations (Figure 6.6).

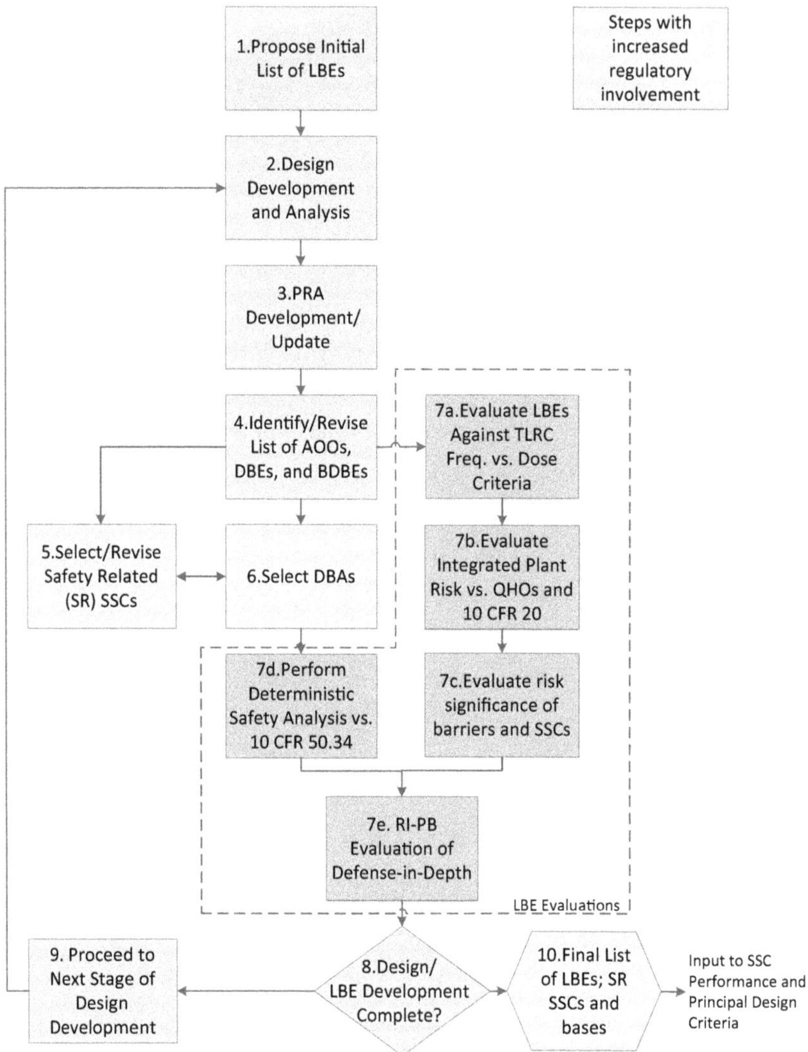

FIGURE 6.6 Process for selecting and evaluating licensing basis threats. "Modernization of Technical Requirements for Licensing of Advanced Non-Light Water Reactors Selection of Licensing Basis Events Draft Report Revision 0"; Prepared for the U.S. Department of Energy, Office of Nuclear Energy, Under DOE Idaho Operations Office, Contract DE-AC07-05ID14517, April 2017, p.5.[11]

The majority of physical barriers are considered passive and include (but are not limited to): fuel itself (i.e., fission product holdup in fuel); fuel cladding; reactor vessel and reactor coolant system piping; and containment structures. Whereas passive structures do not rely on component response or operator actions, active systems do require operator actions and/or a multitude of systems, structures, and components to initiate on demand in response to some initiating event. Passive and automatic system responses are designed into many nuclear generation technologies, but in many DBE scenarios, operator actions and active system responses are essential to preventing core damage.[12]

Similar to safety assessments, the primary goal of cybersecurity plans and control method implementation is to protect the NPP from malicious attacks on safety systems. The subtlety of the safety and security function relationship should not be overlooked. Although cybersecurity requires unique tools, capabilities, and expertise, cybersecurity goals for NPPs share the goals of the safety assessments: ensure the plant can perform its fundamental safety functions. Thus, cybersecurity plans should leverage existing safety and risk assessments to the extent possible when developing cybersecurity strategies.

6.6 REGULATION APPROACHES

One of the common concerns from industry is government regulation. There is some justification in this concern, because regulation can be executed in different ways.

In the UK, industries dealing with major accident hazards (such as offshore oil and gas, nuclear power, and high-risk chemical plants) are required to submit a safety case to demonstrate risk management and compliance with Health and Safety Executive (HSE) regulations. The safety case process ensures that risks are identified, assessed, and controlled to protect workers, the public, and the environment.

The requirement for a safety case is determined by legislation such as the Control of Major Accident Hazards Regulations which applies to high-risk chemical facilities.

The first step is identifying major hazards associated with the operation. This includes process hazards (e.g., chemical releases, explosions, fires), structural hazards (e.g., equipment failures, loss of containment), and environmental hazards (e.g., oil spills, radioactive contamination).

The methods described in this chapter, such as HAZOP, fault tree, and bowtie, are used to analyze potential failures.

A risk assessment is required, including likelihood and consequence analysis and identification of preventive and mitigation controls. The ALARP principle is used to ensure risk reduction measures are cost-effective.

The safety case must describe the Safety Management System (SMS) in place to ensure compliance with safety regulations, train employees and contractors, monitor safety performance and incident reporting, and maintain ongoing risk management and regulatory compliance.

A safety case document must be submitted that includes:

- Description of the facility and operations;
- Hazard identification and risk assessment;
- Preventive and mitigation measures;
- Emergency response plans; and,
- SMS details.

The completed safety case is submitted to HSE for review. HSE evaluates the safety case against regulatory standards, checking:

- Adequacy of risk assessments and control measures;
- Effectiveness of emergency response plans; and,
- Competence of personnel and safety culture.

Companies must review and update their safety case periodically, especially after major incidents, process changes, or new regulations. Regular HSE inspections and audits ensure ongoing compliance. Lessons learned from safety incidents are incorporated into continuous improvement processes.

Note that HSE does not provide a prescriptive list of regulatory requirements for the asset owner to implement. Instead, the onus is on the asset owner to satisfy HSE that it understands its risk and is managing it accordingly.

Failure to comply with HSE regulations can result in significant penalties:

- Financial penalties (Unlimited Fines) of £1 million to £10 million+ for large organizations in serious cases and £100,000 to £1 million for medium-sized companies.
- Criminal prosecution and imprisonment for company directors, safety officers, or responsible managers. Negligence or failure to act on known risks could lead to corporate manslaughter charges.
- HSE inspectors can issue prohibition notices resulting in an immediate shutdown of unsafe operations.
- Victims (workers, contractors, or the public) can sue for damages if non-compliance leads to injury or loss.

Now compare this to a prescriptively managed approach, such as that used in the North American electricity sector—NERC CIP.

The NERC CIP Standards are a set of mandatory cybersecurity regulations designed to protect the power grid and bulk electric system (BES) from cyber threats. These standards apply to power generation, transmission, and supporting entities in the United States, Canada, and parts of Mexico.

The NERC CIP standards focus on identifying, protecting, detecting, responding, and recovering from cyber incidents in the electric sector. Key areas covered include:

- Asset identification and classification;
- Access controls and physical security;
- Cybersecurity policies and personnel training;
- Incident response and recovery planning; and,
- Ongoing compliance and auditing

Entities must identify critical assets and categorize them based on their impact on grid reliability. Once categorized, organizations must implement security controls as outlined in specific NERC CIP standards, such as:

- CIP-002: Identify and categorize BES Cyber Systems.
- CIP-003: Establish cybersecurity policies and governance.
- CIP-004: Implement personnel training and risk assessment.
- CIP-005: Secure electronic perimeters and access controls.
- CIP-007: Apply system security controls (patching, antivirus, logging).
- CIP-008: Develop an incident response plan for cyber events.
- CIP-009: Implement recovery plans to restore operations after an attack.

Entities must document all security measures, policies, and incident response plans to demonstrate compliance with NERC CIP.

NERC conducts regular audits to verify compliance. Non-compliance can lead to penalties of up to $1 million per day per violation. Self-reporting and continuous monitoring help mitigate risks and reduce penalties. Organizations are also required to:

- Conduct regular security assessments and penetration testing.
- Update cybersecurity measures in response to new threats.
- Participate in industry-wide incident response exercises.
- Stay informed about NERC CIP updates and evolving cyber regulations.

The NIS2 Directive (Network and Information Security Directive 2) is an EU-wide cybersecurity regulation that strengthens the security requirements for critical and essential entities (EEs) across various sectors. It replaces the original NIS Directive (2016) and introduces stricter risk management, reporting obligations, and enforcement measures. NIS2 applies to sectors such as energy, healthcare, transport, digital infrastructure, banking, and public administration, ensuring a high common level of cybersecurity across the EU.

Before achieving compliance, organizations must determine if they are a covered entity—NIS2 categorizes organizations as either EEs or Important Entities (IEs) based on their sector and size. Small businesses below a certain threshold are generally exempt unless they are high-risk organizations.

- EEs are large organizations in critical sectors (e.g., energy, transport, finance).
- IEs are medium-sized companies in key industries (e.g., food production, chemicals, waste management).

Organizations must implement risk management measures across the following areas:

- Governance and Cyber Risk Management
- Incident Response and Business Continuity
- Access Control and Data Protection
- Supply Chain and Third-Party Security
- Security Monitoring and Threat Detection
- Cybersecurity Awareness and Training

NIS2 introduces strict cybersecurity incident reporting obligations. Failure to report cyber incidents on time can lead to severe penalties.

Organizations must prepare for regular audits and regulatory oversight by:

- Conducting internal cybersecurity audits.
- Maintaining detailed documentation of security policies and risk assessments.
- Cooperating with EU and national cybersecurity authorities during inspections.

Penalties for failure to comply with NIS2 regulations are significant:

- EEs: Fines up to €10 million or 2% of global annual turnover.
- IEs: Fines up to €7 million or 1.4% of global annual turnover.
- Senior executives can be held personally liable for cybersecurity failures.

In addition to NIS2, the Cyber Resilience Act (CRA) is a proposed regulation by the European Commission that establishes mandatory cybersecurity requirements for hardware and software products sold in the EU. Its goal is to improve the cybersecurity of digital products across their lifecycle—from design to end-of-life. It complements NIS2 as well as the EU Digital Operational Resilience Act (for financial services) and General Product Safety Regulations.

The CRA applies to "products with digital elements" (e.g., IoT devices, industrial controllers, software) and enforces secure-by-design principles.

One of the requirements is to perform risk assessments. It also introduces reporting obligations for incidents and vulnerabilities and mandates CE marking based on cybersecurity compliance.

There are penalties for non-compliance including fines of up to €15 million or 2.5% of global annual turnover (whichever is higher).

Table 6.2 summarizes the pros and cons of these three approaches. Given the nature of cybersecurity, an approach akin to NIS2/CRA or the HSE safety case is recommended. The rigid and bureaucratic nature of regulations like NERC CIP is not recommended because:

- They encourage organizations to achieve the minimum possible requirements, not to seek greater levels of maturity in their risk management.
- They fail to empower the organization to take ownership of their risk.
- They are not adaptable to the changing aspects of cybersecurity risk.

6.7 REASONING BEHIND RISK ASSESSMENTS

OT cybersecurity risk assessments are about understanding the real-world impact of threats on industrial processes. Unlike IT systems, OT environments manage physical processes, meaning that risk impacts can extend beyond data loss to safety hazards, environmental damage, and operational disruption. The reasoning behind conducting OT risk assessments goes far deeper than compliance—it's about ensuring resilience, reliability, and safety.

The NERC CIP approach is beneficial in that it mandates specific security controls, and this reduces ambiguity for asset owners. However, applying this "one size fits all" approach is focused on vulnerabilities, not risk. The HSE safety case approach encourages asset owners to consider their risk and apply the controls that are necessary to manage that risk,

TABLE 6.2 Comparison of Regulatory Approaches

Regulation	Pros	Cons
HSE Safety Case (UK)	Proactive and site-specific—Companies must prove their own safety measures	Complex and resource-intensive—Requires extensive documentation and evidence
	Focuses on prevention rather than just compliance	Lack of standardization—Risk control measures vary across companies
	Encourages innovation—Companies can develop customized risk controls	Slow enforcement—Effectiveness depends on regulatory oversight and inspections
NIS2/CRA Directives (EU)	Mandatory risk management and incident reporting ensure early response	Implementation varies by country—Each EU state has different enforcement mechanisms
	Aligns with EU-wide cybersecurity strategy for consistency	Focuses only on cybersecurity, not broader operational safety
NERC CIP (North America)	Strictly defined security controls reduce ambiguity	Rigid and bureaucratic—Compliance requires extensive audits and documentation
		Slow to adapt to new threats—Regulation updates take time
		Focuses only on cybersecurity, not physical safety risks

but while this gives the asset owner the flexibility to manage risk, rather than focusing on compliance, it is essential to identify a structured, contextual, and iterative process for identifying and managing risk.

The NIS2 directive approach provides a middle ground between the rigid and bureaucratic NERC CIP and HSE safety case methods. NIS2 also focuses on risk assessment to identify the required controls, but it also requires the compliance against international consensus-based standards, such as ISO/IEC 27001 and ISA/IEC 62443, and these standards provide the structured framework that introduces consistency into the process.

ISO/IEC 27001 and ISA/IEC 62443 are globally recognized, consensus-driven standards designed to help organizations manage cybersecurity risks in a systematic, scalable way. Both are developed through international committees composed of stakeholders from industry, academia, and government, ensuring a broad and balanced perspective that reflects real-world challenges and evolving threats. This consensus-based development process lends credibility and global applicability, making these standards widely accepted benchmarks for cybersecurity practices.

The core of ISO/IEC 27001 is the requirement to perform a risk assessment to identify threats to the confidentiality, integrity, and availability of information assets. Based on this assessment, organizations apply appropriate, context-specific controls selected from ISO/IEC 27002 or other sources. ISO 27001 does not dictate specific technical measures but rather emphasizes that controls must be justified by risk, which supports scalability across industries and organizations of all sizes.

ISA/IEC 62443 is tailored specifically to the needs of industrial automation and control systems and like ISO/IEC 27001, the core principle is that security requirements should be defined by the potential impact on the process or mission. ISA/IEC 62443 provides specific roles for asset owners, system integrators, and product suppliers, with clear guidance on performing risk assessments, establishing security levels (SLs), and selecting appropriate countermeasures.

The risk-based nature of both standards means they are adaptable, context-aware, and focused on prioritizing resources where they matter most. Instead of applying controls blindly, organizations are expected to understand their operational context, assess threats and vulnerabilities, and make informed decisions based on actual risk exposure. This is especially important in OT environments, where overly aggressive security can disrupt critical operations, and underestimating risk can have catastrophic consequences.

A well-defined risk assessment process should start with clear scoping—identifying assets, systems, and interconnections within the OT environment. In the ISA/IEC 62443 method, the asset owner identifies a system under consideration (SUC). The next step is to perform a high-level (or initial) risk assessment. It is this assessment that is distinct from other methods, as this focuses on consequence.

Based on this initial risk assessment, the asset owner then divides their SUC into zones. Zones can be created to define specific functions (e.g., safety), or can be providing specific services (e.g., wireless, remote access), or may be a specific vendor solution that is distinct from other solutions in the SUC. The objective is to identify the security controls needed by zone, as these may vary depending on the contents (and function) of the zone. For example, a safety zone will have a higher consequence if it is compromised and so will need additional controls compared with a zone providing local control of a low-risk process. The ISA/IEC 62443 method uses a concept called SL to quantify the security need for a zone. This SL is akin to safety integrity level in process safety, with 1 being the lowest level and 4 being the highest. This approach allows the asset owner to apply more controls to those zones where they are needed, and fewer to lower-risk zones.

The connections between zones are called conduits, and these will also be assessed to ensure appropriate security controls are in place.

Once the SUC is zoned, the asset owner performs a detailed risk assessment. This includes threat identification, vulnerability analysis, impact evaluation (based on process consequences), and likelihood.

6.8 RISK ASSESSMENT VERSUS CHECKLIST

The key outcomes from an OT cybersecurity risk assessment should include:

- A prioritized list of risks with context-specific impact(s)
- An understanding of residual risk after current controls are applied
- Requirements for cybersecurity controls.

A checklist might verify that certain controls or policies are present, but it doesn't necessarily account for the specific context, threats, and consequences of the environment being assessed. A true assessment requires analytical thinking, multi-stakeholder engagement (e.g., operators, engineers), and an understanding of process criticality.

Checklists are a systematic approach to identifying steps for organizing tasks, ensuring all steps have been completed for a given process; they are particularly effective for straightforward tasks, quick evaluations, or when time constraints prohibit or limit the ability to conduct a full assessment, they may serve as a practical tool securing that key elements are not overlooked, which may allow for better monitoring and management of processes.

This may include creating a detailed list of items or actions that may need or are required to be addressed, or which may be particularly useful in complex projects or activities where multiple components must be managed. By using checklists, organizations (and their teams) can enhance their efficiency through basic review, minimization of any risk of oversight, while maintaining a clear focus of their objectives. Under these circumstances, they may be more suitable for regular, more routine evaluations, or when there is a need for ensuring that essential criteria are met without delving excessively into too extensive of detail.

Unfortunately, most asset owners focus on "checklisting"[13] as opposed to conducting real assessments. There are a variety of reasons for this:

- There is a push for a silver-bullet solution. "Just tell me what I need to do to manage my risk" is the common demand. There can be no silver-bullet solution, cybersecurity is unique to everyone and must be treated as such.
- There is a tendency to want to avoid "all the work required" to follow the risk-based approach. Even supposed OT cybersecurity experts will claim that standards like ISA/IEC 62443 are just too complex and there "must be a simpler method."
- Many governments push for standardized approaches like NERC CIP which makes their regulatory task easier but fails to fully address asset owner risk in the most effective way possible.

The concept of using checklists extends far beyond mere task management; it serves as a cognitive tool aiding decision-making and prioritization tasks for management. In many industries that are attempting to solving complex problems to one or more problematic areas, checklists are utilized to standardize procedures and safety outcomes. Using this methodology allows project teams to systematically validate specifications for each critical element that has been considered and addressed, henceforth, fostering accountability and thoroughness in their work outcome.

And, checklisting may be adapted to suit different needs, making it a versatile tool; and whether it is for daily/weekly/monthly processes, special events, or a complex project implementation, checklists can help streamline those processes. Decomposition of diving larger tasks into smaller more manageable "chunks," individuals can approach their responsibilities with greater clarity and confidence, ultimately leading to better outcomes. This takes away appearance(s) of the tasks at hand being ominous and daunting, making them appear to be more manageable and easier to comprehend. However, that is where its usefulness ends.

Checklists may be detrimental when performing risk audits for several reasons. First, they generally promote a superficial approach to risk evaluation, encouraging auditors to check off items without engaging in further or deeper analysis. This may lead to a false sense of security, as critical risks may be overlooked simply because they are not explicitly listed on the checklist. The reliance on these predefined items can stifle creativity and critical thinking, which are essential for identifying unique as well as emerging risks which may not fit neatly into any of the established categories.

Next, checklists may create a false dichotomy between what is considered "acceptable" versus "unacceptable" risk. This binary thinking may limit the auditor's ability to assess any nuances of risk scenarios, leading to an oversimplified understanding of (very) complex situations. In dynamic environments,[14] where risks are constantly evolving, a rigid checklist may become quickly outdated, failing to capture the current landscape of threats and vulnerabilities. As a result, organizations may find themselves ill-prepared to respond to any unforeseen challenges.

And last, the use of checklists may foster a culture of (reactive) compliance rather than one of proactive risk management. When teams focus on completing checklists, their sole objective may be to prioritize meeting regulatory requirements over genuinely understanding and mitigating risks. This compliance-driven mindset can hinder the development of a robust risk management framework encouraging continuous improvement and adaptation. While checklists may serve as useful tools for certain contexts, their limitations in risk audits warrant careful consideration and, where possible, would require a more holistic approach to risk evaluation.

One prevalent pitfall is the tendency to adopt a checklist mentality aimed at minimizing effort. In this scenario, the primary goal shifts to merely passing an audit or meeting regulatory requirements. When asset owners take this route, they may overlook significant vulnerabilities that could jeopardize their security posture. It is crucial to understand that compliance does not equate to security.

Although adhering to standards and regulations may be essential, the real benefit arises when evaluations lead to informed decisions rather than mere adherence to a checklist. A common trap is to rely on the checklist approach with a view of doing as little work as possible. The objective simply becomes a task of merely passing an audit or satisfying a regulator. When asset owners follow this approach they're risking themselves by missing the real vulnerabilities. And—to re-iterate, again—compliance is *not* security.

While the alignment with standards and regulations is necessary, the true value comes when performed assessments driving a risk-based process that results in well-informed decisions—not just simply performing "checkbox compliance."[15]

Asset owners may implement a risk-based approach; however, this strategy may deteriorate over time if there is not a continuous effort to critically evaluate underlying assumptions, prioritize actions based on their real-world impacts, and adapt them accordingly. Without this ongoing scrutiny and adjustment, the effectiveness of the risk management framework may diminish, leading to potential failures, perhaps resulting from vulnerabilities, perhaps from something else.

Maintaining a proactive stance is essential for ensuring that the risk-based methodology remains relevant and robust in the face of new challenges.

OT systems are in a constant state of flux, with new devices being integrated or swapped out, connections changed, and most importantly, threats continuously adapting. Therefore, conducting a risk assessment should be viewed as a critically integral component of an ongoing risk management cycle rather than a one-time "one and done"[16] evaluation. Although this process can be labor-intensive, it is crucial to periodically revisit these assessments—regularly—to ensure that they remain applicable and effective in addressing the current landscape of risks that exist.

The dynamic nature of OT systems necessitates a proactive approach to risk management. As organizations incorporate newer technologies, newer approaches and processes, they also face new and emerging threats; thus, the risk landscape shifts, making it imperative to regularly perform risk assessments. This ongoing evaluation and re-evaluation allows organizations to identify vulnerabilities and implement necessary controls, while enhancing their overall security posture.

Incorporating a continuous risk management strategy not only helps in identifying potential threats but also fosters a culture of vigilance within the organization. With committing to regular assessments, organizations may prepare better for any potentially unforeseen challenges, and thus, can ensure that their risk management practices will evolve in tandem to their operational environment. Adopting this strategy results in the development of more robust systems and enhances the ability to withstand potential disruptions; however, it may require significant investments of additional time and resources; this especially includes financial considerations as many industrial operations usually operate at maximized operational efficiencies, and any additional fiduciary costs will take away from current revenue obtained.

A more effective method for fostering continuous improvement might involve implementing incrementally stepped changes that focus on efficiency and adaptability, rather than solely on faults and disrupted operations. Doing so would allow organizations to evolve without incurring significantly excessive costs or delays.

Prioritizing small, manageable adjustments rather than sweeping overhauls, organizations can create a culture of ongoing enhancement that encourages innovation while minimizing any operational disruption.

This approach not only conserves resources but also enables teams to respond swiftly to emerging challenges that may result from any changes implemented, ensuring that improvements are sustainable and aligned with the organization's long-term goals, not to mention, maintaining safety protocols.

Comprehensive assessments are essential for newly implemented systems as well as any substantial modifications made to existing ones. It is important to conduct regular re-evaluations of these systems on regular and predetermined intervals—usually every three to five years—based on an organization's risk tolerance levels; some sectors may perform and act upon assessments quicker than others, and when safety and performance are critical, time periods in between assessments performed may lengthen.

It is important to understand that checklists should not be regarded as simply substitutes for comprehensive assessments—there aren't. They are part of a collection of many tools available, and it should be emphasized that they are part of a broader set of resources rather than the entirety of the toolkit. A humorous anecdote in many industrial sectors is that—when only a hammer is used, everything appears to be a nail.

A significant drawback of placing excessive reliance on checklists is that they fail to offer a comprehensive view of the underlying issues. Frequently, checklists are associated with vulnerability assessments, which are commonly mistaken for risk assessments. These two concepts are uniquely distinct and serve different purposes. The use of checklists can further exacerbate this confusion, leading to a lack of clarity in understanding any nuances between the two forms of assessments.

Understanding the distinctions between vulnerability assessments and risk assessments is crucial for effective risk management. A vulnerability assessment focuses primarily on identifying and evaluating weaknesses within a given organization, operation, system, or process which could be exploited by threats, known or newly discovered. This type of assessment aims at pinpointing specific vulnerabilities, such as outdated software, inadequate security protocols, or physical security lapses, which may provide a clearer picture on where improvements may be needed to bolster better defense posturing. In contrast, a risk assessment takes a broader approach by not only identifying vulnerabilities but also evaluating any potential impacts, along with their likelihood if those threats are exploited using those vulnerabilities. This process involves analyzing any consequences discovered from different risk scenarios, perhaps considering factors such as the value of an asset at stake, the potential financial losses resulting from such an impact, or the reputational damage which may occur. In the likelihood of such an event, and if its potential impact were to happen, risk assessments could help organizations prioritize their security efforts and allocate resources more effectively.

Another example can be seen in the realm of compliance checks, in which a checklist might ensure that certain regulatory requirements are met. While this is important for legal adherence, it does not necessarily reflect the actual risk landscape of the organization. A risk assessment would delve deeper, analyzing the specific threats that could exploit those vulnerabilities and the effectiveness of existing controls. Thus, relying solely on checklists can lead to a superficial understanding of security issues, ultimately hindering an organization's ability to effectively manage and mitigate risks.

Probably the most significant observation is that checklists might appear to serve as a reflection of an individuals' understanding of the relevant issue or topic. This situation can be exacerbated by those conducting assessments who often possess minimal or no expertise in the specific subject matter. Consequently, this lack of knowledge can intensify any existing challenges presented by the checklists. The reliance upon these checklists may then lead to superficial or misleading evaluations, as assessors might overlook critical nuances which may or would require a deeper introspective understanding of the topic. This knowledge gap not only undermines the effectiveness of the assessments but may also raise concerns about the accuracy of any conclusions drawn from them. The combination of inadequate knowledge among assessors and the limitations of checklists developed as a result of their lack of knowledge can create a cycle of misunderstanding as well as misrepresentation of whatever issues may exist at the time. Addressing these deficiencies is essential for ensuring evaluations are thorough and informative, thereby enhancing the overall quality of the assessment process.

Determining the appropriate time to conduct a comprehensive assessment as opposed to utilizing a checklist involves careful consideration of the specific context and objectives at hand. A full assessment is typically warranted when the situation requires an in-depth analysis, such as evaluating complex issues, understanding multifaceted problems, or when significant changes have occurred that necessitate a thorough review. This approach allows for a detailed exploration of various factors, providing a holistic view that can inform decision-making and strategy development. It is essential that they are reviewed when there are significant changes in the operational environment, such as the introduction of new processes, technologies, or regulations, as these changes can have a significant impact on safety. Additionally, if there is an increase in the scale or complexity of operations, or if past incidents have highlighted vulnerabilities, a comprehensive evaluation of risks is necessary to ensure that all potential hazards are identified and mitigated effectively. A full risk assessment is crucial when embarking on new projects or initiatives that may expose the organization to unforeseen risks. Situations where there is a potential for high-impact events, such as natural disasters, cybersecurity threats, or significant financial investments, all fall within scope of these classifications of impacted events. As with conducting any assessment, organizations can develop strategies to minimize risks and safeguard their assets, employees, and stakeholders.

As with anything else, checklists can sometimes lead to a false sense of security, as they may not capture all relevant factors or emerging risks that could arise in rapidly dynamic settings. Regulators strongly encourage, if not often mandate, a proactive approach to risk management, fostering a culture of continuous improvement and vigilance by requiring full risk assessments through comprehensive methods that not only identify existing risks but also anticipate future challenges, ensuring that organizations are better prepared to respond to unforeseen events. Many who perform such assessments often indicate that regulators have unreasonable expectations as they are representative of what regulators want, not what actually exists; meaning, regulatory auditors may dictate "wish lists" through mandated requirements or controls that prove to be unrealistic or incapable of reaching. This is one of the largest downsides of checklists.

As such, checklists should never be seen as a replacement for formal assessments. A checklist is a tool—not the whole toolbox.

Formal assessments notwithstanding, when a problem or control is not recognized on a specific checklist, it is essential to determine any subsequent steps which may be needed in addressing any situation. First, a thorough review of the checklist should be conducted to ensure that all items have been accurately assessed and that nothing is overlooked. This may involve consulting with team members or stakeholders who are familiar with the checklist's purpose and the context in which it is used.

Next, once the review is complete, the next course of action involves identifying potential gaps in the checklist itself. This could mean revising the checklist to include additional controls or issues that may have been overlooked initially. Engaging in discussions with relevant parties can provide insights into what might be missing and how to enhance the checklist for future use. It is crucial to implement a follow-up process to monitor the effectiveness of the revised checklist. This may include setting up regular reviews or audits to ensure that all controls are being identified and addressed appropriately.

As much as our position to perform full risk assessments is preferred, with regulatory audits, due to complexities and the overwhelming amount of controls and requirements that may exist, it may not be timely enough to perform complete assessments; thus, use of these checklists may be more preferred. And again, it is strongly recommended to perform thorough review of these checklists by matching them (as best as possible) against regulatory requirements. Overlooking critical compliance requirements or procedural steps may attract further, more detailed scrutiny from regulatory bodies. The consequences of such findings can be significant, potentially resulting in penalties, mandated corrective actions, or even reputational damage to the organization involved. Failure to properly review these checklists can also lead to long-term implications for an organization's operational integrity. Regulatory findings may necessitate extensive post-audits or investigations, diverting resources and attention away from core business activities, not to mention the overarching complexities and length of time required to perform subsequent audits. Repeated infractions can result in heightened regulatory oversight, which may impose additional burdens on the organization and hinder its ability to operate efficiently.

Essentially, performing regular assessments, even if it means reviewing checklists, allows the organization to prioritize areas in need of (immediate) attention and improvement. The dynamic nature of operational environments necessitates ongoing assessments of risk factors. Changes in technology, regulatory requirements, and operational processes can introduce new vulnerabilities that may not have been present during previous evaluations. Regularly updating risk checklists allows organizations to adapt to these changes proactively, ensuring that their risk management strategies are aligned with current best practices and industry standards. This proactive approach not only enhances the security posture of OT but also fosters a culture of continuous improvement and vigilance within the organization.

Compliance, not security, dictates the need for checklists as opposed to full-scaled assessments. It pollutes the meaning and context behind actual assessments and only enables adherence to requirements of whatever regulation is being evaluated. Neglecting to perform a comprehensive review of a given checklist before an assessment, even if it isn't as comprehensive as it should be, can lead to several significant repercussions. The absence of a meticulous examination may result in overlooked critical criteria, especially specific areas of interest by regulatory auditors, which could compromise the integrity and accuracy of the assessment itself. This overlooked aspect can lead to incomplete evaluations, ultimately affecting the outcomes and decisions based on the assessment results. Failing to adhere to a thorough checklist review can create inconsistencies in the assessment process. Such inconsistencies may not only confuse the evaluators but also diminish the credibility of the assessment in the eyes of the stakeholders. When key elements are missed, it can lead to a lack of trust in any of the findings, which, when presented to auditors, could have long-term implications for the organization. As such, the repercussions of skipping this essential step can extend beyond immediate assessment outcomes. It may result in increased costs and time delays as issues arise that could have been identified and addressed beforehand. In the long run, the failure to conduct a thorough checklist review can hinder progress, affect team morale, and potentially lead to reputational damage for the organization.

Risk managers work with both compliance and security staff and contractors. Many times, regulators will state that security is compliance, and vice versa. This is far from the truth. Compliance represents minimum requirements defined by a criteria set that includes both private- and public-sectored organizations. It is supposed to be a cooperative effort—a compromise, if you will—between the regulator and the asset owner. More than often, it is not.

There will always be one or more finding(s), there will always be one or more non-compliance violation(s), and there will be multiple area(s) to re-evaluate through significantly more thorough investigation(s) and review(s). There is always work to perform and areas in need of attention, especially when it comes to OT and their operational environments that they support.

The constant involvement between regulatory bodies and asset owners is diplomatic relations with compromises allowed or denied, given or taken, by both sides. This dance, if you will, between the regulator and the asset owner is what we refer to as "regulatory purgatory."

6.9 WHEN CHECKLISTS FAIL

A core assumption underlying the use of checklists is that the systems, processes, or operational scenarios being reviewed are proscribed. Unfortunately, in many OT environments, that assumption does not hold. Industrial processes are often custom engineered or have evolved over time, resulting in site-specific configurations and undocumented practices.

In such cases, applying a generic checklist can not only be misleading., but it can also be detrimental to the risk assessment process. The checklist may prompt the assessor to verify compliance with controls or configurations that don't exist in the current setup—not because of non-compliance, but because the process deviates from pre-conceived assumptions. Worse still, the checklist may skip over unique risks that fall outside this predefined structure. This can result in a false sense of security. A lack of gap does not automatically imply a lack of risk.

A classic example in OT environments is for a checklist to ask, "Are all network connected devices running anti-malware protection?" Firstly, many OT environments will be operating with network connected devices that are incapable of running anti-malware protection (e.g., many PLCs or controllers). Their lack of anti-malware protection does not automatically constitute a gap—to understand the risk, the assessment should consider what types of malware could infect the device and how that malware could be deployed on the device.

Conversely, an operational facility may have devices that should incorporate anti-malware protection but are not considered "networked equipment." Examples include legacy workstations or servers that are connected to proprietary networks of sensors or actuators, but isolated from the wider facility network. These workstations and servers could still be infected by malware (e.g., via infected portable device) and this could result in a loss of view or control.

Another major limitation of fixed checklists arises when risk scenarios fall outside the anticipated bounds or constraints of the checklist.

Checklists work best in bounded problem spaces, where risks, controls, and mitigations are well understood and relatively static. Cybersecurity risk, be it IT or OT oriented, is not static. It is affected by emerging threats, techniques, and practices and new vulnerabilities. In OT environments, there can be even more variation due to site-specific conditions and process interdependencies that cannot be fully captured in a checkbox.

6.10 IS MORE DATA BETTER?

For safety-based considerations, more datapoints are suggested. The rationale behind this recommendation stems from the need to enhance the robustness of any findings by ensuring that all potential risks are adequately addressed. Additionally, inclusion of more data points can significantly improve the reliability of any conclusions drawn from the analysis. A larger dataset allows for a more nuanced examination of trends and patterns, which can be instrumental in identifying underlying issues that may not be apparent with a limited number of observations. This thorough approach not only bolsters the credibility of the results but also fosters a proactive stance in mitigating potential hazards. The integration of additional data points is not merely a quantitative enhancement; it also enriches the qualitative aspects of the research. By capturing a wider array of scenarios and conditions, the analysis can better reflect real-world complexities.

The qualitative enhancement derived from integrating diverse data sources can lead to a more holistic interpretation of whatever findings are discovered. When researchers consider various types of data, they can contextualize their results within a broader framework, thereby enriching the narrative surrounding their research. This multifaceted approach not only strengthens the validity of the conclusions drawn but also enhances the overall impact of the study, making it more relevant and applicable to real-world scenarios. The interplay between quantitative and qualitative data fosters a dynamic research environment where findings can be cross-validated and explored from multiple angles. This synergy not only bolsters the credibility of the research but also encourages innovative thinking and exploration of any new hypotheses that may have been conceptualized.

This expanded perspective allows for a more nuanced understanding of the subject matter, facilitating a comprehensive analysis that can lead to more robust conclusions. As such, the depth of insight obtained becomes invaluable insofar as to developing more sound business practices and strategies that effectively address safety concerns, ultimately leading to more secure outcomes in practice.

Simply put, if you have more data, you have better resolution and less quantization of any error(s) introduced. When it comes to data analysis and processing, the quantity of data plays a crucial role in determining the quality of the results. Essentially, having a larger dataset allows for a finer resolution in the outcomes, which means that the details captured are more precise and nuanced. This increased volume of information enables analysts to discern patterns and trends that might otherwise remain hidden in smaller datasets. Consequently, the richness of the data contributes significantly to the overall accuracy of the analysis. Larger datasets help to minimize quantization errors, which is the discrepancy that arises when continuous data is represented in a discrete format. When there is an abundance of data points, the likelihood of misrepresenting the underlying continuous phenomena decreases. This is particularly important in fields such as signal processing and digital imaging, where the fidelity of the representation can greatly impact the effectiveness of the analysis or the quality of the output. By reducing quantization error, one can achieve results that are not only more reliable but also more reflective of the true nature of the data being studied.

In industries governed by strict compliance regulations, the use of checklists can be subject to various constraints that must be carefully navigated. These constraints often arise from the need to adhere to specific legal and regulatory standards, which can dictate the format, content, and frequency of checklist usage. For example, organizations in sectors such as healthcare, finance, and pharmaceuticals are required to follow rigorous protocols to ensure safety, accuracy, and accountability. Consequently, checklists must be meticulously designed in alignment to these standards, ensuring that all necessary compliance elements are addressed while also facilitating efficient operational processes. In these situations, the importance of using critical thinking cannot be overemphasized.

Risk assessors must engage in context-driven analysis, looking beyond simply answering "yes/no" questions to understand risk, not just vulnerability. Key aspects are how threats might manifest themselves, and what real-world consequences could be.

Assessors must ask themselves the following questions:

- "What is different about this environment?"
- "What assumptions does this checklist imply that are non-applicable here?"
- "Is there more information that the individual isn't telling or sharing with me?"
- "Is the individual telling me what I want to hear?"

Unfortunately, the "yes/no" format of the checklist does not lend itself to critical thinking.

The assessor may not have the knowledge to ask the probing questions that are required, and the assessed party may not be inclined to provide too much detail for fear of creating more work for themselves. Perhaps the most profound limitation of checklist-driven risk assessments is what can be called the "flattening effect"—this is when risk is reduced to a binary evaluation, all risks are treated as equal. In reality, risk is highly differentiated—in applicability, likelihood, and consequence.

Since "flattening" the decision-making process, decision-makers are ruling out a more comprehensive approach, and therefore, are actually introducing risk (in the form of increased error(s) through either assumed or miscalculated results), rather than eliminating it.

Risk management is all about calculating odds:

- What are the odds that something bad will happen?
- If so, when, where, and who will be impacted?

In order to calculate these odds, there should be sufficient data to substantiate the odds of impact. It's all about statistics. The more data is acquired, the better the chances of the odds being more fair. If there isn't substantial data provided, the odds will become skewed. You're not looking at something bad that will happen; you're looking at whatever mechanisms you have in place that will prevent something bad from happening.

By introducing other methods of calculating risk, executives can make much better decisions that are fair and more accurate, rather than "coin-tossing" as are to "yes" or "no" answers. In other words, by creating checklists that are simply "yes" or "no," they're limiting themselves more, rather than doing additional work to introduce more datapoints instead of less. More datapoints means that the amount of error introduced is reduced—the greater the number, the better the result; however, as with anything whereby more datapoints introduced, this can lead to a backlash whereby more risk is introduced rather than eliminated.

Individuals engaged in the process of checklisting often struggle to distinguish between two or more specific data points. This difficulty can arise from several factors, which may include the complexity of the data itself or the manner by which it is presented. When using multiple datasets, the nuances that differentiate these points may become obscured, leading to potential errors in their interpretation as well as application. As a result, the effectiveness of utilizing the checklisting process may be compromised, which may possibly affect any outcomes of the tasks used. The inability to differentiate between these data points can have significant implications for decision-making and its operational efficiency. In environments where precision is paramount, such as in healthcare or engineering, misinterpretation of data can lead to serious consequences. The reliance solely on checklists, while having good intentions of streamlining processes and enhance accuracy, may inadvertently introduce confusion if users are not adequately trained to recognize and analyze any distinctions between similar datasets. This highlights the importance of those who utilize it possess a clear understanding of the underlying data.

6.11 CATERING TO MANAGEMENT THROUGH CHECKLISTS

Many corporations often have management review meetings whereby a department reviews their progress from the previous to the current month. Data is usually collected and statistical methods are utilized to illustrate and demonstrate advancement of any initiative being implemented within the organization. To show progress, data is categorically placed into groups that are color-coded: red for critical, yellow for concern, and green for acceptable.

In reality, no one really understands the statistics shown—all they know is how much red, yellow, and green is displayed during the presentation(s). This is a prime example of how little organizations understand their own internal processes, and in many cases, how irrelevant whatever checklists they use. Additionally, since executive management are generally attending these meetings, the data will often be skewed to show as much green as possible; essentially, telling executive management what they want to read and hear—that everything is "OK." Thus, the usefulness of using both assessments—as well as checklists—now becomes moot, as their utility of existence is merely to demonstrate compliance to executive management's directives.

Management should not be reviewing data that's all green; their roles and responsibilities lie with their decision-making capabilities based on the accuracy and validity of the data presented; however, if the data is skewed or has been custom-tailored to the executive management's directives, then this will nullify whatever decision(s) they make. Similar to the assessors or regulators, executive management should ask the same questions as outlined in the aforementioned page.

To mitigate these challenges, organizations should consider implementing training programs that focus on data literacy and critical analysis skills. By equipping individuals with the tools necessary to interpret data accurately, the likelihood of misidentification can be significantly reduced. Also, enhancing how checklists are designed to incorporate visual aids or clearer categorizations may assist users for making better distinctions. Thus, fostering a culture of data awareness and competence will lead to more effective checklisting practices and improved overall performance.

However, when a checklist is used in isolation, it often fails to reflect the nuanced variation of impacts between one risk and another. For instance, the lack of a firmware update on a non-critical device might be scored the same as poor access control on a safety-critical system. This flattening results in misleading prioritization, where resources may be spent fixing low-risk issues while high-risk issues are then ignored and overlooked.

6.12 USING ASSESSMENTS FROM OTHER COMPANIES

To some degree, utilizing cybersecurity risk assessments taken from other companies, from other critical infrastructure sectors, and from AI business-modeling applications introduces a plethora of issues, some of which teeter on illegal activity. It should be noted that this section, and the subsequent three sections, not only support the negative impacts associative from the use of AI, but from their use in-general.

It is not only a common, but growing, practice among companies, especially companies who are tightly regulated, to use parts of, entire sections of, or the entire content itself of existing cybersecurity risk assessments. This could be due to the lack of knowledge of the company's primary purpose, its role(s) as a critical infrastructure company, and most importantly, the OT and control systems' environments that operate and support the critical functions of those companies. Many of the contributing factors to this growing lack of knowledge of companies' internal workings is discussed throughout this book.

Some of the main reasons why using another company's risk assessments (and their results) include (but are not limited to) the following:

- **Lack of Contextual Relevance**—An assessment taken from another company may not accurately reflect specific threats or vulnerabilities of the company's current threats or vulnerabilities; meaning, items and factors used from another company's operations (or even critical infrastructure industry, such as a company within the electric industry using assessments from the healthcare industry), their metrics (KPIs), how their operations are engineered and implemented, how they're managed and maintained, and (overall) how they operate, may be partially or completely applicable, thereby making whatever data gleaned deemed as inapplicable.
- **Inaccurate Ratings/Different Risk Appetites**—Some risk assessments may rely on subjective judgment(s), and different companies may have varying metrics for what they consider critical, high, medium, or low risk. Companies of entirely different industries, in which one clearly utilizes objective analysis, versus another industry which may utilize more subjective or observed analysis, will (obviously) cause issues. The data will not only be incorrect, it will be non-applicable.

- **Different Risk Footprints**—Additionally, their footprints may vary for different areas of operation, such as remote access, malware detection, and logging; for example, logging practices of all activities of a nuclear power generation facility will be completely different from a hospital's critical care unit. Differing footprints, using the drastic example mentioned, includes factors, such as (but is not limited to):
  - Criticality of that operation;
  - Importance of the information produced from the operation;
  - Timeliness of the information based upon the impact to the operation; and,
  - Scalability of the operation (nuclear is a bigger footprint, and has much, much longer lasting impacts due to radiation, than a CCU).
- **Information Accuracy**—Assessments from company to company are dynamic; that is, their necessitation for performing their risk assessments—whether full or partial—as well as its time of year performed, how often it is performed, and duration of the assessment, are all reflective of that particular company's business management model. Additionally, IT cybersecurity risk assessments might not need to be performed as regularly, and as often, not to mention, as thorough, as opposed to OT or control systems' environments, especially where safety is an integral part of one or more critical operations of that company performing the assessment.
- **Regulatory Requirements**—Regulatory auditors move from company to company throughout a given yearly cycle. During their visit to a company, if they determine that the company being audited has not only reviewed, but performed the same or similar assessment compared to another company within that industry, there could be potential findings, perhaps fines or other legal consequences.

6.13 USING CUSTOM ASSESSMENTS

Why would utilizing custom[17] assessments be considered bad?

First, the number one issue with utilizing a completely custom (not customized) assessment process would pertain to compliance and regulatory requirements' issues. Companies that operate in heavily regulated environments, such as energy and oil/gas refinement, are given very little capacity or license to negotiate their operational position, especially when it pertains to critically important environments, often operated with very strict safety protocols. There is very little negotiating power that the company says—either they operate as to how the regulatory body specifically tells them, or risk being shut down. Even if the company's custom assessment included portions of the regulation as part of their assessment process, they are risking the very financial success of the company. Essentially, using a completely custom assessment process in these types of industries would be a complete waste of time, and would not only upset the regulatory body, but the company's shareholders and board of directors. For these industries, safe is better; meaning, follow what the regulators administer.

Second, custom risk assessments often are inconsistent, not only within their own companies, but their industries. There is a lack of standardization; again, meaning that custom assessments aren't modeled after a baseline, standard, etc. Custom assessments may lack the structured modeling offered through standards and their frameworks, which, in turn, can lead to inconsistencies.

For example, authentication used for vendor access by one internal department may utilize one method, but another department may utilize a completely different method. If the custom assessment focuses on remote access, could there be a risk in the assessment process itself? And again, it depends; what this means is, how detailed does the company wish to delve with just this one control requirement? If the assessment simply skims over the requirement, or uses a simple checklist, then explaining any detail specifics to an auditor will become far more complicated.

With such inconsistencies, critical information may be ignored or omitted. Missing information not only skews the end result of such an assessment, it may completely make the entire assessment null and void; meaning, the assessment is invalid and inaccurate, and may require a reassessment. This wastes time and money, as those who were audited before now need to account to (possibly) new(er) questions, and thus, the end result may be completely opposite from its initial result; or, worse yet, may further drive the risk factor from a lesser severity to one of greater severity.

Inconsistent evaluations across a company's enterprise will make it very difficult to prioritize and allocate financial resources accordingly, and thereby, cause potential in-fighting between internal departments (or perhaps, even entire divisions). Thus, through this use, has now caused a ripple effect which will completely politicize the entire company, now making it an unsavory environment to work in. Key or long-term workers, familiar with the guts of the company, will leave, now causing our next factor.

Third, it's called "tech debt," and it's a growing problem not only in IT, but also OT. Within OT-based environments, technical debt (or "tech debt") pertains to additional or extra work being performed on an OT system.

Tech debt accrues "interest over time"[18] and could have possible consequences, such as the accidental exposure of the OT or control system device to potential security risks; though, there are other factors that contribute to tech debt as an integral part, the primary focus here is the accidental exposure to increased risk. For example, introduction of a performance-enhancing product to monitor temperature and pressure of an electrical transformer, but is installed outside of the company's firewalled enterprise, while having a direct, unsecured connection from the internal enterprise network to the vendor supporting the product, has now introduced new, higher risk factors into what would have been already categorized as low risk.

Tech debt includes (but is not limited to) the following factors:

- **Maintainability**—Implementation of a device, software, or product, along with its manageability, through (too) rapid of an installation, without full considering of all potential consequences, often may lead to disastrous conditions, such as regulatory violation(s), lowered safety conditions, etc.
- **Cost Management**—Attempts at cost-cutting too much to the point of where cuts can now include newly introduced security vulnerabilities for potential attacks, again, without any consideration (usually due to shortened installation schedules).
- **Scalability**—Using the example above concerning the transformer monitoring system, where a lack of thorough evaluation, perhaps due to cost-cutting efforts, time schedules, or lack of employee/contractor resources, has caused a potential bypass condition in which the monitoring system inside the company's network is directly connected to an outside resource (via the Internet), completely bypassing any security measures or countermeasures (such as firewalls). This has now raised what was otherwise a low-risk environment to a critical risk environment.

Fourth, when key or long-term workers leave a company en masse, usually there is a reason. Whatever that reason may be, this causes internal parties to hold back any information, positioning themselves for future fights. Welcome to the "siloed community."[19] Internal assessors now have to fight with workers for information; and, if a regulated industry, definitely does not bode well for either the company—or the workers—as auditors will have many findings based on *their* own risk assessment audits. This often continues in a downward spiral until executive management begin intervening with actions such as budget cuts; or worse, layoffs.

Fifth, custom assessments become "islands";[20] that is, their end result usually is convoluted, complex, and difficult to comprehend. Additionally, these same assessments (generally) won't work with other or similar assessments if conducted. This now makes it difficult to accurately measure risk as one assessment may indicate a critical risk factor, but another may not. Integration no longer is possible as almost all interested parties are fighting among themselves that there is zero cohesion, cooperation, and community.

Sixth, when all of the prior factors are faced by executive management, there are (generally) two options:

1. Layoff all workers, and completely outsource the entire department, or if too widespread, perhaps the entire division.
2. Or, if outsourcing would be considered too expense, layoff most of the workers, and hire contractors to replace them.

However, this now introduces what was discussed earlier in the book—lack of ownership. Neither an outsourced company, or a contractor, will really take ownership and responsibility for their actions and how they perform regular operations.

Additionally, outsourced organizations and/or contractors often will bring into the company outsourcing their own management styles and models. If it is a regulated company, this will often conflict between the company's compliance department(s) and the outsourced workers. Some (maybe even all) of the processes introduced by the outsourced workers may now introduce new risk into the environment, as it had worked at a prior company; however, that company's metrics and KPIs are (more than likely) measured differently than the outsourcing company.

6.14 STAFF TURNOVER ISSUES

Adding to the limitations of checklist-based approaches is the growing impact of corporate turnover, outsourcing, and workforce specialization. Many organizations today structure their teams around narrowly defined skill sets, assigning staff or contractors to single-purpose roles—PLC programming, firewall configuration, or instrumentation—without broad visibility into the wider operational context. This over-specialization may hinder cross-functional thinking that robust risk assessments demand. Individuals focused solely on task execution often lack the mandate—or the experience—to connect technical issues to broader operational risks. Using this model, checklists become the default mechanism for driving action, because workers aren't expected (or enabled) to exercise deeper analytical judgment.

Meanwhile, frequent staff turnover, particularly among contractors and temporary personnel, leads to a steady erosion of institutional knowledge. When those individuals leave, they take with them a rich understanding of historical information, decisions made, known system configurations, vulnerabilities, and prior incident responses—often without proper handoff or documentation. The next person inherits a checklist but not the reasoning behind the past risk decisions.

This creates a shallow assessment culture, where "doing the checklist" is seen as sufficient, even when the systems, personnel, and threats have changed significantly. In contrast, long-tenured employees—the so-called "greybeards"—often retain invaluable knowledge about operational quirks and hidden risks that cannot be captured in a checklist alone. Their insights into what could go wrong and why are rooted in experience, not procedure(s).

Without mechanisms to capture and contextualize this knowledge—such as formal risk registers, post-mortems, or living asset documentation[21]—the organization becomes vulnerable to repeating same or similar mistakes or missing any evolving risks.

6.15 CRITICAL THINKING

One of the most, if not *the* most, important factors to risk management is to identify, process, analyze, and report logically, and with substantiated merit. Called "critical thinking," it is a method by which all data, no matter how relevant or irrelevant, is considered as part of the overall analytical method. The point is to view analytics openly, and most importantly, broadly from a wide-angled lens in an effort to perceive as many factors, as much data, as possible, which can then be included as part of this process. As such, it is thought of as a crucial method for analyzing an unknown number of factors which may be considered for any perceived or projected outcome or consequence.

This is particularly useful with risk management when there is insufficient data available to provide a substantiated conclusion. Often thought of as "big picture thinking," it represents all aspects from tactical to strategic level techniques of thought and perception.

With it, this enables corporations to ask the following questions:

- What are the possible outcomes?
- What are the possible consequences?
- If there are any consequences, how will this impact our business?
- Will there exist any legal repercussion(s), financially, reputationally, or both?
- Based on which questions are asked, and what outcomes may result from them:
    - How much will this cost (time, resources, financial)?
    - What is my estimated recovery time?
    - What else may be impacted?
    - Who else may be impacted?

- And will there be any potential future repercussions?

Critical thinking is simply not about identifying and analyzing one possible conclusion. It involves the assertion as to why that conclusion was determined, what biasness may exist (if any), how it was determined, and if there were any previous circumstances, events, incidents, or outcomes which may have contributed to the conclusion.

One other aspect for perceiving critical thinking is applying the "drill down"[22] approach to problem solving. Again, this involves utilizing as much data as possible to ascertain a possible conclusion. From there, it may be necessary to continue drilling down by asking "why," "what," "where," and "how" in order to simplify the process for capturing the essential (primordial) reasoning. This perception is extremely useful when conducting recovery methods to a given operational incident because: every situation is different.

The prescriptive processes that are provided are intended to guide organizations. Unfortunately an unintended consequence is that users get blinded by the minutia of the process itself, rather than focusing on the goal. As a result, the goal becomes the completion of the process, not the objective of the process, that is, to understand and reduce risk.

Reconsider the Oldsmar incident. The current processes fail to reveal the hidden risks the organization faced. None of the questions in assessments would have uncovered that the SCADA system allowed users to set dangerous chemical dosing levels. Critical thinking, however, would prompt reviewers to examine all aspects of the operation closely, ultimately identifying a gap. Another review at a different organization may not yield the same gap(s), and that is the point of critical thinking versus applying prescriptive checklists. Checklists ask for answers to specific questions; critical thinking starts by asking what could go wrong, irrespective of predefined questions.

6.16 DYNAMIC THINKING

Dynamic thinking, on the other hand, is the complete opposite of critical thinking. It is probably best observed as a "drill up"[23] approach to problem solving. This methodology, too, has its usefulness with risk management in several ways. This thought process focuses on how change of an operational process may continue and evolve over a period of time. This contrasts with static thinking which pertains to focusing on either the current or past state of an operational process and fixating at a specific reference or point in time. Static thinking may alternatively be described in terms of stateful processing whereby one state of a process or operation then leads to the next, and so on and so forth.

Unlike where critical thinking may be utilized in a situation, or is used in response to an event, occurrence, condition, or incident that has yet to happen, dynamic thinking realizes that whatever is being reverse-analyzed has already happened. In simple terms, dynamic thinking is taking an already determined conclusion, but working upwards (or backwards) to determine which factors existed or were used to ascertain the already created/generated conclusion. This is evidentiary when conducting post-regression analysis, which are statistically determined outcomes through substantiated and attestable data.

Dynamic thinking is useful with risk assessments insofar that past events, occurrences, incidents, outcomes, or consequences are incorporated as part of a new risk assessment for predictive analysis of either current or potential risks moving forward. Although dynamic thinking, by itself, can be used solely as a risk management tool, in most circumstances, it is an integral part of the critical thinking process of current and potential risk analysis.

6.17 CHALLENGE-RESPONSE/CHECKBACK

One very important method of ensuring that an operation is not disrupted is by performing a challenge-response, or "checkback." Although this may be considered more of an operational security-based method, it can very well apply to cybersecurity as well. The process in of itself implies what it means, what it does, and why this an important step to any process, cyber or otherwise.

For cybersecurity, it ensures that certain controls—measures and countermeasures—are implemented, or in most circumstances, any modifications made, such as through an update, or a complete upgrade, checkbacks are a way of ensuring that what was set or configured before remains the same after said activity. And, even if the current operational environment is being completely overhauled with a newer environment, newer system, or newer software (or firmware), the checkback process still ensures that whatever design was engineered remains consistent to the specifications designed.

For example, if an upgrade to an existing piece of software remains the same per design specification(s), but is merely a security patch upgrade, there are a series of steps, some of which are nothing short of using common sense; whereas, other steps may or may not apply based on the industry, and more to the company using that system. It is crucial that for such operational environments where safety, reliability, and performance, or all three, are considered critical, conducting a checkback *must* be performed; otherwise, unexpected consequential events may occur, and a backout process(es) *may not* be possible unless a checkback process is performed. For the checkback process to work, it operates on a buddy system; that is, two individuals who are knowledgeable of the operation being modified, cross-check each other's work.

The following series of steps may (or may not) include (but are not limited to) the following steps. The example is non-industry specific. The process being performed here is a minor update to several new sensory devices that were installed as part of a cooling system. The sensors measure pressure, temperature, rate of flow, and check for cavitation (preventative measure to alleviate a "water hammer" from forming). Two sensors, A3H115 and AYB1011, are being added.

ENGINEER #1 TO ENGINEER #2: This is Work Order #911567, connecting Sensor A3H115 and AYB1011 to PLC #23.

ENGINEER #2 TAKES THE WORK ORDER, READS THROUGH IT, AND IF ACCURATE, ACKNOWLEDGES: Confirmed.

ENGINEER #1: Wire P334 is connected to Sensor A3H115.

ENGINEER #2: Confirmed.

ENGINEER #1: Sensor setpoint set to +5V.

ENGINEER #2: Confirmed.

ENGINEER #1: Checkback—Wire P334 connected to Sensor A3H115, set to +5V.

ENGINEER #2: Confirmed.

ENGINEER #1: Wire P347 is connected to Sensor AYB1011.

ENGINEER #2: Confirmed.

ENGINEER #1: Sensor setpoint set to +5V.

ENGINEER #2: Confirmed.

ENGINEER #1: Checkback—Wire P347 connected to Sensor AYB1011, set to +5V.

ENGINEER #2: Confirmed.

ENGINEER #1 TO ENGINEER #2: OK, we're good here. I will sign first, followed by you.

Both engineers sign the work order form, and each notarize the form with their PE number.

This is how a checkback process works. The same would hold true if cybersecurity was being applied. When conducting a cybersecurity risk assessment for software and equipment located within operational environments that are crucial or critical to the overall operation, use of the checkback is *strongly* recommended.

A checkback is important in terms of cybersecurity, as many operational environments, especially small to medium-small operations, lack sufficient budgets and personnel to operate their own environments. Oftentimes, they use freelance contractors or contracting companies. Contractors typically won't be completely familiar with the history of the operational environment, and in many circumstances, the site's operations manager may not have a full grasp or understanding of their own environment. Using contractors does not imply that, in general, all contractors perform poorly for their clients. This is merely meant as a demonstrating factor of a growing crisis that many public municipalities or utilities (such as cooperatives) lack the funding and/or personnel to perform processes that enhance and instill safety, reliability, and performance for any given operational environment.

6.18 CONCLUSION

Risk assessments are like ordering food at a fast chain restaurant. You can either take a meal plan (including fries), or you can piecemeal separate, specific food items. Utilizing this thought process, the same holds true with risk management—no one size fits all. What adds to the conundrum and misrepresentation of cybersecurity is that the focus is more so on the evaluative process (or the analytical methodology), rather than the ultimate goal(s) (and their conclusions).

For conducting a risk assessment, the overarching methodology (and its processes) should include all aspects of an operational environment—including cybersecurity assessments; thus, meaning, cybersecurity does not dictate how an operational environment should be defined; rather, cybersecurity is defined by the operational environment. This method or perception of thinking has been lost over the past several decades, primarily due to the advent of a Worldwide network ("The Internet"). Rather than addressing the problem with operations and engineering, the preferred method today is to contact IT/OT personnel, who will, more than likely, have little to no knowledge of the specifics of the operational environment(s). Operational processes should define how cybersecurity is used and deployed, not the other way around.

And last, though checklists can and may serve as a useful tool, again, it should be integrated as part of an overall risk assessment process—not be the sole or entire risk assessment process. Additionally, dependency upon a checklist does not allow for dynamic thinking, and instead, focuses on static references or occurrences that will—more than likely—change (if not rapidly) over a period of time.

NOTES

1 Edward Marszal and Jim McGlone, *Security PHA Review for Consequence-Based Cybersecurity*, Research Triangle Park, NC: ISA [International Society of Automation], 2019.

2 Edward Marszal and Jim McGlone, *Security PHA Review for Consequence-Based Cybersecurity*, Research Triangle Park, NC: ISA [International Society of Automation], 2019.

3 The term "all-hazards" or "all-hazards approach" is used (quite) extensively with the emergency preparedness and incident response communities. Its meaning suggests the development of comprehensive plans to address an assortment of emergencies resulting from a wide range of threats which may come from emerging risks, new or old, of a given operational environment, generally one that is hazardous or where safety is critically important. This approach is indicative of the critical infrastructure protection (CIP) community and *is not* associated with the NERC CIP program provided by the North American Electric Reliability Corporation (NERC).

4 The term "center of the universe" is a slang term often used within the context scientifically, spiritually, metaphorically, and methodologically. The premise behind the term is that the universe is infinitely expanding, of which there is no central point of reference, from where it originated; thus, the term implies aligning oneself as seeing oneself or themselves as the focal point of reference of their own reality and point of origin. This concept may be viewed as conceited and very self-centered.

5 https://safeche.engin.umich.edu/tutorials/lopa-tutorial/#:~:text=A%20Layers%20of%20Protection%20Analysis%20(LOPA)%20is,safeguards%20to%20prevent%20against%20a%20given%20risk.&text=A%20HAZOP%20identifies%20potential%20hazards%2C%20while%20a,mitigation%20measures%20that%20guard%20against%20the%20hazard.

6 The term "deterministic" refers to a philosophical doctrine by which all events, causes, and resultants, both human and automated by action, are determined by causality; that is, for every outcome, something has had to have caused it, or was responsible, in some form, for its (eventual) outcome or consequence.

7 Used here within this chapter, and for the remainder of this book, our primary example of defense-in-depth, LOPA, and deterministic analysis will utilize the nuclear electric generation industry as its basis.

8 Design basis means that information which identifies the specific functions to be performed by a structure, system, or component of a facility, and the specific values or ranges of values chosen for controlling parameters as reference bounds for design. These values may be (1) restraints derived from generally accepted 'state of the art' practices for achieving functional goals, or (2) requirements derived from analysis (based on calculation and/or experiments) of

the effects of a postulated accident for which a structure, system, or component must meet its functional goals.", p. 2, "Enclosure 1 - Background: Design-basis Events, Design-basis Information, and External Events", U.S. Nuclear Regulatory Commission, no date, URL: https://www.nrc.gov/docs/ML1432/ML14328A170.pdf (alt URL: http://riskbook.infracritical.com/book1/chapter6/ch6ref1.pdf).

9 The term "design basis event" (alternatively "design basis accident") is not to be confused with "design basis threat"; and, represents a potential event or accident, in which its design and construction must be capable of withstanding loss of any/all systems, structures, and components that would ensure the continued health and safety of site personnel and general public. URL: https://www.nrc.gov/reading-rm/basic-ref/glossary/design-basis-accident.html; https://www.nrc.gov/reading-rm/basic-ref/glossary/design-basis-threat-dbt (alt URL: http://riskbook.infracritical.com/book1/chapter6/ch6ref5.pdf).

10 The term "what if?" is a supposition utilized through questioning the potential possibility of a future occurrence, outcome, or consequence, particularly negative in nature. This term is often used for highly consequential or catastrophic events which may, or may not, ever happen.

11 https://www.nrc.gov/docs/ml1710/ML17104A254.pdf (alt URL: http://riskbook.infracritical.com/book1/chapter6/ch6ref3.pdf)).

12 https://info.ornl.gov/sites/publications/Files/Pub108669.pdf (alt URL: http://riskbook.infracritical.com/book1/chapter6/ch6ref2.pdf).

13 The term "checklisting" refers to conducting an assessment in a systematic approach that involves creating a list of tasks, items, or steps to ensure that all necessary actions have been completed.

14 The term "dynamic environment" refers to a setting or operation in which contributing factors, and their conditions, are constantly changing and in a state of flux. This type of operational environment is often indicative of many industrial operations in which both safety and performance are critically important.

15 The term "checkbox compliance" is directed specifically at heavily regulated industries, such as the energy and healthcare sectors, in which complex regulatory rules and requirements often cause asset owners to adopt a checkbox approach in which simply marking or checking off a task as being completed (even though it may not have been fully evaluated); thus, the asset owner is "secured"—again a misleading idealistic misnomer by many.

16 The term "one and done" pertains to the misnomer that performing a single assessment, if successful, will guarantee that an environment is "secure"; however, as cybersecurity is ever-changing, it may be "secure" at the time of the post-audit, but, this does not mean that it

will be "secure" if future threats and vulnerabilities are found. Many executive managers fall into this bad business practice whereby they now have a false sense of security, when in fact, they do not.

17 Not to be confused with "customized"; meaning, "customized assessments" use an already established baseline or assessment process that is currently in use, as opposed to custom, which completely ignores all standardized assessment processes out there. An example of a customized assessment would include using ISA/IEC 62443, and tweaking some of the control requirements, or adding additional controls; a custom assessment is completely "home-grown" and does not utilize a standardized assessment process as its baseline.

18 The term "interest over time" does not pertain necessarily to financial cost alone; the term refers more so to reviewing measurable metrics, which can include financial costs, resource allocation, etc. through trending analysis; that is, it is the acquisition of meaningful, trackable data that can be analyzed.

19 A "siloed community" can be a single team within a department, group of individual departments, sites, or entire divisions (if large enough) in which there is complete isolation (zero communication out/from their community to others), lack of collaboration and coordination, ineffective and inefficient business management (often duplicated processes due to lack of collaboration, coordination, and communication), missed opportunities (whereby, if one group can benefit from a new opportunity, resulting in increased revenue or reduced expenses, other groups may benefit as well, but are missed due to lack of cohesion), and "tech debt" (in which allocation of funds is mismanaged due to lack of knowledge distribution, communication, and leadership).

20 In this example, the term "island" pertains to a non-continuous data flow resulting from a custom assessment versus all of the other risk assessments performed. This mismatch of results (if you will) may show or demonstrate the company's lack of internal coordination, communication, and its overall responsibility to the industry. As a result, regulatory auditors may scrutinize their own assessments more carefully and intensely than what they may typically perform at other companies.

21 The term "living asset document" refers to the library of documentation that is continuously updated reflecting the current status of relevancy to business assets, both tangible (such as equipment, property, inventory) and intangible (such as intellectual property, goodwill, brand reputation). It is an alternative approach to conducting asset tracking and management.

22 The term "drill down" refers to a top-down perceptive thought methodology whereby large amounts of data are collected, examined, and analyzed, providing a single deterministic result, outcome, or conclusion (of one, many) has not or may yet happen.

23 The term "drill up" refers to a bottom-up perceptive thought methodology whereby a single deterministic result, outcome, or conclusion (of one, many) that has already happened is used to determine relating factors (often through causal analysis).

CHAPTER 7

Emerging Risks in OT Cybersecurity and the Growing Need for Risk Assessments

7.1 INTRODUCTION

As operational technology (OT) environments evolve through digital transformation and increasing integration with information technology (IT), the cybersecurity risks they face grow in both complexity and scale. While traditional IT security models often fall short in addressing the unique characteristics of OT systems—such as long equipment lifecycles, safety-critical operations, and legacy architectures—the need for tailored and proactive cybersecurity risk assessments has never been more urgent. This chapter examines the emerging risk factors that threaten the resilience and integrity of asset-intensive sectors, including the rapid adoption of new technologies, shifting organizational structures, and increasing reliance on opaque software supply chains. Through real-world examples and analysis, the chapter emphasizes the critical importance of consequence-focused risk assessments as a means of safeguarding operational continuity and public safety in the face of evolving cyber threats.

7.2 EMERGING RISKS

Although the continued comingling of OT and IT remains a major factor in cybersecurity risk, several new and emerging threats are transforming the risk landscape for OT environments. These evolving challenges must be incorporated into risk assessments:

DOI: 10.4324/9781003610557-7

- Supply Chain Vulnerabilities—OT systems increasingly depend on complex, global supply chains for hardware, software, and maintenance services. Compromise at any point—hardware implants, firmware backdoors, or unverified third-party integrators—can create long-term, undetected vulnerabilities. Nation-state actors are known to exploit supply chains to pre-position malware in critical systems.
- Legacy Systems with Insufficient Security Controls—Many OT environments still run on systems that are decades old and lack essential security features. These systems are difficult to patch or secure, making them vulnerable to attackers or insider threats. Examples include unsupported PLCs with Telnet access or HMI panels with hard-coded default admin credentials.
- Remote Access and Cloud Adoption—OT systems now often include remote monitoring, vendor support portals, or cloud-based analytics. Weak VPN setups, poor identity and access management, or exposed APIs can create vulnerable points in OT networks. Misconfigured remote access during the COVID-19 pandemic greatly expanded the attack surface, and many of these vulnerabilities still exist today.
- Insecure Protocols—Protocols like Modbus, OPC-DA, and PROFINET were not designed with security in mind. These protocols are not limited to brownfield sites; many greenfield projects still incorporate these protocols. Attackers can spoof, replay, or inject commands into OT communications due to lack of authentication or encryption. Research has shown that attackers can manipulate valve states or falsify sensor data using unsecured industrial protocols.[1]
- OT-Targeted Ransomware—Ransomware campaigns are now specifically targeting OT environments, recognizing that downtime pressures operators to pay. Even if OT systems are not directly encrypted, the lack of IT visibility for safe operation can lead to shutdowns. Norsk Hydro's aluminum operations were forced into manual mode due to ransomware. "The overall cost of the attack was estimated at 550–650 million NOK (≈ $60–70 million USD)."
- Insider Threats—An aging OT workforce, increasing outsourcing, and a lack of cybersecurity awareness heighten insider risk. Sabotage or unintentional misconfigurations can go undetected due to insufficient monitoring and logging in OT systems. The Maroochy Shire sewage attack (2000) remains a classic example of insider misuse of remote access.[2] More recent examples include an incident at the Kuwait Oil Company in February

2023, where a disgruntled former contractor was alleged to have intentionally manipulated systems causing the shutdown of field production equipment and disruption to operations.[3]

- Organizational Changes—Many asset-intensive sectors are seeing pressure to reorganize and, in some cases, consolidate. In many cases, this is driven by financial factors. For instance, in the UK, the water industry regulator OFWAT is pressuring water and sewage companies to improve their performance after they have failed to achieve customer service and other operational targets.[4] In the United States, smaller water systems are being acquired by larger operators. For example, the City of Pittston, serving 4,400 customers, was sold to American Water.[5] There are many factors impacting cybersecurity here, including lack of infrastructure funding, regulatory pressure, and demands to reduce operating costs.
- Technology Changes—Industry 4.0 offers organizations the promise of efficiency improvements, cost savings, and more rapid response to change. Organizations seek to use IIoT and edge computing to monitor where it was previously cost-prohibitive to do so, cloud computing to save on on-premise infrastructure and support, and artificial Intelligence (AI) to mine their vast quantities of data and identify patterns that can help them improve their operations. The step change in processing capability that quantum computing offers will help further enable this information processing, but will also help adversaries in their mission to crack passwords and encryption.

All these changes further emphasize the need for organizations to conduct regular risk assessments. While the potential consequences may remain unchanged, threats, vulnerabilities, and exploits change as organizations deploy new technology, reorganize, or make changes to their operations. The negative impact of these changes should be factored in to any business decision before it is made.

7.3 HOW WILL CYBERSECURITY RISK ASSESSMENTS EVOLVE?

Cybersecurity risk assessments serve as a foundation for identifying, understanding, and mitigating threats before they impact operations. In OT environments, where systems directly control physical processes, the consequences of a cyber incident can extend beyond data loss to include environmental damage, equipment failure, financial loss, or even threats to human life. This reality makes risk assessments not only a cybersecurity exercise but a fundamental aspect of process safety and operational resilience.

In 2021, the Colonial Pipeline[6] ransomware attack resulted in a temporary shutdown of fuel distribution across the southeastern United States. Although the attack originated in the IT environment, the company shut down OT systems as a precaution due to uncertainty about the extent of the compromise. A structured risk assessment could have helped clarify interdependencies and response protocols to reduce the impact of the incident.

Unlike IT systems, OT systems often rely on legacy hardware, proprietary protocols, and operate in environments where uptime is critical. These systems were not designed with cybersecurity in mind. This is one of many reasons why risk assessment, not gap assessment, is so critical. Gap assessments will tell you if a control is in place or if a vulnerability exists. It will not, however, identify the consequences of that gap. Furthermore, to prepare for incident response, it is critical that the potential consequences are understood. Mitigation controls, such as mechanical failsafes and manual procedures, can only be in place if failure scenarios are understood.

The 2017 Triton/Trisis[7] malware incident targeted safety instrumented systems[8] (SIS) at a petrochemical facility in Saudi Arabia. The attackers gained access to engineering workstations and attempted to disable SIS controllers—posing a direct risk to human life and facility integrity. A gap assessment could have identified that there was a lack of segmentation between networks, a lack of electronic access controls, and a failure to maintain the controller key in the correct ("RUN") position to prevent it from being reprogrammed. The gap assessment would not have quantified the potential consequences of the controllers being compromised, which in this case was fortunately limited to a plant shutdown. Such a shutdown is significant to a petrochemical refinery, but far more severe consequences could have occurred, including fire or explosion, loss of containment, harm to people, and damage to equipment. In fact, the failure to maintain the controller key in the correct position is a common gap found in OT environments. The rationale for this is that it is inconvenient and time-consuming for personnel to walk to the device (which can be some distance from the engineering workstation used to administer the device), turn the key to "PROGRAM," return to the workstation, perform the reprogramming, and then revisit the device and put the key back into the "RUN" position. The lack of risk assessment is clear here, since a value judgment is made without consideration of the risk of leaving the device in a mode that allows it to be maliciously reprogrammed.

Historically, OT has been treated as an isolated domain, but that is no longer viable. As critical infrastructure sectors—such as energy, water, transportation, and manufacturing—become more digitized, OT must be viewed as a frontline asset in cybersecurity planning. Elevating its importance involves recognizing that OT cybersecurity risk is safety and process risk and treating it as such. This means elevating these risks to the same level as other safety and process risks and managing these risks with the same level of commitment.

In 2021, a water treatment plant in Oldsmar, Florida,[9] experienced an incident where a remote user increased the level of sodium hydroxide in the water to dangerous levels. The incident was originally assumed to be an intentional attack but after investigation the FBI concluded there was no evidence of this. As with most cybersecurity incidents, it was most likely caused by human error. The toxic level of sodium hydroxide was corrected well before it reached the public, but the incident highlighted the lack of mitigation controls to prevent such a serious incident from occurring because of a simple human error. For example, the SCADA system did not prevent a user from entering a value representing a dangerous level of chemical, and although Oldsmar claimed it had failsafes in place it is not clear what these were.[10,11] At best there may have been daily water quality testing, which could still have resulted in toxic water reaching some members of the public.

While the fundamentals of risk assessment remain constant, the landscape in which these assessments are performed continues to evolve. The potential consequences of an incident in OT environments (such as a loss of control, unplanned shutdown, or hazardous condition) do not change. What changes, and continues to change, is the number and variety of potential causes that can lead to these consequences.

In the past, many OT systems were isolated, hardwired, and relied on bespoke equipment with well-understood failure modes. Today these systems are increasingly software-driven, networked, and dependent on third-party software elements, from operating systems and device drivers to cloud services and, especially recently, AI-based analytics platforms.[12] Modern control systems may incorporate a wide array of external software libraries, communication stacks, middleware components, and firmware supplied by multiple vendors, often with little transparency into how those components are constructed, maintained, or secured.

This growing software supply chain complexity significantly complicates risk assessment. Most users, integrators, and asset owners have no direct insight into the source code, design decisions, or vulnerability management processes of the third-party software embedded in their systems. Even if they maintain good cybersecurity hygiene for the components they directly manage, they may still be exposed to risks buried deep within proprietary or open-source dependencies—risks that can remain hidden until exploited.

An example of this was the Log4j[13] vulnerability (Log4Shell),[14] which affected millions of systems worldwide because a widely used logging component contained a critical flaw. Many organizations were unaware that this library was included deep within the software stacks of their control systems, exposing them to unexpected and hard-to-detect risks. Similarly, supply chain attacks like SolarWinds and CloudStrike demonstrated how trusted software updates could result in loss of function.

These examples underscore the reality that the number of potential causes of an OT cybersecurity incident is expanding, not because the fundamental processes are changing, but because the underlying software ecosystem is becoming more complex and increasingly opaque. The more complex the system, the more difficult it becomes to map dependencies, validate software integrity, and ensure that every element meets the required security standards.

An essential principle in managing this growing complexity is reducing unnecessary software and hardware dependencies, incorporating only the modules and libraries that are required for system function. Every additional component introduces potential failure paths, whether through unpatched vulnerabilities, poorly maintained code, or insecure update mechanisms.

The development and adoption of the Software Bill of Materials (SBOM) and Hardware Bill of Materials (HBOM) are critical steps in supporting this objective. An SBOM provides a structured inventory of all software components, their versions, and their origins, allowing organizations to identify and track dependencies across the software supply chain. This enables faster vulnerability response when issues are discovered in common components, such as the aforementioned Log4j vulnerability. Similarly, the HBOM catalogs hardware components, including manufacturers, firmware versions, and critical dependencies, helping to identify risks from counterfeit parts, compromised hardware, or supply chain attacks.

However, even with detailed SBOMs and HBOMs, it is impossible to predict every potential failure or threat vector. This is why effective risk assessment is not about enumerating every specific attack or failure scenario, but instead about focusing on the consequences of failure, regardless of cause. By centering the assessment process on what could go wrong and what the impact would be, organizations can prioritize controls that are robust across a wide variety of potential causes, whether those causes arise from malicious intent, human error, equipment failure, or hidden vulnerabilities in third-party components.

For example, the same loss of control over a critical valve could result from a cyberattack exploiting a software vulnerability, a misconfigured firmware update, or a failed sensor input. The risk assessment process identifies this potential loss of control as the consequence of concern and focuses on implementing layered controls—such as physical interlocks,

SISs, alarm functions, and manual overrides—that can mitigate the consequence no matter the trigger.

This consequence-first approach acknowledges that the number of possible failure modes is continually expanding, particularly in highly integrated OT systems where software, hardware, and network layers are deeply intertwined. It shifts the focus from chasing every new threat to building resilient systems that maintain safety, reliability, and operational integrity under a wide range of conditions.

Without evolving risk assessment practices to reflect these realities—including the complexity introduced by modern supply chains and embedded software ecosystems—organizations risk underestimating their true exposure, even when their traditional safety protections appear unchanged. By leveraging tools like SBOM and HBOM and maintaining a focus on consequences and layered risk mitigation, organizations can navigate this complexity and remain prepared for both known and emerging threats.

7.4 BOMS

Software and hardware bills of materials are established concepts. The SBOM has been in use in software engineering since the early 2010s, but it gained official recognition within cybersecurity through the U.S. Department of Commerce's National Telecommunications and Information Administration (NTIA). In 2018, the NTIA initiated the multi-stakeholder process on software component transparency, which defined and promoted SBOMs as a key element of software supply chain security. A May 2021 Executive Order 14028 (Improving the Nation's Cybersecurity) mandated the use of SBOMs in government procurement.

An SBOM is a structured list of all software components—libraries, modules, and dependencies—contained in a software product. It functions like an ingredients list for software and is critical for:

- Identifying known vulnerabilities (e.g., via CVEs).
- Tracking open-source software usage and licenses.
- Facilitating patch management and incident response.

HBOMs predate SBOMs in manufacturing and engineering, where they have been used for inventory, sourcing, and compliance. However, the concept of HBOM for cybersecurity has emerged more recently, around 2020–2021. Since then, HBOMs have been discussed more formally in critical infrastructure and Department of Defense supply chain risk management, especially as part of zero trust and hardware integrity initiatives.

An HBOM is a detailed inventory of all hardware components in a system or device, including embedded chips, boards, processors, memory, and interface components to help:

- Manage supply chain risks (e.g., counterfeit or insecure components).
- Identify obsolete parts and vendor dependencies.
- Assess hardware vulnerabilities (e.g., firmware-level backdoors).

7.5 CERTIFICATION

A positive trend in OT is the increase in product and system certifications. The ISASecure program is an internationally recognized certification framework based on the ISA/IEC 62443 series of standards, which defines security requirements for ACS (also known as industrial automation and control systems, or IACS in the standards series).[15]

The insecure nature of products and systems begins much earlier in the supply chain. For example, a lack of awareness of security issues among developers can result in poorly designed software in components and systems. These technical vulnerabilities can later be exploited in cybersecurity attacks or may unintentionally cause incidents due to human error. Vulnerabilities are also present in processes, procedures, and in operational personnel training and oversight, which can also lead to incidents.

ISASecure provides three primary certification schemes (certification programs):

- Product Supplier Security Development Lifecycle Assurance—Ensures vendors follow secure development practices.
- Component Security Assurance—Verifies the security of individual system components, including off-the-shelf IIoT devices.
- System Security Assurance—Validates the security of integrated systems and configurations, including off-the-shelf solution products.
- Site Security Assurance—Validates conformity to ISA/IEC 62443 for an entire IACS-based facility, which includes all policies and procedures, service providers, and technical security controls.

The ISA/IEC 62443 utilizes a risk-based approach to security management. The risk assessment process identifies key aspects of the asset owner's IACS, such as the zone and conduit arrangements and their associated target security levels. This then determines the necessary technical security capabilities required in hardware and software for these zones and conduits to effectively manage the risk. The ISASecure ACSSA evaluation process starts with reviewing the asset owner's risk assessment process and its results.

7.6 THE POSITIVE ROLE OF AI IN RISK MANAGEMENT

Despite many common reservations about its use, AI can be a valuable tool in enhancing the effectiveness of OT cybersecurity risk assessments and operational resilience. When properly integrated and governed, AI technologies can provide capabilities that go beyond traditional manual analysis, particularly in environments characterized by large volumes of data, complex system interdependencies, and time-critical processes.

Some key areas where AI can strengthen OT cybersecurity risk management include:

- **Improved Situational Awareness through Data Correlation**—OT environments generate vast amounts of data from alarms, system logs, network traffic, and sensor outputs. AI can help automate the correlation of these diverse data streams, detecting patterns that may indicate multi-stage attacks or abnormal system behavior. For example, an AI system might recognize that a series of failed authentication attempts on a remote access gateway, combined with unexpected changes in PLC configurations, could signal an active intrusion attempt.
- **Accelerated Incident Response with AI-Assisted Threat Analysis**—Machine learning models can classify threats and prioritize alerts based on historical incident data, contextual awareness, and threat intelligence feeds. By filtering out false positives and focusing analyst attention on high-probability events, AI-powered systems can significantly speed up threat detection, triage, and containment. This capability is particularly useful in environments where cybersecurity resources may be limited, and response time is critical.
- **Risk Scoring and Asset Prioritization**—AI algorithms can assist in dynamically scoring asset risk based on vulnerability data, exposure, operational criticality, and real-time threat activity. This enables more targeted and effective allocation of cybersecurity resources, ensuring that the most critical systems receive the highest levels of protection.

7.7 THE NEGATIVE ROLE OF AI IN RISK MANAGEMENT

While AI provides powerful new capabilities, it also introduces new risks if not properly governed. For example, in manufacturing environments, AI-based predictive maintenance systems have been exploited in red-team simulations where attackers injected false-positive data into sensor streams ("data poisoning"), effectively suppressing legitimate maintenance alerts. By causing the system to incorrectly classify failing equipment as healthy, these manipulations created a false sense of security that could lead to process disruptions or safety incidents.

Additional concerns about the use of AI in OT environments include:

- **Increase in attack surface**, by incorporating external data inputs or cloud-based training mechanisms.
- **Lack of transparency**, the opaque nature of AI logic makes it difficult to understand how decisions are made, potentially complicating incident response and forensic analysis.
- **Exploitation through adversarial attacks**, this may result from reverse engineering an AI engine and specifically focusing on an organization's risk assessments, identifying which site or facility has an exploitable weakness.
- **Introduction of operational risk**, if the results of AI recommendations are relied upon without due diligence, effective oversight, or adoption of necessary failsafe mechanisms.
- **Use of poor quality or inappropriate data**, for instance, training AI models on poor quality risk assessments from other organizations, or risk assessments that do not apply to the organization or sector and its risk. The quality and applicability of AI recommendations depend on the data it consumes.

This illustrates why AI systems themselves must be treated as risk-bearing components within the assessment process. Risk assessments should include evaluation of the following for any AI-enabled system:

- Integrity of training data
- Protection against data poisoning
- Model transparency and auditability
- Failsafe mechanisms and human-in-the-loop oversight
- Regular retraining and validation of AI models

Many students today are now utilizing AI to completely write (i.e., 100% of their report is completely written) their report for submission. Many academic institutions have become aware of this practice; and, as far as they are concerned, this is plagiarism. And what is the reason? Today's "AI" is not as smart as the vendors or application authors claim them to be; in fact, they steal ideas, concepts, values, terminology, entire web sites, and entire books or copywritten material, and through the combination of extremely complex algorithms, produces output that appears to be unique, but in fact is not.

When a student utilizes AI, the end result produced is what many refer to as a "derived work";[16] that is, someone else has modified, either partially, heavily, or completely, based on someone else's work. This is a serious issue when it applies to written or other forms of artistic work.

The same holds true with performing a cybersecurity risk assessment using AI. The results produced from utilizing an AI engine for a cybersecurity risk assessment will not be unique to the organization performing that assessment, as much of the inputs ingested into the AI engine will not be unique and would be considered similar to using another company's assessment results (see Chapter 6 discussing issues with risk assessments and checklists).

Ultimately AI is like an instrument in a control system. Like any instrument it must be used appropriately, for its intended purpose and environment, and its output must be calibrated periodically.

Today's definition of AI is merely a rebranding of a slow progression of an architecture that started as far back as the 1960s. Referred to as "neural networks," the premise was to create "smart programs" that could, instinctively, obtain meaningful thought processes for solving complex human issues. That same goal still exists today, but rebranded.

With the advent of the Internet and upgrades made to ingestion engines, AI companies have consumed exabytes worth of data for training their AI engines. This also includes privately used AI engines; at some point, data—enormous amounts of data—must be gathered from somewhere to allow AI to perform its calculations for the complex problems being presented to it. The fact is, data has to be fed, then manipulated—by humans—for the final result. This engine is a product of humans, written by humans, modified and custom-tailored by humans; none of this is done by a machine, which is what AI is supposed to represent.

While AI engines are nothing more than sophisticated modeling programs, this does not exclude nor discount the fact that there are similar modeling or business intelligence applications which exist, which may or may not use AI engines, but do not necessarily require massive amounts of external data to be ingested. Those applications also apply here.

There are several rather significant risks for using AI engines for performing cybersecurity risk assessments. They are listed (though not limited to) as the following:

- **Malclassification**[17] **Attacks**—AI engines may be tricked through manipulated input data, causing them to misclassify legitimate input data as malicious or vice versa. Misclassification of data for malicious purposes is a method by which several subset attacks may be applied individually or through various combinations:
  - **Model or Data Poisoning**[18] **Attacks**—Are methods by which input data is manipulated to avoid detection by (essentially) pretending to be valid data. The sole purpose of this is to provide invalid data via the ingestion process into the AI engine

to either create bypass conditions to exist, thus, making it easier to penetrate a targeted company; or (which is the most common method) generate invalid or incorrect results (aka "false positive"[19] or "false negative"[20]).

- **Evasion[21] Attacks**—These attacks are utilized once invalid data has already been ingested into the AI model by requiring adversaries to provide alternative or modify datasets for their expected results.
- **Model Exfiltration Attacks**—Also referred to as "model extraction attacks,"[22,23] are attacks used to steal the AI engine's model(s) and use them to conduct attacks at either the targeted company where it was taken from or elsewhere. At the time of writing this book, there are cases in which, through the emergence of autonomous vehicles, AI models have already been stolen and used elsewhere, involving incidents such as reprogramming vehicles or manipulating location services, etc. For cybersecurity risk management, whatever model is currently used by a company can then be exfiltrated, and then applied against either the same company or another company. Remember the concern about using assessment models from other companies? In those circumstances, if one company "borrowed" from another company, their business model would be same because their assessment models would be the same; in comparison, this would be very similar to using the same password on every PC.

- **Data Breaches**—The large datasets at the heart of generative AI may contain sensitive or proprietary information about an organization—its intellectual property, recipes, designs, or risks. If these datasets are not properly protected, they become a prime target for attackers seeking to exfiltrate confidential data, including network topologies, incident response procedures, employee behaviors, or security vulnerabilities. Moreover, training data that includes real-world incident records may inadvertently expose details about past breaches or internal weaknesses.

7.8 THE IMPACT OF ORGANIZATIONAL CHANGES

The consolidation of asset-intensive organizations, such as water utilities, electric cooperatives, and municipal infrastructure systems, into larger for-profit companies has accelerated in recent years. Public-private partnerships are another reaction to changing regulatory and governmental objectives.

The primary business reasons for this are to achieve operational efficiencies and realize economies of scale. Some regulated industries may experience consolidation as a result of regulatory pressure, as smaller operators struggle to fund the necessary activities to achieve compliance.

While the business benefits may be clear, the negative impact on cybersecurity posture may not be considered. Firstly, the infrastructure is already likely underfunded. This implies legacy equipment, insecure architectures, and poor security practices. At the same time, the drive to achieve economies of scale and operational efficiencies means these consolidated organizations will want to deploy (or scale up) digital transformation, such as smart metering, remote operations, and predictive maintenance. These technologies themselves introduce new vulnerabilities and increase the attack surface, but if not carefully considered, their impact can be even more detrimental to an organization's cybersecurity posture. For example, rolling out new remote operations solutions on top of insecure OT equipment can severely impact the vulnerability of an organization.

Newly acquired organizations will likely have vastly different cybersecurity maturity levels and will have varying policies and controls. Training of the workforce, especially in cultural aspects, should not be underestimated but usually is. This is not limited to an organization's workforce. Each acquisition brings new third-party vendors, integrators, and contractors.

In short, while a small utility may struggle with managing their cybersecurity risk, acquisition by a larger parent company does not necessarily resolve this struggle.

The parent company will usually face higher regulatory expectations, and acquiring non-compliant entities increases its liability and reporting obligations.

Although arguments for new investment will be made prior to acquisition, it is not uncommon for private equity and for-profit utilities to acquire critical infrastructure and drive down investment in areas such as cybersecurity, which are usually seen as cost centers.

From a nation's perspective, centralized ownership of multiple critical infrastructure systems may increase the impact of a cyberattack.

Some considerations for acquisitions are provided in Table 7.1.

7.9 THE IMPACT OF TECHNOLOGY CHANGES

Asset-intensive industries are rushing to deploy Industry 4.0 solutions that promise to improve their operations.

Legacy control systems limit the options for monitoring additional process variables. In many cases it has been cost-prohibitive to collect

TABLE 7.1 Cybersecurity Considerations for Acquisitions

Phase	Cybersecurity Considerations
Pre-acquisition	• Conduct cyber due diligence (asset inventories, known vulnerabilities) • Review incident history and regulatory compliance • Evaluate network architectures
Post-acquisition (integration)	• Isolate legacy OT systems until risk is understood • Conduct risk assessments • Begin migrating to centralized monitoring and access controls
Long-term operations	• Standardize cybersecurity policies across the enterprise • Conduct regular red-teaming or tabletop exercises • Engage local teams in cybersecurity awareness and culture-building

sensor data—either because of cable length, power source, or device limitations—and often the processing of this data needs to be performed outside the control system (e.g., vibration signatures), but no connectivity is available to support this. A combination of IIoT, edge computing, and cloud computing now makes such requirements feasible.

Risk assessment continues to take a back seat in the rush to deploy these solutions. Organizations see the potential benefits (reduced costs, increased uptime, faster response) but fail to balance them with the added risk:

- Increase in attack surface through new communication conduits. In many cases, organizations are using existing IT networks to support this new OT traffic, without considering the implications of comingling such traffic.
- Use of inherently insecure products, often based on standard hardware and firmware containing hard-coded passwords and running insecure services (e.g., Telnet).
- Potential impact on business processes with these new solutions. While existing processes and procedures have been refined over many years, the introduction of new technology should necessitate updates to these processes and procedures to accommodate new failure scenarios.

Since the launch of ChatGPT in 2022, interest in using all forms of AI has increased exponentially—often with conflation of terms such as generative AI and other approaches such as Machine Learning. AI has been used in automation since the 1960s, when expert systems were first developed to emulate human decision-making processes. In the 1980s, AI techniques such as fuzzy logic and neural networks were applied to control systems, enhancing their adaptability and robustness. The current wave of AI interest is focused on generative AI, systems that create information or predict sequences based on enormous training datasets and vast amounts of compute resources, allowing AI to generalize information and make predictions. Implementing AI in industrial environments requires careful consideration due to several critical factors, including human safety, system reliability, information protection, and transparency. Just as with IIoT, edge computing, and cloud computing, organizations must properly assess the risks associated with deploying any AI approach before doing so.

Quantum computing also offers the promise of significant benefits to asset-intensive organizations, particularly in areas such as complex system optimization, predictive maintenance, and real-time decision-making. Quantum computing uses the principles of quantum mechanics to process information. Unlike conventional computers, which represent information using two states (0 or 1), quantum computers use qubits, which can be both 0 and 1 simultaneously due to a phenomenon known as *superposition*. They also utilize entanglement and quantum interference to perform complex calculations significantly faster than traditional computers for specific types of problems, such as cryptography. This means quantum computing has the potential to dramatically enhance the efficiency of asset-intensive operations by solving analysis problems that are currently computationally intractable with conventional computers.

This step change in computation capability could potentially be deployed in cybersecurity, for instance, leveraging quantum-enhanced machine learning to detect network or host anomalies earlier and allocate resources more effectively.

Conversely, quantum computing increases cybersecurity risk. The dramatic increase in computational capability means that cracking encryption codes and brute-forcing passwords—tasks that would take conventional computers years or even centuries to accomplish—could potentially be done in minutes or hours using sufficiently powerful quantum algorithms. This poses a major threat to secure communication, financial transactions, and critical infrastructure protections that rely on current encryption and password methods.

For example, a 2048-bit RSA encryption key—currently considered secure and used widely in public key infrastructure—would take classical computers trillions of years to break using brute force. However, with Shor's algorithm, a quantum computer with a few thousand stable qubits could theoretically factor that key in hours.

Similarly, complex passwords (e.g., 12-character combinations with a mix of letters, numbers, and symbols) are currently too complex to brute-force. Even with high-performance GPU clusters, cracking a strong password might take hundreds of years. A quantum computer running Grover's algorithm, however, could reduce the time needed to brute force such a password in a few hours.

To address the emerging cryptography threat, cybersecurity experts and standards bodies are developing and testing post-quantum cryptography (PQC)—encryption methods that are designed to resist both classical and quantum attacks. These include lattice-based, hash-based, and code-based cryptographic algorithms. NIST is actively finalizing a set of quantum-resistant algorithms for widespread adoption. Organizations are being encouraged to begin planning for cryptographic agility—that is, preparing their systems to transition to PQC once it is standardized.

Addressing the password cracking threat requires a different approach. Multi-factor Authentication (MFA) is already highly recommended (and in some cases required by regulation) for user accounts. However, like many cybersecurity controls, the implementation of MFA is not yet universal. At the time of writing, large organizations (employing 10,000 or more employees) have an 87% adoption rate, but small and medium businesses (SMBs) are only at 34%.[24] Even without quantum computing, a lack of MFA is a serious vulnerability in any organization—and these SMBs likely form part of a supply chain for the larger organizations. If businesses have not yet implemented MFA, will they be any more likely to do so when the risk of password cracking increases exponentially?

7.10 CONCLUSION

The cybersecurity landscape for OT systems is undergoing a fundamental transformation, driven by technological innovation, increased digital interconnectivity, and the evolving tactics of adversaries. While the potential consequences of failure—such as physical damage, environmental harm, and human safety risks—remain constant, the pathways leading to such outcomes are becoming more varied and less predictable. Addressing this complexity requires a shift from static, control-focused assessments to dynamic, consequence-first risk management strategies. By incorporating tools like SBOMs and HBOMs, adopting certification frameworks, leveraging AI responsibly, and preparing for quantum-era threats, organizations can build layered defenses that are resilient to both current and future challenges. Most critically, organizations must recognize that cybersecurity in OT environments is not simply a technical issue—it is a core component of operational safety and business continuity. Regular, informed, and integrated risk assessments are essential to navigating this evolving threat landscape with confidence and clarity.

NOTES

1 Krotofil, M., & Larsen, J. *Rocking the Pocket Book: Hacking Chemical Plants for Competition and Extortion*. Black Hat USA, 2015. https://media.blackhat.com/bh-us-15/Krotofil/bh-us-15-Krotofil-Rocking-The-Pocket-Book-wp.pdf
2 Slay, J., & Miller, M. *Lessons Learned from the Maroochy Water Breach*. In *Critical Infrastructure Protection* (pp. 73–82). Springer, 2007. https://doi.org/10.1007/978-0-387-75462-8_6
3 *Security Middle East Magazine*, March 2023: https://www.securitymiddleeastmag.com/kuwait-oil-co-hit-by-insider-sabotage/
4 https://www.ofwat.gov.uk/waterstory/i-didnt-realise-a-power-shower-used-so-much-more-water/ (alt URL: http://riskbook.infracritical.com/book1/chapter7/ch7ref1.pdf).
5 https://smartwatermagazine.com/news/american-water/pennsylvania-american-water-signs-agreement-purchase-city-pittstons-wastewater
6 On May 7, 2021, the Colonial Pipeline Company proactively shut down its pipeline system in response to a ransomware attack. On May 13, 2021, Colonial Pipeline announced the company restarted their entire pipeline system and product delivery commenced to all markets. URL: https://www.energy.gov/ceser/colonial-pipeline-cyber-incident (alt URL: https://web.archive.org/web/20210511171309/https://www.epa.gov/sites/production/files/2021-05/documents/colonialpipelineemergencyfuelwaiver.pdf ; URL: https://www.energy.gov/ceser/colonial-pipeline-cyber-incident; URL: https://www.cisa.gov/news-events/news/attack-colonial-pipeline-what-weve-learned-what-weve-done-over-past-two-years (alt URL: http://riskbook.infracritical.com/book1/chapter7/ch7ref2q.pdf).
7 The HatMan malware affects Triconex controllers by modifying in-memory firmware to add additional programming. The extra functionality allows an attacker to read/modify memory contents and execute custom code on demand through receiving specially crafted network packets. HatMan consists of two pieces: a PC-based component to communicate with the safety controller and a malicious binary component that is downloaded to the controller. Safety controllers are used in a large number of environments, and the capacity to disable, inhibit, or modify the ability of a process to fail safely can potentially result in physical consequences. This report discusses the components and capabilities of the malware and some potential mitigations. Media reporting also

refers to this malware as both TRITON and TRISIS. URL: https://www.cisa.gov/sites/default/files/documents/MAR-17-352-01%20HatMan%E2%80%94Safety%20System%20Targeted%20Malware_S508C.pdf; URL: https://www.cisa.gov/sites/default/files/documents/MAR-17-352-01%20HatMan%20-%20Safety%20System%20Targeted%20Malware%20%28Update%20B%29.pdf (alt URL: http://riskbook.infracritical.com/book1/chapter7/ch7ref3a.pdf, http://riskbook.infracritical.com/book1/chapter7/ch7ref3b.pdf, http://riskbook.infracritical.com/book1/chapter7/ch7ref3c1.pdf, http://riskbook.infracritical.com/book1/chapter7/ch7ref3c2.pdf); URL: https://www.ic3.gov/CSA/2022/220325.pdf (alt URL: http://riskbook.infracritical.com/book1/chapter7/ch7ref4.pdf); https://hdiac.dtic.mil/articles/cyber-physical-systems-and-critical-infrastructure/ (alt URL: http://riskbook.infracritical.com/book1/chapter7/ch7ref3.pdf).

8 A "safety instrumented system" is "a system that is composed of sensors, logic solvers, and final control elements whose purpose is to take the process to a safe state when predetermined conditions are violated. Other terms commonly used include emergency shutdown system (ESS), safety shutdown system (SSD), and safety interlock system (SIS)." URL: https://nvlpubs.nist.gov/nistpubs/SpecialPublications/NIST.SP.800-82r3.pdf (alt URL: http://riskbook.infracritical.com/book1/chapter7/ch7ref4.pdf).

9 URL: http://scid.infracritical.com/pages/scid-00113.

10 Al Braithwaite, the city operations manager of Oldsmar, Florida, at the time of the "incident," indicated that the conclusion offered by the FBI and DHS was that the incident was not a cyber attack; rather, it was a typographical error made by the employee responsible for managing the city's water system at the time of the incident and represented an overreaction by local city officials and law enforcement, thus gaining national attention when no such incident existed. It was considered a "non-accident," meaning it was classified as an "event" caused by a minor fault due to operator error. URL: https://www.tampabay.com/news/pinellas/2023/04/11/oldsmar-cyberattack-water-supply-poisoning-fbi-update/; URL: https://www.wusf.org/local-state/2023-04-13/official-hack-oldsmar-city-water-treatment-plant-2021.

11 The City of Elgin, Texas, indicated in a public memorandum that their SCADA system would never have controlling capabilities to modify access to safety-based preset amounts of chemicals (such as sodium hydroxide); URL: https://www.elgintexas.gov/AgendaCenter/ViewFile/Item/2774?fileID=10891 (alt URL: http://riskbook.infracritical.com/book1/chapter7/ch7ref5.pdf).

12 URL: https://cyote.inl.gov/content/uploads/24/2025/04/21-50125_02_CyOTE_Fact-Sheet_rev1_Oct2023-FINAL-1.pdf (alt URL: http://riskbook.infracritical.com/book1/chapter7/ch7ref6.pdf).

13 Apache Log4j is an open-source Java-based logging framework that collects and manages information about system activity. URL: https://www.cisa.gov/sites/default/files/publications/CSRB-Report-on-Log4-July-11-2022_508.pdf (alt URL: http://riskbook.infracritical.com/book1/chapter7/ch7ref8a.pdf)

14 URL: https://www.cisa.gov/news-events/cybersecurity-advisories/aa21-356a (alt URL: http://riskbook.infracritical.com/book1/chapter7/ch7ref8b1.pdf); URL: https://www.cisa.gov/news-events/cybersecurity-advisories/aa22-174a (alt URL: http://riskbook.infracritical.com/book1/chapter7/ch7ref8b2.pdf).

15 https://isasecure.org/certification

16 A "derivative work" (alternatively "derived work") is a work based on or derived from one or more already existing works. URL: https://www.copyright.gov/circs/circ14.pdf (alt URL: http://riskbook.infracritical.com/book1/chapter7/ch7ref9.pdf).

17 Although the word "malclassification" does not exist, the use of this word is more appropriate given the malicious intent of misclassifying data; however, the correct term to use for these sorts of attacks is "adversarial attacks" ("Defending Against Adversarial Examples," Austin Short, Trevor La Pay, Apurva Gandhi, p. 3; URL: https://www.osti.gov/servlets/purl/1569514 (alt URL: http://riskbook.infracritical.com/book1/chapter7/ch7ref10a.pdf); URL: https://nvlpubs.nist.gov/nistpubs/ai/NIST.AI.100-2e2025.pdf (alt URL: http://riskbook.infracritical.com/book1/chapter7/ch7ref10b.pdf).

18 For "data poisoning attacks," adversaries can deliberately introduce malicious data samples during the training phase of an AI engine to manipulate how the AI model "thinks," and in doing so, change the generated predictions. "Just How Toxic is Data Poisoning? A Unified Benchmark for Backdoor and Data Poisoning Attacks", Avi Schwarzschild, Micah Goldblum, Arjun Gupta, John P. Dickerson, Tom Goldstein, p. 1; URL: https://par.nsf.gov/servlets/purl/10315225

19 A "false positive" is a circumstance whereby a security mechanism accidentally has detected a specific threat, when in fact, no threat exists. URL: https://csrc.nist.gov/glossary/term/false_positive (alt URL: http://riskbook.infracritical.com/book1/chapter7/ch7ref11a.pdf); URL: https://doi.org/10.6028/NIST.SP.800-83r1 (alt URL: http://riskbook.infracritical.com/book1/chapter7/ch7ref11b.pdf); URL: https://doi.org/10.6028/NIST.SP.800-61r2 (alt URL: http://riskbook.infracritical.com/book1/chapter7/ch7ref11c.pdf).

20 A "false negative" is a circumstance whereby a security mechanism that is intended to detect a specific threat fails to identify it. URL: https://csrc.nist.gov/glossary/term/false_negative (alt URL: http://riskbook.infracritical.com/book1/chapter7/ch7ref12a.pdf); URL: https://nvlpubs.nist.gov/nistpubs/SpecialPublications/NIST.SP.800-83r1.pdf (alt URL: http://riskbook.infracritical.com/book1/chapter7/ch7ref11b.pdf); URL: https://nvlpubs.nist.gov/nistpubs/Legacy/SP/nistspecialpublication800-86.pdf (alt URL: http://riskbook.infracritical.com/book1/chapter7/ch7ref12b.pdf).
21 "Poisoning Attacks Against Machine Learning: Can Machine Learning Be Trustworthy?", Alina Oprea, Anoop Singhal and Apostol Vassilev, p. 95; URL: https://tsapps.nist.gov/publication/get_pdf.cfm?pub_id=934932 (alt URL: http://riskbook.infracritical.com/book1/chapter7/ch7ref13.pdf).
22 "DisGUIDE: Disagreement-Guided Data-Free Model Extraction", Jonathan Rosenthal, Eric Enouen, Hung Viet Pham, Lin Tan, p. 2, URL: https://par.nsf.gov/servlets/purl/10438329
23 "Play the Imitation Game: Model Extraction Attack against Autonomous Driving Localization", Qifan Zhang, Junjie Shen, Mingtian Tan, Zhe Zhou, Zhou Li, Qi Alfred Chen, Haipeng Zhang, p. 3-5; URL: https://par.nsf.gov/servlets/purl/10477442
24 https://expertinsights.com/user-auth/multi-factor-authentication-statistics?utm_source=chatgpt.com

CHAPTER 8

Regulation, Culture, and Governance

8.1 INTRODUCTION

As industrial systems increasingly integrate, and the distinction between Information Technology (IT) and Operational Technology (OT) continues to diminish, the necessity for reliable, repeatable, and risk-informed cybersecurity assessments in the OT domain has transitioned from being a mere option to an absolute requirement. This shift is driven by the growing complexity of interconnected systems, which heightens the potential for cyber threats that can disrupt operations and compromise safety. Organizations must recognize that robust cybersecurity measures are not just a technical necessity but a fundamental aspect of their operational framework, ensuring resilience against evolving cyber risks. Despite ongoing evolution of regulatory frameworks aimed at enhancing cybersecurity standards, the effectiveness of these measures largely hinges on the organizational culture and governance strategies in place. A proactive approach to cybersecurity must be embedded within the organizational ethos, transcending the notion of compliance as a mere checkbox exercise. When cybersecurity is treated as a vital component of operational integrity, it fosters a culture of vigilance and accountability, empowering employees at all levels to prioritize security in their daily activities and decision-making processes. Ultimately, the success of cybersecurity initiatives within the OT landscape is contingent upon a holistic governance approach that aligns with the organization's overall mission and values. By cultivating an environment where cybersecurity is viewed as integral to operational success, organizations can not only meet regulatory requirements but also enhance their resilience against potential threats. This alignment ensures that cybersecurity efforts are sustained, evolving in tandem with technological advancements and emerging risks, thereby safeguarding the organization's assets and reputation in an increasingly interconnected world.

DOI: 10.4324/9781003610557-8

8.2 THE INCREASING NEED FOR OT CYBERSECURITY RISK ASSESSMENTS

Risk assessments serve as a critical tool for organizations seeking to identify and understand their vulnerabilities and the potential consequences that may arise from them. By systematically evaluating these risks, organizations can pinpoint the necessary controls to mitigate them effectively. This process goes beyond merely cataloging vulnerabilities; it also involves a thorough analysis of the potential impacts. It is essential to recognize that two environments may exhibit similar technical weaknesses, while the associated risks can differ significantly based on contextual factors and the importance of the systems involved. This nuanced understanding is vital for developing a robust risk management strategy.

The growing complexity of regulatory frameworks and policies highlights the need for a more advanced approach to risk assessment. Standards such as ISA/IEC 62443, frameworks like the NIST Cybersecurity Framework (CSF), and regulations like NIS2 stress the importance of conducting context-aware and consequence-driven evaluations. These frameworks promote a thorough understanding of the operational environment, emphasizing that risk assessments should not only identify vulnerabilities but also assess the specific impacts of those vulnerabilities in various situations. This move toward a more holistic view of risk is crucial for effective governance in OT cybersecurity.

By prioritizing an understanding of vulnerabilities and their potential consequences, organizations can develop tailored strategies that address their unique risk profiles. This approach not only enhances the effectiveness of cybersecurity measures but also helps organizations align with regulatory expectations, ensuring that organizations are better prepared to manage risks in a dynamic, yet often unpredictable environment. Thus, the emphasis on context and consequence focused within risk assessments will provide a better and more solid foundation for resilient cybersecurity practices.

8.3 SECURITY NOT "REGULATORY PURGATORY"

The challenge of compliance often detracts from the fundamental objectives of cybersecurity risk management. While the intention behind regulatory frameworks is to enhance security measures, the reality usually differs. Organizations may find themselves caught in a cycle of fulfilling regulatory requirements, leading to a situation where the focus shifts from genuine risk mitigation to merely satisfying compliance mandates. This shift can dilute the effectiveness of cybersecurity strategies, as teams may prioritize meeting regulatory standards over addressing actual vulnerabilities.

As a result, the implementation of security controls can devolve into a bureaucratic process, where actions are taken primarily to check off boxes on a compliance checklist. This approach can create a false sense of security, as organizations may believe they are adequately protected simply because they have adhered to regulatory guidelines.

The term "regulatory purgatory" effectively embodies the phenomenon of stagnation experienced by many organizations. This condition arises when entities find themselves ensnared in a perpetual cycle of compliance with policies and superficial reporting practices. In this scenario, the focus shifts away from addressing the underlying issues that could potentially trigger a cyber incident. As a result, organizations may become complacent, prioritizing the appearance of compliance over the substantive measures necessary to enhance their cybersecurity posture. This overlooks the dynamic nature of cyber threats, which require a more proactive and adaptive response.

In this environment, the critical relationship between security and operational safety becomes increasingly strained and tenuous. Organizations often treat security measures as mere formalities, leading to a disconnect between the theoretical frameworks established by regulations and the practical realities of their operational environments. This detachment can result in a false sense of security, where risk assessments are conducted more as a checkbox exercise rather than a genuine evaluation of vulnerabilities, threats, and their potential impacts if not properly addressed or at all. Consequently, the effectiveness of these assessments diminishes, leaving organizations ill-prepared to respond to actual cyber threats.

The implications of deciding to remain in "regulatory purgatory" are profound. Organizations may find themselves vulnerable to cyber incidents that could have been mitigated through proactive and meaningful risk management strategies. By prioritizing compliance over genuine security practices, they risk not only their operational integrity but also their reputation and trustworthiness in the eyes of stakeholders. Security teams may find themselves overwhelmed by the demands of documentation and audits, diverting their attention from critical tasks that could lead to meaningful risk reduction. To break free from this cycle, organizations need to shift their focus from mere adherence to regulations toward fostering a culture of security that emphasizes continuous improvement and real-world applicability, while striking a balance between meeting compliance requirements and implementing robust risk management practices. By prioritizing genuine security outcomes over mere compliance, organizations can better protect themselves against evolving threats and ensure that their cybersecurity efforts are both practical and sustainable.

This realignment necessitates a shift in perspective regarding regulatory compliance; rather than viewing regulations as the ultimate goal, organizations should consider them as a foundational baseline. This baseline serves as a starting point for developing robust security strategies that not only meet compliance requirements but also enhance overall security posture. It is essential for organizations to critically evaluate their security assessments, policies, and controls. If these elements do not demonstrably contribute to a reduction in risk, they should not be accepted without scrutiny. Instead, organizations should adopt a proactive approach, questioning the effectiveness of existing measures and making necessary adjustments. This could involve revising outdated policies or replacing ineffective controls with more innovative solutions that better address current threats and vulnerabilities. Therefore, the goal is to foster a culture of continuous improvement within a given security framework. When prioritizing the alignment of security programs with organizational objectives and emphasizing the importance of measurable outcomes, organizations can create a more resilient operational environment. This approach not only enhances compliance but also empowers organizations to respond more effectively to emerging risks, ensuring that security remains an integral part of their mission rather than a mere checkbox in a compliance checklist.

In recent years, industries driven by compliance have emerged as a direct response to the increasing complexities of regulatory frameworks and the growing imperative for organizations to adhere to rigorous legal and ethical standards. Critical infrastructure sectors such as finance, healthcare, and pharmaceuticals exemplify this trend, where adherence to compliance is not just regarded as a best practice but as essential for their operational viability. The stakes are particularly high in these fields, as the potential for significant financial losses and other implications involving capital gains necessitate a robust compliance strategy. Organizations operating within these domains must navigate a labyrinth of regulations that govern their activities, making compliance a cornerstone of their business models.

The transformation of compliance-driven industries has been significantly shaped by a series of high-profile scandals and crises that have underscored the severe consequences of failing to comply with established regulations. These incidents have not only eroded public trust but have also prompted regulatory bodies to tighten their oversight, leading to the introduction of more rigorous compliance requirements.[1] As a result, companies are now faced with the dual challenge of maintaining operational efficiency while simultaneously ensuring that they adhere to an ever-evolving set of rules. This heightened scrutiny has compelled organizations to reassess their compliance frameworks and implement more comprehensive measures to mitigate risks associated with non-compliance.

In response to these challenges, businesses within compliance-driven sectors have made substantial investments in developing robust compliance programs, enhancing employee training, and adopting advanced technologies designed to streamline compliance processes. These initiatives aim to foster a culture of compliance that permeates every level of the organization, ensuring that all employees are equipped with the knowledge and tools necessary to uphold regulatory standards. Through prioritizing compliance with regulatory requirements, organizations not only safeguard themselves against potential penalties and legal repercussions but also enhance their reputations and build trust with stakeholders. Thus, the commitment to compliance has become a defining characteristic of successful organizations in these critical infrastructure sectors.

Technological advancements, alongside regulatory pressures, have significantly influenced the landscape of compliance-driven industries. The emergence of advanced data analytics, artificial intelligence, and automated compliance solutions has transformed how organizations oversee their operations. These innovations empower businesses to conduct more thorough monitoring and swiftly address potential compliance challenges. As some companies may decide to leverage these technologies, these companies can implement real-time reporting mechanisms and conduct comprehensive risk assessments, which enable them to pinpoint vulnerabilities before they develop into more serious issues. Because of these advancements, the perception of compliance has shifted dramatically. What was once viewed primarily as a reactive obligation has now become a strategic priority for many organizations. Companies are increasingly aware that establishing robust compliance frameworks not only mitigates risks but also enhances their overall reputation in the marketplace. This proactive approach to compliance fosters trust among stakeholders, including customers, investors, and regulatory bodies, thereby reinforcing the organization's credibility and integrity. As such, the integration of technology into compliance practices has proven to be a catalyst for business success. Organizations that prioritize compliance as a strategic element are better positioned to navigate the complexities of regulatory environments while simultaneously driving operational efficiency. By recognizing the value of a robust compliance framework, businesses can leverage it as a competitive advantage, ensuring long-term sustainability and growth in an increasingly complex and evolving landscape.

In terms of how this fits within OT and operational environments, safety once again plays a critically important role in this massively complex equation. If the safety of a for-profit industrial plant's operation is compromised or has suffered a degradation to its operation, this affects the net outcome, which in turn affects the revenue stream, and ultimately the profit margin(s) of the organization. In today's tight and highly competitive markets, the difference of only a few percentage points on the stock market can either make or break a corporation. Again, as financial loss and capital gain are impacted, compliance-driven solutions are further imposed and enforced. While intentions related to safety management are genuine, for-profit corporations must also generate a profit.

However, without safe and relatable industry-based practices in place, the corporation cannot be profitable. This further reinforces our term "regulatory purgatory" as this part of the corporation is in a constant dance between regulators, compliance assessors and auditors, security, and ultimately, executive management.

It should be noted that industries driven by regulatory requirements often face heightened risk levels due to the complexity of their frameworks that they must navigate. As mentioned earlier, specific critical infrastructure sectors, including finance, healthcare, and energy, are subject to stringent regulations that dictate how they manage data and security protocols. The focus on compliance can inadvertently lead to a false sense of security, as these organizations may prioritize meeting regulatory requirements over implementing robust cybersecurity measures. This can inadvertently create vulnerabilities, as the emphasis on compliance may overshadow the need for proactive risk management and adaptive security strategies.

Consequently, these industries can become more susceptible to cyber threats, as they may not invest adequately in innovative security solutions that go beyond mere compliance. To those industries, the words "security" and "compliance" are often used interchangeably, sometimes together. Though many may parrot that "security" will always take precedence over "compliance," the meaning and its implementation are often the complete opposite. Some regulatory bodies, through their auditors, usually enforce strict adherence to requirements that they have set, imposed, and are enforcing. These requirements are "defined by committee," with many participants having little or no actual technical knowledge of whatever restrictive controls are being implemented or altered. The regulatory bodies consist of legal and policy managers who are familiar with methods of ensuring that the regulatory body remains intact, further exhibiting their influence over those industries upon which they impose their doctrine.

However, in contrast to what has been stated thus far about compliance-driven industries, those industries outside this compliance category often enjoy greater flexibility in their operational practices, allowing them to adopt more dynamic and comprehensive cybersecurity measures and countermeasures. Without the constraints of strict regulatory oversight, these organizations can prioritize their security posture based on their unique risk profiles and emerging threats that pertain specifically to them. For example, a tech startup may choose to implement cutting-edge cybersecurity technologies and practices tailored to its specific needs, rather than adhering to a one-size-fits-all compliance-based framework. This adaptability can lead to a more resilient security posture, as these companies are better equipped to respond to any evolving cyber threats and vulnerabilities.

8.4 CONTEXT NOT CONDITION

Organizations must learn to navigate the evolving landscape of cybersecurity threats by integrating context-aware risk assessments into their governance frameworks, as this is becoming increasingly crucial. By being context-aware, our focus is not solely based on the method of evaluation, but also on considering each specific situation in the environment being assessed. What this means is that any given assessment does not rely solely upon any standardized test(s) or predefined criteria, but instead incorporates other factors such as a location within a facility, function or process applied, operating system, access methods, points of entry, etc. Incorporating these factors into an assessment can enhance the evaluation by making it more meaningful and relatable.

For example, while maintaining the anonymity of the story being told, one instance involves an engineer who was summoned to a conference room by several individuals, including several regulatory auditors. A question was raised as to why a particular cybersecurity configuration was not implemented on a piece of plant equipment. The engineer carefully attempted to explain their reasoning, such that the cybersecurity configuration in question, although possible, was unnecessary and was intended for another type of device crafted by another manufacturer, involving a completely different architecture. Although it would satisfy the regulatory requirement, it was deemed completely unnecessary. The auditors, without any hesitation, insisted that the engineer implement the cybersecurity configuration regardless of the condition, and that the engineer had a predetermined set period to complete and provide a record of completion to the auditors, or the company would face further questioning and perhaps receive a fine.

Another example involved a similar situation in which regulatory auditors questioned why additional cybersecurity measures and countermeasures were implemented on a different piece of plant equipment, and that, in its current state of operation, was deemed "non-compliant" based on several specific regulatory controls. The engineer stated that the additional cybersecurity provisions were added as a secondary defensive method since the device was located at near-fringe locations. The auditors objected and demanded that the device be placed precisely as it was before the additional modifications, and that there were no compliance-based reviews that could indicate any additional benefit resulting from the modifications. Similar conditions existed, and the device was retrofitted with its prior and original configuration.

In both examples, the rigidity of the regulatory auditors' circumstantial interpretations and their lack of technical knowledge demonstrate that, in those situations, "compliance" overshadowed "security." Not all examples (such as those above) represent a draconian approach to cybersecurity; in many cases, situations involving poor or missing secure configurations, improper asset identification, and other compliance-based issues have been helped by audits.

Regulations will always be with us, even if their content varies. However, rather than blindly following regulations, organizations should follow a risk-based approach that can provide their necessary security protections but also be used to demonstrate compliance to applicable regulations.

The approach must be consequence-based, so that organizations evaluate the likelihood of various incidents but also consider their potential impacts arising from those incidents on their people, environment, operations, reputation, and stakeholders.

Using national or international standards or frameworks adds credibility to the result, but organizations should still not simply implement everything that is specified in a particular standard or framework.

For example, the NIST CSF establishes a baseline that would satisfy almost all regulatory requirements. The NIST CSF is a framework, not a regulation. The NIST CSF, in turn, refers to other standards and guides (such as ISA/IEC 62443, which explicitly addresses the security of industrial automation and control systems) that provide specific guidance on the implementation of controls. Following NIST CSF (and its underlying standards and guides) assures that the organization is implementing the controls correctly.

ISA/IEC 62443 defines requirements for organizations to conduct a high-level risk assessment to identify consequences and impacts, and a detailed risk assessment to incorporate threats, vulnerabilities, and exploits. This leads to the identification of a specific security level (SL), which in turn determines the security controls required to meet that level.

Once an organization has employed the risk-based methodology and implemented the necessary controls, it can identify any remaining gaps related to applicable regulatory requirements. For example, within the electric industry, under transmission, there are specific requirements for the placement of equipment used at the transformer level versus the switch house level.

Some organizations are now doing just that and are standardizing their baseline controls and matching them against their regulatory requirements, focusing more on the specific technical cybersecurity aspects to OT environments for that particular industry. Some industries are cooperating with regulators better than others. Nonetheless, although slow, it is still progress.

Companies are struggling with finding suitable risk management models and frameworks[2] to use within their specific industry, and many utilize (or appear to be or allow) what regulators impose control over how risk is discovered and managed.

Applying the NIST CSF and/or ISA/IEC 62443 is non-trivial, and many organizations complain that they are "too complex." As a result, they are tempted by the apparent simplicity of frameworks that define a fixed set of controls. This approach may appear more straightforward on the outset, but it sets the organization down the road to regulatory purgatory, as explained above. Even if not regulated, the organization will tend to focus more on compliance with the chosen checklist than security itself.

In some cases, regulators dictate how entire industries should operate, from start to finish, which includes open market trading, and even financial planning—every aspect is carefully "observed" by outsiders who do not have a detailed insight into the intricacies of how organizations operate and what specific risks they may carry.[3] For each regulatory requirement, there is a cost involved; the more controls that are required, the greater the cost. Regulators may not consider how much it will cost an organization to implement and maintain controls to meet the regulations. A risk-based approach will enable the demonstration of the risk-reward tradeoff for implementing or not implementing a control.

In some sectors, regulatory bodies use the term "risk management" but often misuse it. In most cases, it refers to vulnerability or gap assessment. In some cases, the criticality of a vulnerability is considered a risk. This misuse of the term hinders the effective implementation of the most crucial aspect of cybersecurity management.

Organizations must recognize that a singular focus on risk assessment can overlook the broader implications of potential security incidents, which can have far-reaching consequences, and can lead to a narrow perspective that fails to account for the wider implications of potential security incidents. While risk assessment is a crucial component of an organization's security strategy, it often emphasizes quantifying and mitigating specific threats without considering the broader context in which these threats exist. This limited focus can result in a lack of preparedness for incidents that, while not immediately apparent in risk assessments, could have significant repercussions on the organization's operations, reputation, and stakeholder trust.

Incorporating remediation methods based on risk assessment is crucial for enhancing an organization's overall cybersecurity posture. Remediation strategies should be custom-tailored to address the specific consequences identified during the assessment process. This allows organizations to implement targeted measures that could mitigate those risks while also preparing ahead to prevent potential incidents. This holistic approach not only strengthens the organization's defenses but also fosters a culture of resilience, enabling teams to respond swiftly and effectively when faced with cybersecurity challenges. Engagement means involving various departments and/or stakeholders in discussions about potential risks and their broader implications.

8.5 THE PRESSURE TO COMPLY

One of the most damaging cultural problems in cybersecurity governance is the tendency to assert compliance even when it does not reflect operational reality. Declaring compliance without evidence or assurance creates a dangerous illusion of security and can arise for various reasons: pressure from leadership to show success, fear of regulatory penalties, or simply the desire to pass an audit—for example to avoid "extra work" closing audit findings.

This problem leaves an organization vulnerable to incidents that it has falsely convinced itself it is protected against. This, in turn, undermines the trust of regulators and insurers who rely on accurate reporting to assess risk. It further reinforces the culture that "all that matters is passing the audit," not taking security seriously. This can increase the likelihood of an incident as employees cut corners and pay lip-service to policies and procedures.

Rather than ask how to "look compliant," organizations should ask: "Are we truly reducing our risk?" Transparency, accountability, and evidence-based governance must replace check listing and "compliance theater."[4] OT environments deserve better than security policies that exist only on paper. The right culture—supported by the right leadership and governance structures—will treat cybersecurity as a shared responsibility rooted in integrity, not paperwork. In doing so, they will be better prepared not only to comply with regulations, but to protect what matters most: human safety, operational continuity, and public trust.

As stated previously, a regulated for-profit company's primary objective is to make a profit. It makes sense to do as little as possible in maintaining adherence to regulatory requirements, but this is often left up to interpretation, as companies will go to great lengths to justify their reasons to auditors on how they've continued to be compliant, when in fact, that observation may be questionable. Rather than investing in security initiatives, these companies often spend the same amount—or more—on compliance-driven programs instead, due to stiff penalties and fines that are imposed if found non-compliant, especially in key-critical areas vital to not just the company, but to the Nation.

For example, following the September 11th 2001 event, airport security was revamped, and the U.S. federal government took control (and responsibility) of security checkpoint screening of passengers and their baggage at all airports. However, the U.S. Transportation Security Agency, since its inception up to present, has been under constant scrutiny for a plethora of serious issues including (but not limited to) the following:[5,6]

- Detection equipment not regularly calibrated, maintained, and certified;
- TSA screeners lacking proper training; and,
- TSA screener candidates being improperly vetted (hiring of convicted felons).[7]

Though there were additional issues, the three issues outlined above are considered the most important ones as they misrepresent assurances that their security practices are thorough and would stop would-be adversaries from boarding a commercial aircraft.

8.6 SECURITY ASSESSMENTS NOT VULNERABILITY ASSESSMENTS

Most organizations today focus and have prioritized their security programs more on vulnerability scanning rather than gap assessments, rather than performing actual, regular security assessments. In most cases, these acts of securing their environments are rooted primarily from the regulatory-compliance mindset, such that, if vulnerabilities are addressed the organization is "secure." This mindset and culture is prevalent within OT environments as hardware/software architecture enhancements, updates, or upgrades are often discouraged, perhaps even prohibited if operations are deemed critical, and instead will apply "secondary controls"[8] within those environments.

Regulated organizations tend to be pressured to meet key performance indicators agreed by corporate stakeholders, board members, and stockholders. These organizations may also face increasing pressure from regulatory bodies to meet cybersecurity requirements based on "best practices," often set by the regulator itself. The pace of regulatory update cannot match the pace of change in technology, organizational change, and geopolitical state and as a result the requirements will be constantly lacking.

Regulatory bodies and corporations within heavily regulated industries, such as energy and water, often use the term "best practice" when referring to the requirements they identify. Even outside of those heavily regulated industries, the term best practice is widely used. Like checklists and prescriptive requirements, the use of the term best practice can be detrimental when used in cybersecurity management.

These best practices are typically developed through committees of interested stakeholders. Through this process, the committee-defined approach helps establish a set of best practices that incorporates both standards and known frameworks. However, the effectiveness of these best practices is impacted by who is involved and how they identify what is needed.

Crucially, calling something a best practice signals that it should be followed by everyone; not doing so implies a failure to meet expected standards. This does not mean that these best practices are bad. For example, the CISA Cyber Physical Goals checklist identifies 35 best practices. These are categorized within the NIST CSF core functions. Some best practices are essential for any organization—for example "incident planning and preparedness"—but some are extremely narrow in their specificity or effectiveness—for example "deploy security.txt files." To imply that all organizations must implement all 35 controls or they are not "following best practice" would be misleading. Worse still, the 35 best practices omit critical controls for asset-intensive organizations—for example, deployment of mechanical failsafes or implementation of manual procedures. This creates an even more misleading situation: meeting all the best practices (if feasible) would not guarantee an organization is managing their cybersecurity risk.

Table 8.1 summarizes the objectives of these best practice methodologies, considering what was intended and the reality. There is nothing inherently wrong with the idea of best practices, just how they are identified, documented, and interpreted.

As already noted, organizations that prioritize vulnerability assessments over larger-scoped assessments, particularly due to their practicality, cost (which is very important), and focus on actionable areas of concern, will state that performing these assessments enables them to continue to be secure. The use of vulnerability assessments is particularly attractive to corporations because they're easier to implement and manage, more cost-effective, and don't require as many staff to operate. Although performing vulnerability assessments does have its merits by identifying any weaknesses that would-be attackers could exploit, it does not consider the other elements of the risk equation: threat and consequence.

Here are a few issues with performing only vulnerability assessments within OT environments:

- Regardless of the staffing count, focusing solely on vulnerability assessments is a financial drain on the organization, particularly when it encounters a plethora of low-risk vulnerabilities. When

TABLE 8.1 Objectives of Best Practices

Objective	What Should Happen	What May Not Happen
Definition and utilization of comprehensive and well-documented standards and frameworks.	Through these committees, a wide range of experts (involving those who've worked at a particular company for an extended period, as well as others) produce a more thorough and well-thought-out compliance framework (often under the moniker of another name, such as "security framework" or "risk framework") in addressing the industry's vulnerabilities and potential threats.	Those who attend consist of compliance, legal, and policy development—all non-technical. Those who do attend with technical roles are often instructed to observe only and to debrief the active attendees in a private teleconference call.
Increased buy-in from industry leaders and its adoption.	Executives from key-critical stakeholders, representing the significant share of the effort performed, foster a sense of ownership and contribution, thus increasing the likelihood of widespread adoption and adherence to newly established standards and frameworks.	Executives from key-critical stakeholders representing the significant share of the effort performed may feel threatened if there are no compromises, potentially performing actions that could have a negative impact.
Define methods of reducing risk footprints while improving security postures.	Through the widely used and accepted standards and frameworks, which include "best practices" and proven security controls, the overall security posture of the industry will improve.	Remediating risk footprints and security postures based on "best practices" addresses the symptoms and not the problem.

(*Continued*)

TABLE 8.1 (Continued)

Objective	What Should Happen	What May Not Happen
Creates an enhanced sense of trust.	Adherence to regulatory requirements and "best practices" within and throughout the community appeals to the organizations' customers, partners, and their regulators.	Use of groupthink may not necessarily provide suitable results that would be beneficial to the community at large, as many members from these committees may follow a selected few who are the most prevalent key-critical players of that industry (e.g., Shell versus Ma's Oil).
Regulatory requirements cut costs by streamlining risk and cybersecurity efforts through the use of standardized documentation.	Combined use of "best practices," known standards, and frameworks reduces costs applied to risk management and cybersecurity.	Increased regulatory costs and other expenses are actually killing regulated industries; costs are incurred through a cascaded effect: • More controls mean more staff; • More staff mean more procedures; • More procedures mean slower processing; • Slower processing means less produced; • Less produced means less revenue.

attention is focused on all vulnerabilities, particularly the low-risk items, rather than the more critical ones, the organization spends more time and money remediating those low-risk vulnerabilities. By failing to address more serious issues correctly, the organization continues to be exposed to risk, often of a more severe nature.

- Through vulnerability assessments, scanning tools used in vulnerability management have a limited scope. They may miss zero-day exploits or newly discovered vulnerabilities not added to those scanning tools' datasets. Furthermore, in OT environments, it may not be feasible to scan some hosts or networks, and some equipment may not even be on a network. Having a successful vulnerability scan should not be taken as a sign that there are no vulnerabilities.
- There is a potential for both false positives and false negatives, which can sometimes result from improper scanning methods or incomplete vulnerability datasets. For false positives, if a scanning tool is unable to ascertain if a device or piece of software is vulnerable, it may flag it as vulnerable when, in fact, it is not. The same may be said for the condition in which a device or piece of software is not identified as vulnerable due to incorrect, missing, or improper vulnerability datasets.
- Vulnerability scanning tools may accidentally scan a device that does not meet IETF standards (such as one with a non-standard TCP/IP stack) which may cause the device to fail, often requiring either a restart of the device (or software) or reload of the configuration file(s) to reinstate previously normal operation.

Unfortunately, the checklist and best practice environment that exists rewards proactivity of any kind, even if it is not the best use of resources or does not adequately identify the organization's real risks. Organizations may also encourage positive reports and discourage the identification of issues as these will require time and money to remediate.

This climate of checklists and best practices does not encourage organizations to use critical thinking skills and follow their own path. The weight of support lies with those who follow best practices and utilize checklists to demonstrate their security compliance. Even for sectors that use external cybersecurity consultants—because they lack the in-house capability—the result is likely the same. No one wants to recommend deviation from the best practices and checklists any more than anyone would recommend something other than IBM.[9] This lack of critical thinking continues to impact cybersecurity risk reduction in IT and OT.

8.7 MONITORING AGAINST POLICY

A cybersecurity policy is not something that is written and filed away. The purpose of a cybersecurity policy is to define the necessary activities and behaviors to manage the associated risks. Therefore, this policy should be at the forefront of the governance process. It provides a yardstick for the organization's performance.

Every organization is different. Cybersecurity policies should reflect these differences, but all will contain several key sections:

- Security Policy
- Risk Assessment and Management
- Organizational Security Policies and Procedures
- Physical, Environmental, Personnel, and Vendor Security
- Continuous Improvement and Maturity Management

It is not enough for an organization to monitor its performance against its own policy. Without reference to external measures, there is no way of knowing how good this performance really is. Unfortunately, many organizations track their own performance with little or no reference to external measures. They become convinced they are doing well, when in reality they may be at risk. Tracking compliance will help an organization understand where it is with regard to the overall industry.

8.8 MATURITY MODELS

One approach to tracking against industry performance is to use a maturity model. Maturity models provide a structured framework to evaluate an organization's capabilities over time. This benchmarking can help prioritize investment and align cybersecurity with business objectives.

Common maturity models include:

- **C2M2 (Cybersecurity Capability Maturity Model)**: Developed by the U.S. Department of Energy, C2M2 provides a scalable model for assessing maturity across domains such as risk management, asset identification, threat detection, and incident response. C2M2 has three maturity indicator levels (MILs) in its model, MIL1 (initial or ad hoc practices, limited cybersecurity capabilities), MIL2 (documented, repeatable practices with assigned responsibilities), and MIL3 (institutionalized practices with metrics and continuous improvement).
- **ISA/IEC 62443 Security Maturity Model**: This model assesses maturity across foundational (technical), procedural, and

governance dimensions. It enables asset owners to define target maturity levels based on risk and operational context and defines five levels: initial, managed, defined, quantitively managed, and optimizing.

- **NIST CSF Implementation Tiers:** While not a strict maturity model, the NIST CSF includes four tiers (Partial, Risk-Informed, Repeatable, Adaptive) that describe the degree to which cybersecurity risk management is integrated into organizational culture and business processes.

Maturity models support continuous improvement by:

- Enabling gap analysis between current and target states.
- Providing a roadmap for cybersecurity program development.
- Facilitating cross-functional understanding of cybersecurity progress.
- Supporting evidence-based discussions with regulators, insurers, and stakeholders.

Unfortunately, even maturity models can fall foul of the cultural issues already described. The desire to overstate maturity can mean organizations will claim they are performing better than they really are.

8.9 TO REGULATE, OR NOT TO REGULATE

Since the incident at the City of Oldsmar, the U.S. EPA has made efforts to address the growing cybersecurity threat to the U.S. water and wastewater sector.[10]

Federal agencies as well as several other organizations have attempted to create the water sector's cybersecurity program, but have been reporting numerous challenges such as workforce skills gaps as well as attempts at securing older technologies (specifically control systems) that are difficult to update with modern-day cybersecurity protections. Based on several reports, the sector has made limited investments in cybersecurity protections as those organizations' water systems have been prioritizing funding to meet regulatory requirements for clean and safe water, while any cybersecurity improvements have been voluntary. "In a May 2024 alert, the Environmental Protection Agency (EPA) said it planned to increase enforcement activities to ensure drinking water systems now address cybersecurity threats."[11]

Since 2003 similar to many of the other critical infrastructure federal stakeholders, the EPA is required by law, under National Security Memorandum 22 (NSM-22),[12,13] to "identify, assess, and prioritize water sector risk."[14] Furthermore, from these reports, the agency has indicated that, although they have performed analyses to all threats, vulnerabilities, and consequences, they have yet to integrate any of the resulting work into a comprehensive assessment program. "Without a risk assessment and strategy to guide its efforts, EPA has limited assurance its efforts address the highest risks."[15]

The agency has faced numerous legal challenges by overstretching its existing legal authority to mandate a cybersecurity program.

> In March 2023, EPA interpreted existing legal requirements to include cybersecurity assessments at drinking water systems but withdrew the requirement seven months later after facing legal challenges. Previous requirements and NSM-22 direct EPA to identify the authorities it needs to compel the sector to address risks. In July 2024, EPA officials said they had evaluated their authorities and would release the evaluation in 2025 with their risk assessment and strategy. Doing so and seeking additional authority as necessary can help EPA ensure the water sector is better prepared for any future cyberattacks.[16]

It should be noted that much of this action was due to the City of Oldsmar's incident. At the time of the incident, it was considered a targeted attack by an unauthorized user exploiting an insecure remote access service. Two years after the incident, the U.S. Federal Bureau of Investigation (FBI) concluded that there was no evidence of an external unauthorized user. The incident was therefore likely one of the most common causes of a cybersecurity incident—a non-malicious authorized user making a mistake. The strategy for cybersecurity management did not change as a result of this conclusion from the FBI. This is the very essence of risk management—understanding the consequences and threats, not just vulnerabilities, and managing accordingly.

To reinforce this point, the

> EPA has not conducted a comprehensive sector-wide risk assessment of the water sector's cybersecurity risk or used a risk-informed strategy to guide its actions, which our past work has shown is a basic underpinning for better managing federal programs and activities. Additionally, EPA's efforts to ensure water and wastewater systems take action to improve their cybersecurity have been met with legal and other challenges from the water sector. However, EPA has not fully evaluated the sufficiency of its existing legal authorities for achieving widespread implementation of key cybersecurity requirements for water and wastewater systems or taken action to identify and address any gaps in its authority.[17]

Since the "EPA has not conducted a comprehensive sector-wide risk assessment or used a risk-informed strategy to guide its actions to improve the water sector's level of cybersecurity," the General Account Office ("GAO") "found that using a risk-informed strategy can improve the effectiveness of agency efforts to develop critical infrastructure cybersecurity programs."[18]

The key characteristics of an effective risk-based strategy for cybersecurity management would include the following:

- **Risk assessment.** Assesses the risks to critical assets and operations. We have also previously highlighted the importance of performing a cybersecurity risk assessment to help inform the steps that agencies should take when developing a critical infrastructure cybersecurity program[19] through voluntary action that all water utilities need to implement. The current program employs 32 criteria with minimal requirements.[20] The EPA has partnered with CISA to produce a checklist[21] for public utilities to determine if they're vulnerable and require further analysis of securing both their IT and OT environments. Both the EPA and CISA are offering their assistance in evaluating a given public utility's risk footprint. However, this is misleading as it is only a vulnerability assessment, not a risk assessment. No consideration of the risk to critical assets and operations is included in the process.
- **Objectives, activities, and performance measures.** Addresses what the strategy is attempting to achieve, steps to achieve those results and the priorities, milestones, and performance measures that include measurable targets to gauge results and help ensure accountability. When defining the steps to achieve results, we have previously highlighted the importance of agencies determining whether they should act in a regulatory or advisory role.[22] We have also previously highlighted the importance of relying on NIST cybersecurity guidance to identify practices that critical infrastructure owners and operations should follow.[23]
- **Roles, responsibilities, and mechanisms to coordinate efforts.** Identifies who will implement the strategy, outlines their roles, and establishes mechanisms to coordinate their efforts. This characteristic entails identifying the specific federal departments, agencies, or offices involved, and, where appropriate, the different non-federal (e.g., state, local, or private) entities. A strategy should clarify the organization's relationships in terms of leading, supporting, or sharing responsibilities. A strategy should also identify specific processes for coordination and collaboration between responsible entities.
- **Identification of needed resources and investments.** Addresses how much the strategy will cost, as well as identifies the types of resources required, and shows where those resources should be

applied based on risk reductions matched against costs. Specifically, a national strategy should elaborate on the risk assessment mentioned earlier and give guidance to implementing parties to manage their resources and investments accordingly.

Regulators in any sector or country should focus on outcomes, principles, and accountability. They should avoid becoming involved in an organization's operational decision-making. Unfortunately, intentionally or not, prescriptive regulation approaches tend to do the latter. Even the checklist and best practice approach, without the force of regulation, tends to lead to this result. This involvement in operational decision-making has been likened by some as inviting a vampire into your home. What starts as support and guidance can turn into an intrusion, and this intrusion can become increasingly impactful as time goes on. As noted earlier, the focus can shift from managing security to managing compliance. For this reason, it is preferable to keep the vampire out of the home.[24]

8.10 CONCLUSION

As industrial and operational systems continue to evolve within increasingly complex regulatory and threat landscapes, the imperative for organizations to prioritize cybersecurity as a strategic, risk-based endeavor has never been clearer. Throughout this chapter, we have highlighted how the pressures of regulatory compliance—while well-intentioned—can often lead organizations into a cycle of superficial assurance, or "regulatory purgatory," where demonstrating adherence takes precedence over genuine risk reduction.

True cybersecurity maturity cannot be achieved through checklists or prescriptive controls alone. It requires a deep integration of context-aware, consequence-driven risk assessments into governance structures, organizational culture, and daily operations. This shift demands leadership commitment, technical insight, and a willingness to challenge outdated norms and misaligned incentives.

Regulation alone is not the answer. While concerns over critical infrastructure security may suggest that regulation is the only answer, it must be implemented effectively. Prescriptive regulation is not ideal and results in a lack of critical thinking. As demonstrated with the water industry example, the prescriptive regulations fail to prevent the recurrence of prior incidents (e.g., the Oldsmar non-malicious user error).

The most effective type of regulation is one that is risk-based, enabling organizations to identify their specific risks and manage them accordingly. Asset-intensive organizations should be encouraged to adopt this approach and manage their risks in a manner that suits their needs. Regulation should focus on outcomes, principles, and accountability, verifying that organizations have followed a risk-based approach, identified their risks, and are managing them.

Frameworks such as NIST CSF and ISA/IEC 62443 offer robust pathways toward this goal, but only when applied with discernment and tailored to the organization's unique risk profile. Similarly, while maturity models and best practices can guide progress, they must not become ends in themselves. Instead, they should support critical thinking, encourage continuous improvement, and ensure security programs are adaptive, relevant, and effective.

Ultimately, regulation alone cannot secure critical infrastructure. It is only through a unified culture of cybersecurity—one rooted in accountability, transparency, and a commitment to operational resilience—that organizations can meet both their regulatory obligations and their broader mission to protect people, processes, and systems in an increasingly interconnected world.

NOTES

1 One such example has been regarding the securing of control systems in the water and wastewater sector.
2 https://aspr.hhs.gov/cip/hph-cybersecurity-framework-implementation-guide/Documents/HPH-Sector-CSF-Implementation-Guide-508.pdf (alt URL: http://riskbook.infracritical.com/book1/chapter8/ch8ref1.pdf).
3 https://obamawhitehouse.archives.gov/sites/default/files/omb/legislative/letters/cybersecurity-regulatory-framework-for-covered-critical-infrastructure-act-section-by-section-analysis.pdf, p. 5 (alt URL: http://riskbook.infracritical.com/book1/chapter8/ch8ref2.pdf).
4 The term "compliance theater," synonymous with the term "security theater," refers to alluding to the perception that environments are adherent to regulatory requirements; when in fact, they are not (or may not appear to be), giving the regulator a misleading impression of the organization's true state of adherence to its compliancy.
5 "AVIATION SECURITY - TSA Could Better Ensure Detection and Assess the Potential for Discrimination in Its Screening Technologies", U.S. Government Accountability Office (GAO), GAO-24-107094; URL: https://www.gao.gov/assets/d24107094.pdf (alt URL: http://riskbook.infracritical.com/book1/chapter8/ch8ref3.pdf).
6 "TRANSPORTATION SECURITY ADMINISTRATION - Progress and Challenges Faced in Strengthening Three Key Security Programs",

U.S. Government Accountability Office (GAO), GAO-12-541T; URL: https://oversight.house.gov/wp-content/uploads/2012/03/3-26-12-Joint-TI-Lord-Testimony.pdf (alt URL: http://riskbook.infracritical.com/book1/chapter8/ch8ref4.pdf)

7 It should be noted that the hiring practices which accidentally included hiring former convicted felons were quickly remediated shortly after public disclosure. URL: "Report: Felons hired in rush to fill screener jobs", CNN, February 5, 2004; https://www.cnn.com/2004/US/02/05/tsa.felons.screeners/index.html.

8 The term "secondary control" (alternatively called "altered control," "alternate control," or "alternative control") refers to applied alternative security protection mechanisms to secure a given site, facility (if more than one per site), environment, operation, or device. An example would be implementing strong physical protection mechanisms (such as guns, gates, and guards) to prevent any possible external threats from ever propagating into the setup.

9 An unattributed, popular saying from the days when IBM was the safe bet for companies buying servers. IBM has been replaced by others such as Microsoft and Cisco. It can also be phrased as "If it ain't broke, don't fix it."

10 http://scid.infracritical.com/pages/scid-00113.

11 https://www.gao.gov/assets/880/870558.pdf (alt URL: http://riskbook.infracritical.com/book1/chapter8/ch8ref5.pdf).

12 https://bidenwhitehouse.archives.gov/briefing-room/presidential-actions/2024/04/30/national-security-memorandum-on-critical-infrastructure-security-and-resilience/, "National Security Memorandum on Critical Infrastructure Security and Resilience", April 30, 2004 (alt URL: http://riskbook.infracritical.com/book1/chapter8/ch8ref6.pdf).

13 Specifically, within 180 days of the date of the National Security Memorandum (April 30, 2024), Sector Risk Management Agencies shall develop plans to execute the required roles and responsibilities of each Sector Risk Management Agency to ensure a continuity of effort and the coordination of policy and resourcing requirements. Within 270 days and on a recurring basis biennial by February 1 of each year, each Sector Risk Management Agency shall submit its sector-specific risk management plan to the Secretary of Homeland Security, based on guidance developed by the Department of Homeland Security, through their Secretary or Agency Head. The plan shall be informed by the sector-specific risk assessment included as an annex. The White House, National Security Memorandum on Critical Infrastructure Security and Resilience.

14 https://www.gao.gov/assets/880/870558.pdf (alt URL: http://riskbook.infracritical.com/book1/chapter8/ch8ref5.pdf).

15 https://www.gao.gov/assets/880/870558.pdf (alt URL: http://riskbook.infracritical.com/book1/chapter8/ch8ref5.pdf).
16 https://www.gao.gov/assets/880/870558.pdf (alt URL: http://riskbook.infracritical.com/book1/chapter8/ch8ref5.pdf).
17 https://www.gao.gov/assets/880/870558.pdf (alt URL: http://riskbook.infracritical.com/book1/chapter8/ch8ref5.pdf).
18 See, for example, GAO-23-105789; URLs: https://www.gao.gov/products/gao-23-105789, https://www.gao.gov/assets/gao-23-105789.pdf (alt URL: http://riskbook.infracritical.com/book1/chapter8/ch8ref7.pdf). We have also reported that national strategies differ from other federal planning documents such as agency-specific strategic plans that the Government Performance and Results Act of 1993 requires. These strategies are national in scope, cutting across levels of government and sectors and involving a large number of organizations and entities (i.e., federal, state, local, and private sectors). GAO-04-408T; URLs:; https://www.gao.gov/products/gao-04-408t, https://www.gao.gov/assets/gao-04-408t.pdf (alt URL: http://riskbook.infracritical.com/book1/chapter8/ch8ref8.pdf).
19 See, for example, GAO-19-332; URLs: https://www.gao.gov/products/gao-19-332, https://www.gao.gov/assets/gao-19-332.pdf (alt URL: http://riskbook.infracritical.com/book1/chapter8/ch8ref9.pdf); GAO-18-62; URLs: https://www.gao.gov/products/gao-18-62, https://www.gao.gov/assets/gao-18-62.pdf (alt URL: http://riskbook.infracritical.com/book1/chapter8/ch8ref10.pdf); and GAO-23-105789; URLs: https://www.gao.gov/products/gao-23-105789, https://www.gao.gov/assets/gao-23-105789.pdf (alt URL: http://riskbook.infracritical.com/book1/chapter8/ch8ref7.pdf).
20 https://www.epa.gov/sites/default/files/2018-06/documents/cybersecurity_guide_for_states_final_0.pdf (alt URL: http://riskbook.infracritical.com/book1/chapter8/ch8ref11.pdf).
21 https://www.cisa.gov/sites/default/files/2023-03/cisa_cpg_checklist_v1.0.1_final.pdf (alt URL: http://riskbook.infracritical.com/book1/chapter8/ch8ref12.pdf).
22 See, for example, GAO, Regulatory Guidance Processes: Selected Departments Could Strengthen Internal Control and Dissemination Practices, GAO-15-368 (Washington, D.C.: Apr. 16, 2015); URLs: https://www.gao.gov/products/gao-15-368, https://www.gao.gov/assets/gao-15-368.pdf (alt URL: http://riskbook.infracritical.com/book1/chapter8/ch8ref13.pdf).
23 See, for example, GAO-19-332 URLs: https://www.gao.gov/products/gao-19-332, https://www.gao.gov/assets/gao-19-332.pdf (alt URL: http://riskbook.infracritical.com/book1/chapter8/ch8ref9.pdf); GAO-19-48; URLs: https://www.gao.gov/products/gao-19-48,

https://www.gao.gov/assets/d1948.pdf (alt URL: http://riskbook.infracritical.com/book1/chapter8/ch8ref14.pdf); National Institute of Standards and Technology, Framework for Improving Critical Infrastructure; Cybersecurity, version 1.1 (April 16, 2018); and Guide to Operational Technology (OT) Security.

24 This idea became commonly known because of Bram Stoker's novel *Dracula*, when Count Dracula could not enter Lucy Westenra's home without an invitation. It is believed to be rooted in European folklore.

CHAPTER 9

Incident Response and Recovery

9.1 INTRODUCTION

The chapter focuses on the incident response and recovery aspects of OT systems. Incident response planning is essential, but plans must be based on a thorough risk assessment. There is a misconception that incident response is based on a static document created for audits. In fact, effective planning is an ongoing process that must adapt to technological and operational changes. Common gaps in preparedness result in a poor response, which can significantly contribute to the costs of recovery. Aligning incident scenarios with realistic recovery goals, SLAs, and system design considerations can help address this gap.

The main elements of incident recovery include robust backup strategies for OT-specific devices, mechanical failsafes, and system design updates to enhance resilience. Practical issues such as hardware availability, firmware compatibility, and manual procedures must be considered.

Forensic readiness is another critical factor, making sure organizations can gather and preserve digital evidence to learn from incidents and support legal or regulatory processes. Insider threats are different from external ones and need different technical and procedural countermeasures.

The use of the Five Rs of Incident Response—Response, Recovery, Restoration, Remediation, and Reassessment—provides a structured, phased approach to managing incidents effectively and promoting continuous improvement. This discussion should cover escalation protocols, service provider requirements, and methods for testing and evaluating incident response plans through various realistic exercises.

Finally, the importance of tracking and analyzing near misses as early warning signs is essential to strengthening cybersecurity posture. Utilizing proven models from health and safety can provide a predictive and behavioral perspective.

DOI: 10.4324/9781003610557-9

9.2 PLANNING

Incident response plans do not appear in isolation. They are a result of a comprehensive risk assessment. Furthermore, incident response plans are not a one-time exercise, nor are they something that is reviewed every three years or so, when auditors perform their review.

The most common issues with incident response preparedness can be categorized as failure to:

- Assess the risk.
- Prepare a plan to manage the risk.
- Implement the mitigation controls that reduce the impact of an incident.
- Implement the preventive controls that reduce the likelihood of an incident.
- Thoroughly test the plan and address any identified gaps.
- Consider both internal and external changes.
- Continue to improve the preparedness.

Figure 9.1 shows a continuous lifecycle for incident response planning that, if followed, addresses these failures.

Incident response planning cannot commence until a risk assessment has been performed. As already noted earlier in this book, there is a general lack of understanding of what OT cybersecurity risk assessment addresses. Rather than being concerned with the compromise of IT or OT devices, the risk is a failure of a process that can lead to serious consequences such as harm to people or the environment, interruption of production, or damage to machinery.

If performed correctly, the risk assessment will identify:

- Threats, and importantly, will prioritize them. For example, while nation-states may have extensive resources, motivation, and capabilities, the most likely threat remains an insider, either malicious or non-malicious. The risk assessment and the resulting preparedness must reflect this prioritization.
- Incident scenarios with associated consequences and impacts. Understanding these scenarios is crucial to a successful incident response plan. For instance, a compromise of a server or workstation involves restoring from backup, but the scenario is much more than that. The incident could result in a process accident, and the work required to prepare for that is very different.

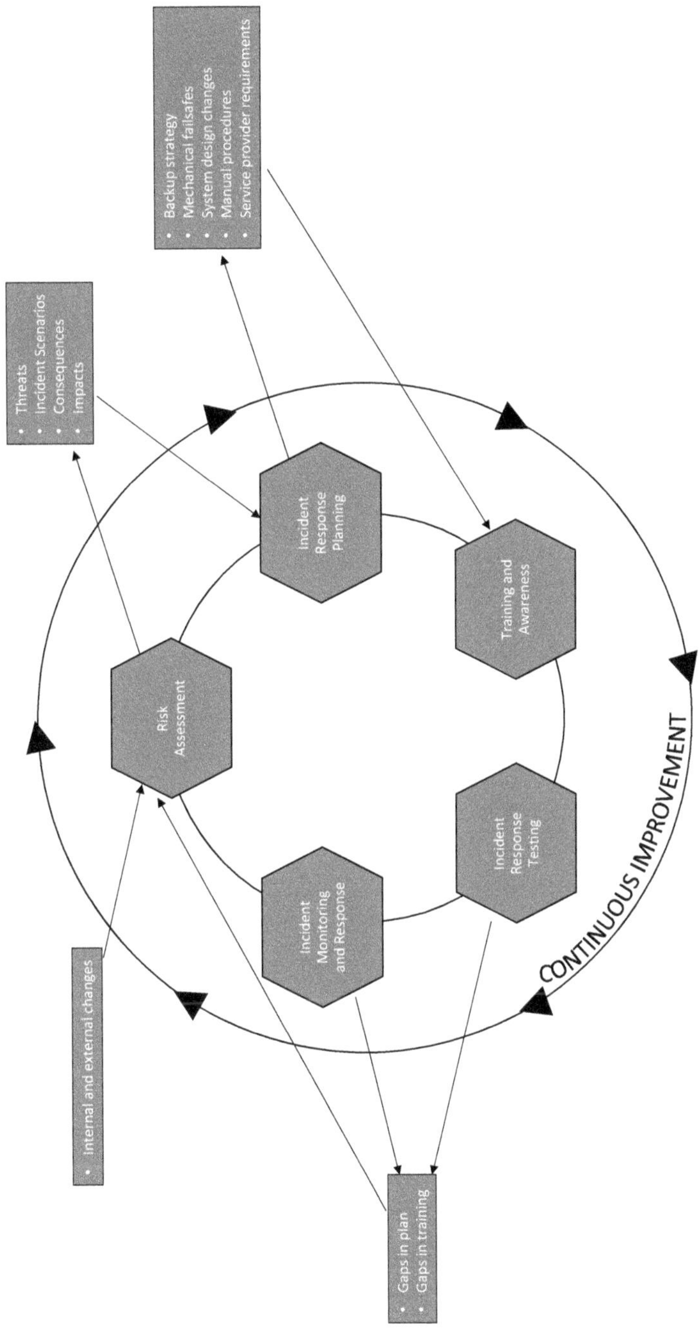

FIGURE 9.1 The continuous incident response planning cycle.

A properly prepared incident response plan will consider the output of the risk assessment process to define:

- Recovery objectives.
- Roles, responsibilities, and levels of authority.
- Communications procedures and contact information.
- Logistics information.

The recovery objectives must be identified for each essential function in the OT environment:

- The recovery time objective—Defining how long the function can be out of service
- The recovery point objective—Defining how much data can be lost in the event of a failure

These objectives are not abstract values. They directly impact some critical decisions that the organization should make:

- Establishing SLAs with vendor(s)
- System design decisions that factor in resilience
- Spare parts, on- and off-site
- What is being backed up, and how often
- Duration of backup and restore, and the backup location(s)

The risk assessment process and incident response planning will also identify controls that are required to mitigate the impact of a cybersecurity incident:

- Mechanical failsafes
- System design changes
- Manual procedures

These controls are commonly overlooked in a cybersecurity incident response plan but are critical to a sound response strategy.

9.3 BACKUP STRATEGY

Backups are an essential protection for OT systems in the event of a cybersecurity incident. In an OT system, backups should be maintained for all programmable electronic elements:

- Process and safety controllers, including programmable logic controllers (PLCs).
- OT-specific devices such as intelligent electronic devices, protocol gateways, and front-end processors.
- Communications devices such as routers, firewalls, and switches.
- Servers and workstations.
- Engineering or technician laptops.

Each equipment type should have a procedure that describes the specific steps taken to perform that backup. Note that some automated backup may be available, either at a system level (entire system) or device level (e.g., via a PLC programming environment).

Restore procedures describe the specific steps needed to restore the system from a backup. These procedures must be tested regularly using real backup files. Testing of this sort provides additional verification that the backup is completing as required and verifies the restoration process.

9.3.1 Backups Are Not Limited to Software

Even in IT environments, a comprehensive incident response plan ensures hardware spares are available to meet recovery objectives.

Maintaining essential hardware spares in an OT environment can be more challenging, but it remains just as necessary. With OT environments, organizations are faced with many challenges:

- The specialist nature of OT hardware means spares may not be readily available when needed.
- Specific hardware builds may become obsolete, and firmware or software compatibility with new builds may be an issue.
- OT hardware lacks the interchangeable features of IT hardware, like servers or workstations.
- Changes to OT hardware may require additional changes, for example, I/O wiring.

While stories about OT environments running Windows XP are familiar, many overlook the equally fragile nature of OT hardware, firmware, and software. For example, a PLC consists of specific hardware versions, and each version supports one or more firmware versions. Each PLC firmware may support communication with one or more versions of programming software. And finally, each programming software version may run on specific operating systems. As a result, updating one aspect may trigger a series of necessary changes. Further complicating the update, these issues must be identified in the ongoing risk assessment process and managed outside the incident response process.

Discovering that significant changes are needed for an installation during an incident is the worst possible time, especially due to the unavailability or incompatibility of OT hardware. The management of this issue is discussed later in Section 9.5 on system design changes.

9.3.2 Recovering a PLC, Controller, or OT-Specific Device from Backup

Unlike IT systems, where automated backups and image restoration are standard, recovering PLCs or controllers is a manual and time-consuming process. Recovery requires:

- Access to the latest known-good logic or program files.
- Knowledge of controller firmware versions and configuration files.
- Vendor tools and engineering software to reload and test the configuration.
- Procedures to validate field device communication, I/O mappings, and safety logic.

If the incident includes malicious tampering, the original configuration may be missing or untrustworthy. In such cases, recovery can only proceed if off-system backups or trusted repositories are maintained. Therefore, secure configuration management and engineering workstation protections are essential components of a resilient OT system.

9.4 MECHANICAL FAILSAFES

Critical infrastructure operators use various mechanical failsafes and safety measures to prevent or mitigate failures, protect public health, and ensure the reliable operation of these systems. It is essential that these are properly maintained. In the event of a cybersecurity incident, they may be the only barrier left to prevent a serious incident affecting the public, the facility, or the environment. Examples include:

- Overflow protection and independent alarms—such as overflow weirs and alarms separate from those in the control or safety system.

- Check valves—also known as backflow preventers—are used to ensure that flow is in only one direction.
- Pressure Relief Valves—designed to release excess pressure in pipelines and tanks. They prevent overpressurization, which can cause equipment failures or ruptures.
- Burst Discs—designed to rupture at a specified pressure to release excess pressure safely.
- Independent sensors and actuators—monitoring pressure, pH, or other process variables and activating actions, such as shutting down pumps, when pressures exceed safe limits.
- Flow Control Valves—regulate flow rate in pipelines and prevent pipe bursts caused by excessive pressure.
- Isolation Valves—placed within distribution systems to isolate sections of pipelines or equipment in case of leaks or emergencies. They allow for the isolation of problematic areas while maintaining service to other parts of the system.
- Float Switches—used to trigger alarms or equipment shutdowns when levels reach a critical point, preventing overflows or equipment damage.
- Air Relief Valves—used to release trapped air pockets in pipelines, preventing airlocks and ensuring a continuous flow of water.
- Bunding Areas, Dams, and Levees—bunding areas, dams, and levees are constructed to contain water, chemicals, fuels, or wastewater to prevent overflows or breaches during heavy rainfall, flooding, or loss of containment.

These mechanical failsafes should be implemented based on process hazard analysis. However, when reviewing cyber causes of process hazards, it is important to verify the presence of mechanical failsafes. Cyber-related causes may lead to scenarios where mechanical failsafes are not included. This is especially true when an organization digitalizes an aspect of their traditional analog control environment, such as replacing relay control of a process with a PLC. This shift moves the organization from a *non-hackable* situation (electromechanical relays with no programming or configuration) to a *hackable* one (a PLC that can be compromised in various ways), so new, non-hackable controls need to be added to provide the independent failsafe.

The ongoing lifecycle outlined in Section 9.1 must include regular inspections, maintenance, and monitoring of mechanical failsafes to ensure they function properly when needed to reduce the impact of a cybersecurity incident.

9.5 SYSTEM DESIGN CHANGES

9.5.1 Common Issues

The risk assessment and incident response planning activities might reveal scenarios that necessitate modifications to the system design. Along with the mechanical failsafes outlined in Section 9.4, Table 9.1 lists common

TABLE 9.1 Common Issues Requiring System Design Changes

Issue	Examples of System Changes to be Implemented
Setpoint Validation and Range Checks	Validate that operator-entered setpoints are within predefined safe limits. Enforce engineering limits on process variables (e.g., temperature, pressure, flow). Reject or alarm invalid entries.
Redundant Sensors and Voting Logic	Use multiple sensors with voting logic (e.g., 2-out-of-3) for critical measurements. Improve reliability and reduce false positives/negatives.
Alarm Management and Prioritization	Implement alarms for abnormal conditions with clear prioritization (e.g., warning, critical). Ensure alarms are actionable and not excessive (avoid alarm flooding). Include acknowledgment and logging mechanisms.
Rate Limiting and Signal Filtering	Apply rate-of-change limits to prevent rapid and potentially hazardous adjustments to control outputs. Filter noise and spikes to avoid spurious trips or actions.
Interlocks and Permissives	Design interlocks that prevent dangerous operations unless conditions are safe (e.g., prevent pump startup if a valve is closed). Use permissives to ensure safe startup/shutdown sequences.
Emergency Shutdown	Include well-defined ESD functions that put the plant in a safe state during critical events. Ensure ESD systems are isolated from basic process control systems.
Watchdog and Heartbeat Monitoring	Monitor system health and detect loss of communication or PLC logic execution. Trigger alarms or safe-state actions if the controller stops responding.
Audit Logging and Event Recording	Maintain records of operator actions, alarms, and system status changes. Use internal diagnostics to detect hardware or software failures. Alert operators and prevent unsafe control behavior.

issues that may not be currently integrated into the system design but should be addressed based on scenarios identified during risk assessment and incident response planning.

Reference should be made to functional safety standards, particularly:

- IEC 61508—Functional safety of safety instrumented systems (SIS).
- ISA 84/IEC 61511—Safety systems for the process industry.
- ISA 18.2—Alarm management lifecycle.
- ISO 13849/IEC 62061—Machine safety control systems.

The Top 20 Secure PLC Coding Practices provide some additional specific guidance on considerations for PLC programs.[1]

9.5.2 Understanding Interdependencies

OT systems do not operate in isolation. Incident response planning must consider interdependencies, such as:

- Power supply, communications, water, heating, ventilation, and air conditioning, and third-party services.
- Cross-site dependencies (e.g., centralized SCADA or historian systems).
- Cyber-physical links, such as networked sensors controlling physical actuators.

Interdependencies should be considered during cybersecurity risk assessments to understand how failure in one area can have a cascading effect on others. This informs prioritization for response planning and may require system design changes as described in Section 9.5.1.

9.5.3 System Availability

The terms availability, reliability, maintainability, and redundancy are often used incorrectly or interchangeably.

Availability is the likelihood that a system works correctly when needed. It is measured as a percentage over a specific period, like daily, monthly, or yearly. Yearly availability is the most common method for assessing a system. An availability of 90% means about 40 days of downtime each year. An availability of 99.9999% (known as six nines) means around 30 seconds of downtime in the same period.

Availability results from the combination of reliability and maintainability. Reliability is a measure of the probability that a component or system will perform its required function in a specific environment for a specified period without failure.

Maintainability measures how easily a product can be maintained and is vital for successful operations. That's why backup recovery time is an essential factor to consider. Having a backup is critical, but knowing where that backup is stored and how long it takes to restore must also be considered to meet recovery objectives. The same applies to hardware spares. If a spare controller is stored in a vendor warehouse in a different city, then restoration time will depend on how long it takes to deliver the controller to the site. In both cases, it is not enough to have a backup or spare in place; it is also necessary to understand the implications of deploying that backup or spare. This is also why incident response testing (described in Section 9.10) is critical, and why realistic tests exercising all aspects, including recovering the backup or spare, are necessary.

Redundancy achieves high availability by replicating hardware so that if one device fails, another can take over. Like mechanical failsafes, it is essential to periodically exercise redundant systems to verify that they will function as intended when needed. This may involve manually switching over to a redundant device or system for a defined period. This can also be tested during incident response exercises.

9.6 MANUAL PROCEDURES

As with mechanical failsafes and system design factors, the risk assessment and incident response planning stages may identify the need for manual procedures. In the event of a serious cybersecurity incident, for instance, one that takes a SCADA system or Distributed Control System (DCS) out of service, it may be necessary for the organization to initiate manual procedures to operate its plant. For example, operate a water treatment plant without automatic control.

Additionally, specific manual procedures may be necessary for routine activities that support the risk management and incident response process. For example:

- Require all site visitors to take a cybersecurity induction that covers the key cybersecurity rules.
- Require all personnel to complete formal training, including ongoing security awareness, and update this training annually to keep up with evolving threats, vulnerabilities, and mitigations.
- Require that all changes involve backups of equipment before and after the change.

- Require that all changes follow a formal change-control procedure that includes updating and approving all documentation.
- Require that all files are transferred using a secure, approved method.
- Require the calibrating and testing of instrumentation or inspection of mechanical failsafes.

These manual procedures must be documented. In most critical infrastructure organizations, they are known as standard operating procedures (SOPs). An SOP defines a step-by-step approach to completing an activity, even if that activity seems trivial or obvious. The primary reasons for documenting these procedures are:

- To minimize the opportunity for error, by prescribing the method and leaving no scope for interpretation.
- To improve consistency and reliability through a well-defined procedure that can be followed repeatedly with the same outcome.
- To improve operational efficiency by identifying the optimal procedure.

SOPs are living documents, subject to revision for a variety of reasons, including:

- To correct errors in the procedure
- To add further detail to clarify the procedure
- To revise the procedure after identifying improvements or efficiencies

These reasons may occur as a result of lessons learned from an exercise or a real incident. This is why it is crucial to test these procedures during exercises.

Another aspect to consider in manual procedures is the *separation of duties*. This is an essential element of secure and safe operations. It involves ensuring that more than one person is required to complete a particular task where safety or security is paramount so that:

- The risk of human error is reduced
- The risk of fraud is reduced

Typical separation of duties may involve:

- Separate electronic authorization for actions, such as changing setpoints in a control system or migrating software between development, testing, and production environments
- The use of multiple security keys, held by separate personnel

Where it is not possible or practical to separate duties, for instance, in very small organizations where skilled personnel are limited, alternate controls should be in place, such as:

- Audit trails to track who took what action, and when
- Periodic supervisory reviews to verify that all tasks are being performed as expected

9.7 SERVICE PROVIDER REQUIREMENTS

Very few organizations can operate without the support of service providers. The risk assessment and incident response planning processes will identify scenarios where these service providers are needed. For example, restoring devices from backups, repairing failed hardware, or manually operating the plant.

Some organizations have formal contracts that clearly outline assumptions and expectations. Others rely on informal arrangements, calling a service provider only when needed. Few organizations can demonstrate traceability from their risk assessment outcomes and incident response plans to their service provider requirements. In many cases, these requirements have been in place for years without review to ensure that recovery objectives remain achievable with the service provider's support.

As with manual procedures, it is essential to document service provider requirements clearly. For service providers, their explicit agreement is also necessary, preferably in the form of a contractual agreement. Key factors that must be in place in any support contract are as follows:

- Support hours—OT systems generally require support 24/7/365. Service provider support must align with this, or the organization's recovery objectives should be adjusted. For instance, if weekend support is unavailable from the service provider, the organization should set recovery objectives for that period, such as "next business day."
- Response time—It is essential to specify the required skills and knowledge to provide support, as well as a time window to ensure the right person is on-site. This is especially true for smaller service providers, who may have limited resources.
- Mean time to repair (MTTR)—This should be agreed upon for all major equipment. The MTTR should be monitored as this metric has a significant impact on system availability.
- Spares—To support the target MTTR, it may be necessary to deploy spares strategically, either on-site or at a nearby vendor location. It is essential that spares are appropriately maintained and accessible when needed.

If service providers are needed in response to specific incident scenarios, they should be included in incident response exercises. This would verify the following, for example, before it is needed for real:

- The service provider answers the telephone when the organization calls.
- The service provider can locate the correct backup and restore it if needed.
- The service provider can identify the correct spare and replace it if needed.
- The service provider can be available on site when needed.

9.8 FORENSICS

9.8.1 The Importance of Forensics in Incident Response

Digital forensics plays a vital role in incident response. Forensic data helps organizations understand what happened, how it happened, and who might be responsible. Without forensics, organizations risk repeating similar incidents. Incident response is an ongoing cycle of testing, reacting, and improving. Forensics can inform organizations about new threats, techniques, and vulnerabilities in processes or systems. Additionally, forensic data provides a foundation for legal actions or serves as evidence for regulatory bodies.

In terms of incident response, forensics helps answer questions such as:

- What systems were affected?
- What data was accessed, modified, or exfiltrated?
- How did the incident occur?

And in the case of unauthorized access:

- How did the threat actor gain access?
- Is the threat actor still active in the environment?

Many organizations still lack the maturity to address these questions. Take, for example, Oldsmar, FL (2021).[2] Due to a lack of forensic data, the initial assumption was that an external malicious actor had intentionally modified the level of sodium hydroxide to toxic levels. It took the FBI two years to conclude that there was no evidence of external malicious action. During that time, the focus was on securing remote access, even though it should have been on making system design changes to reduce the likelihood of an authorized user entering unsafe setpoints for chemicals like sodium hydroxide, as that would still be the most likely cause of a similar incident.

9.8.2 Preserving Forensic Data during Incident Response

Forensic readiness needs to be incorporated into incident response planning to ensure that organizations not only react quickly but also learn from security incidents. To preserve the integrity and admissibility of forensic data, several best practices must be followed during incident response:

- Maintain chain of custody. This includes detailed records of who collected, handled, and accessed evidence. Use standard forms and procedures to track the movement of data and devices.
- Preserve volatile data. Capture data in RAM, process monitors, and network monitors before powering down or rebooting systems, using trusted tools that do not alter system state during collection.
- Create system images of storage devices. These can be copied and used for analysis rather than using the original data.
- Avoid using affected systems for regular operations during the investigation. Disable user access or isolate systems to prevent further damage or loss of evidence.
- Be aware of privacy laws, industry regulations, and data breach notification requirements. Ensure forensic activities align with legal obligations.
- Ensure that forensics is conducted by trained professionals or external experts. Improper handling of evidence can invalidate it or lead to incomplete conclusions.

9.8.3 Is It Cyber or Not?

Identifying the source of an incident is essential for effectively containing it during the response and applying specific mitigations afterward. This attribution is challenging in any environment, but it can be even harder in OT environments because they interact with the real physical world.

For example, in the immediate aftermath of the 2024 Francis Scott Key Bridge collapse in Baltimore, theories emerged that the ship involved (The MV *Dali*, operated by Synergy Marine Group) had been "cyber-attacked." Well-known social media personalities such as Andrew Tate and Alex Jones helped propel the theory to millions of readers around the world.[3] Later, as with Oldsmar, no such threat was found;[4] the incident was a result of loss of electrical power on the ship. As with Oldsmar, such false attribution could have led to a diversion of resources away from the actual root cause and could further result in the introduction of unnecessary controls at the expense of controls that could help mitigate future incidents.

Practical root cause analysis (RCA) depends on precise forensic investigation. This involves operator input, control system status, and maintenance history—all understood within an operational context.

9.8.4 Recovering after Internal Sabotage

Internal sabotage—such as a disgruntled employee deleting control programs, disabling alarms, or corrupting system logic—poses unique challenges for forensic data recovery. Unlike external cyberattacks, internal sabotage involves individuals with legitimate access and, often, detailed knowledge of systems, making their actions more difficult to detect, trace, and prove. Insiders may also cover their tracks by deleting logs, wiping devices, or exploiting gaps in monitoring policies. Consequently, these incidents demand both technical and organizational recovery measures to preserve evidence. Key measures, in addition to the preservation measures listed in Section 9.8.1, are shown in Table 9.2.

TABLE 9.2 Key Technical and Procedural Measures to Preserve Evidence

Technical measures	Log all critical activities (e.g., logic changes, user logins, configuration changes) and use centralized log servers or write-once, read-many storage to prevent tampering. Deploy endpoint detection and monitoring on engineering workstations, HMIs, and PLC programming terminals to detect unauthorized or unusual behavior.
Procedural measures	Apply role-based access controls (RBAC), enforce least-privilege principles, and regularly review and revoke access for former employees or users no longer needing elevated privileges. Segregate duties to ensure no single user has unchecked control over critical systems (e.g., separate configuration, approval, and implementation roles). Train managers and technical staff to recognize behavioral warning signs and escalation paths for potential insider threats.

A case like the Maroochy Shire sewage spill in Australia (2000), where a former contractor remotely manipulated wastewater systems, highlights the damaging effects of insider threats—along with the need for monitoring, revocation of access, and logging. These measures are crucial not only for detecting and preventing incidents but also for gathering evidence afterward, identifying the nature of any sabotage, facilitating rectification, and supporting the successful prosecution of those involved.

9.8.5 Forensics Management in OT

Historically, OT systems were designed for precise, high-availability real-time operations—not for general-purpose use, including data collection for later forensic analysis. Unlike IT systems with detailed event logging and endpoint detection, OT systems often lack:

- RBAC.
- Audit trails and user event logging.
- Tools to safely extract memory or configuration states post-incident.

Without such capabilities, post-incident investigations in OT are often speculative and incomplete. Engineering workstations, historians, network devices, and controllers may provide some evidence, but only if configured and maintained appropriately. To further compound the issue, the high-availability nature of these systems may mean that the priority is to restore operation at the expense of losing forensic evidence. This is another reason why forensic data collection must be factored into system design and incident response planning, so that spur-of-the-moment decisions that can seriously impede RCA are avoided.

Considerations to include are:

- Logging strategies for controllers, firewalls, and HMIs.
- Securing historian and engineering workstation data.
- Capturing network traffic and controller state snapshots.
- Defining roles and escalation paths for investigations.

9.9 RECOVERY

9.9.1 The Five "R"s of Incident Response

Incident response is much more than dealing with the immediate situation. These five stages—response, recovery, restoration, remediation, and reassessment—provide a lifecycle approach that not only addresses the immediate impact of an incident but also supports long-term improvement and risk reduction:

- **Response**—The immediate actions taken to detect, contain, and mitigate the impact of a cybersecurity incident.
- **Recovery**—The process of stabilizing systems, restoring critical operations, and ensuring business continuity following an incident.
- **Restoration**—The full return of systems and services to their normal operational state, including validation and testing.
- **Remediation**—The identification and elimination of the root cause or vulnerabilities exploited during the incident to prevent recurrence.
- **Reassessment**—Not identified through traditional risk management models, the authors felt that this stage should be required—a thorough review and evaluation of the incident response to identify lessons learned and improve future readiness.

9.9.2 Response

The response phase centers on immediate detection, containment, and mitigation. In OT environments, this step requires special consideration due to the potential impact on physical processes, human safety, and production continuity.

Incident responders must quickly verify the situation and evaluate the scope and impact. In OT systems, immediate containment could involve segmenting network zones, switching to manual control, or activating SIS. Such actions will require coordination among control room operators, engineering staff, site leadership, and traditional cybersecurity stakeholders, such as the security operations center (SOC).

Predefined OT-specific response playbooks, such as isolating a PLC or blocking remote engineering workstation access, can help ensure that containment actions do not inadvertently disrupt critical operational processes.

In OT, documenting system status, collecting logs from PLCs or HMIs, and preserving historian data are essential for later forensic analysis. However, site leadership may override specific actions to prioritize personnel and facility safety. Safety always remains the top concern in such facilities. This means cybersecurity stakeholders, including SOC personnel, must be trained to handle these situations appropriately.

For example, while a senior or lead-level SOC analyst procedure might require them to request various forms of ID before investigating an IT incident, there may need to be a faster process for facility leadership to interact. This could involve the use of specific codewords, for instance.

Specially trained OT personnel should be available to interact with the site personnel, and these individuals will be aware of the challenges of responding in an operational facility where safety is paramount.

9.9.3 Recovery

After the initial response phase, the recovery phase focuses on stabilizing and restoring critical business and operational processes. In OT environments, this includes:

- Revalidating the integrity of PLC code. This must include verifying the integrity of the backup program files.
- Ensuring that field devices are communicating correctly. This includes verifying that communications are established and that the correct data is being transmitted.
- Confirming that safety systems are fully operational. SIS or ESD systems may have tripped or have been manually overridden. In some scenarios, the safety system controller(s) may have been intentionally disabled or modified.

Recovery efforts may require coordination with equipment vendors, automation engineers, and maintenance teams. Vendors may be required to restore firmware to embedded devices or replace hardware that has been compromised and cannot be restored. Maintenance personnel may need to physically inspect devices to verify that they have been restored to their normal working state. End-to-end tests may need to be performed, involving multiple parties in different physical locations, for example, remote site, central data hub, and onshore operational management location, to verify the integrity of data throughout the information chain.

In OT environments, recovery priorities must be based on process criticality and safety risk. Essential control systems—such as DCS, PLC networks managing hazardous processes, or real-time monitoring systems—should be restored first. Support systems, such as production reporting, data historians, or optimization dashboards, can be brought online later. For example, recovering a DCS that maintains process temperature and pressure is far more urgent than reactivating the historian used for long-term data analysis.

It may be necessary to conduct testing and validation in a controlled environment, such as an offline setting, before reintroducing systems into active production. Additionally, systems should be closely monitored during the initial period of resumed operation to identify any latent issues or incomplete restoration.

9.9.4 Restoration

Restoration is in transition from recovery to full resumption of operations. This phase focuses on restoring systems to their pre-incident functionality and performance.

In OT environments, this includes thoroughly validating process parameters, safety interlocks, HMI screens, and communication paths between sensors and actuators, as well as the screens throughout the organization.

Once restored, systems must be tested to avoid unpredictable outcomes in real-world processes. For instance, after restoring a SCADA system, operators should verify that alarms are functioning correctly, setpoints are correct, and all monitoring devices (e.g., RTUs) are responding as expected. Restoration also includes re-establishing operator control panels and re-enabling automatic control loops—which may have been changed from automatic to manual—as well as ensuring that compliance monitoring systems are operational again.

9.9.5 Remediation

Remediation focuses on addressing the root causes and vulnerabilities that enabled the incident. In OT, such vulnerabilities can include insecure legacy devices (e.g., hard-coded default passwords), insufficient network segmentation (e.g., co-mingled IT and OT networks), or poor password practices (e.g., shared accounts with old passwords).

To effectively eliminate these root causes, organizations must go beyond surface-level fixes and conduct a thorough RCA. One widely used and effective method in OT environments is the *Five Whys* technique. This approach involves asking "Why?" repeatedly (typically five times) to reveal the actual underlying issue systematically. Consider the example shown in Figure 9.2.

In this example, it would be easy to assume the problem was that the PLC code was overwritten, and now that the code is restored, or even that remote access was the issue. The five whys method reveals that the underlying problem is that risk had not been assessed, and a budget approved for updating a legacy system, and this is what must be done to prevent a repeat of this problem.

Remediation efforts may include patching or replacing compromised firmware, isolating insecure protocols (e.g., Modbus/TCP), updating user authentication schemes, or implementing read-only policies for USB devices.

In complex environments, it may be necessary to re-architect network zones to comply with ISA/IEC 62443 standards. Equipment vendors may need to be involved in firmware upgrades or system hardening.

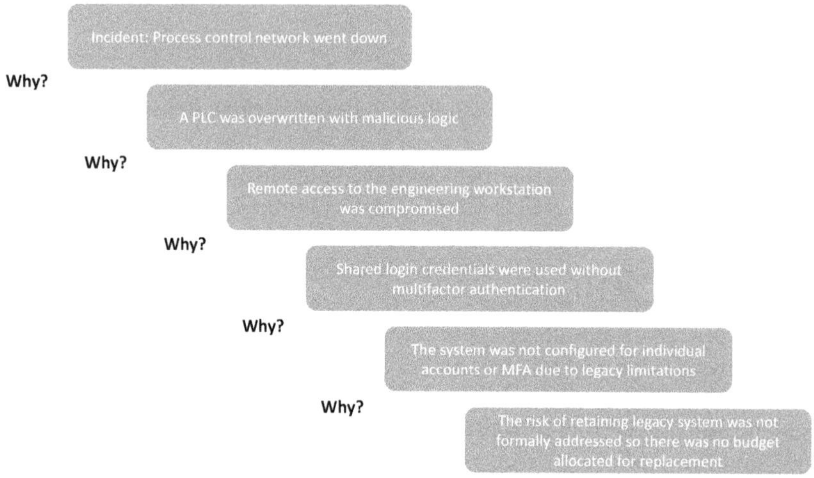

FIGURE 9.2 Five whys example.

In many situations, such changes are difficult or even impossible without major system modifications. Therefore, it may be necessary to implement compensating controls until those system updates can be made. Revised procedures—such as restricting a process control engineering workstation access during normal operations or removing a safety engineering workstation from an externally accessible network—may be needed.

9.9.6 Reassessment

Reassessment is the final stage of the incident response lifecycle, a step that's rarely discussed but essential for continuous improvement in an organization.

In OT environments, the reassessment phase must consider both technical and operational dimensions:

- How quickly were operators alerted to anomalies?
- Were manual overrides successful?
- Did the incident response plan account for physical safety and process continuity?

A post-incident review should include control engineers, OT vendors, operators, IT security teams, and management to evaluate response times, cross-functional communication, coordination of plant and cybersecurity resources, and effectiveness of contingency actions.

Lessons learned should feed into updated incident response plans and improved training for staff. For example, if delays in identifying rogue logic on a PLC led to process upsets, reassessment might lead to new controls for code change notifications and access logging.

This phase may also include tabletop exercises and simulation-based training tailored to OT scenarios. Reassessment ensures that each incident contributes to a more resilient OT environment and a stronger overall security posture.

9.10 ESCALATION

A significant challenge in incident response is determining whether an incident requires escalation. Organizations cannot overreact and treat every report as a significant incident, but at the same time, an underreaction could have significant consequences.

Incident response plans, therefore, need to include clear, predefined criteria for escalation, for instance:

- How to categorize severity to ensure the appropriate response is triggered. The risk assessment process should already identify potential scenarios and associated consequences and impacts.
- When to engage senior executives, legal counsel, or external stakeholders such as regulators or customers. Incident response plans should comply with any regulatory or contractual notification requirements, as well as organization policy requirements.
- Alternative activity paths to take if primary methods fail. What happens if there is no response from the SoC, or no response from legal counsel? The incident response plan may need to define some sort of call tree that is used to address such situations.

9.11 TESTING

Incident response plans must be exercised periodically. Untested plans are not much better than no plan at all. The worst time to discover issues in an incident response plan is during a real incident. Exercising plans not only identify potential gaps in those plans but also provide essential training for individuals who may one day experience a real incident.

Exercises verify that procedures are correct, and documentation provides adequate detail. Varying scenarios should be chosen, and the drills should be as realistic as possible. The frequency of drills will depend on the organization. Many critical infrastructure organizations undertake these drills one to four times a year.

Testing should ensure all five phases of incident response—response, recovery, restoration, remediation, and reassessment—are reviewed.

Several types of incident response exercises can be employed. Table 9.3 highlights three types:

- **Tabletop**—This is the most common method. It is relatively easy to execute, but it is the least effective in terms of training response. The lack of real-world experience does not provide any

TABLE 9.3 Types of Incident Response Exercise

	**Tabletop** • Pre-scripted scenarios and injects • Script and injects are limited and lack unanticipated developments • Creating new scenarios takes significant time and effort • Format fails to replicate the high-pressure, fast-moving nature of real cybersecurity incidents • The format lacks the practical elements of a response
	**Real world** • Realistic environment • Incorporates practical aspects • Limited in scope to avoid impacting live operation • Expensive and complex to execute
	**Virtual** • Large Language Model containing incident data, cyber frameworks, controls • Configurable scenario (industry, size, team details, technology, injects, etc.) • Script and injects update dynamically based on decisions • Immersive 3D rendering to increase realism • Location independent, low cost, and low risk

practical aspects (such as locating the cables needed to disconnect from a corporate or external network).

- **Real World**—This is the most realistic method, but it is expensive and complex to execute. This may limit the frequency with which such a method can be used.
- **Virtual**—This method can involve generative AI to generate scenarios and virtual reality to provide immersive environments. This is much easier to execute and can be used more frequently than other methods. Repeatability allows users to compare and improve their performance over time.

9.12 NEAR MISSES

Cybersecurity incidents are like safety incidents in that near misses occur. Near misses are leading indicators of issues requiring attention. For example, a vendor uses its own USB drive to install software on a system workstation. This action may not infect the workstation, but this near miss is a failure to follow correct procedures. Failing to record near misses can lead to further procedural failures and, ultimately, a cybersecurity incident. Recording the near miss should trigger a review, which may involve retraining users, issuing warnings to vendors, or other actions. The process of dealing with the near miss provides feedback on behavior to help avoid future failings.

In health and safety management, the relationship between leading and lagging indicators for health and safety is shown in the form of *Heinrich's triangle*. The triangle is widely used in industries with health and safety risks. Scientists have calculated the ratios between near misses and workplace accidents and have repeatedly validated the Heinrich model, which shows there are 300 near misses for every 29 minor injuries for every 1 major injury.[5]

Most cybersecurity metrics used today are lagging indicators. They are outcomes, such as the number of cybersecurity incidents experienced or the time it takes to detect, identify, contain, or resolve an incident. To manage cybersecurity, an organization must identify leading indicators that influence the lagging indicators. A security triangle, based on Heinrich's triangle, is shown in Figure 9.3.[6] We can infer that there is a similar relationship between security near misses and major security incidents on the basis that cybersecurity and safety have very similar behavioral aspects. As a result, tracking near misses is more than just improving behavior; it should also help identify when training is needed and help reduce the likelihood of a major security incident.

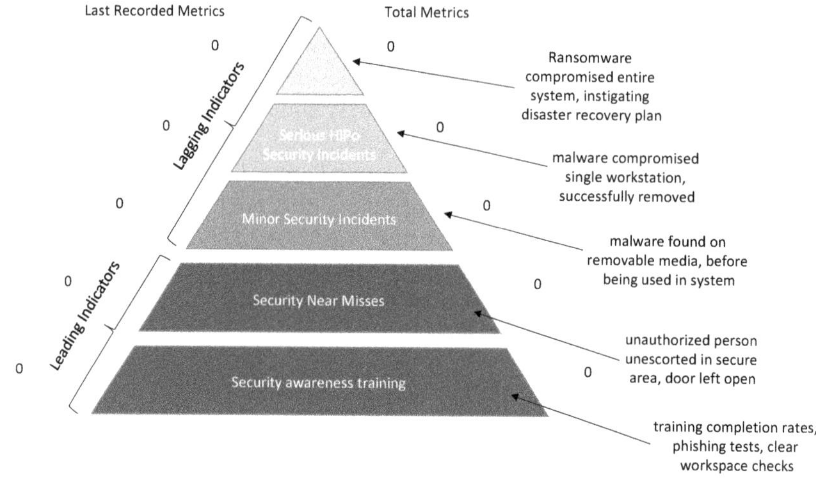

FIGURE 9.3 Security incident triangle.

9.13 CONCLUSION

Planning and detailed components such as backup strategies, system design changes, mechanical failsafes, and manual procedures are essential. The chapter introduces the Five Rs—Response, Recovery, Restoration, Remediation, and Reassessment—as a structured lifecycle for incident management and improvement. It also emphasizes the importance of digital forensics, internal sabotage detection, and coordinated engagement with service providers. By incorporating lessons from safety management and promoting realistic testing and tracking of near misses, the chapter equips organizations with the tools to improve both cyber resilience and operational reliability.

NOTES

1 https://plc-security.com/
2 http://scid.infracritical.com/pages/scid-00113
3 https://www.npr.org/2024/03/27/1241001030/-baltimore-bridge-collapse-conspiracy-theories
4 http://scid.infracritical.com/pages/scid-00113
5 https://www.newea.org/2019/01/07/near-misses-learning-to-protect-ourselves-and-our-utilities-better/?utm_source=chatgpt.com
6 Mustard, S. *Industrial Cybersecurity: Case Studies and Best Practices* (pp. 200–201), International Society of Automation, 2022.

CHAPTER 10

Post-incident Analysis

10.1 INTRODUCTION

Chapter 9 noted that the final stage of incident response should be reassessment, a stage that is very often overlooked. Even when considered, the approach to reassessment may not be sufficiently comprehensive to ensure that future incidents are avoided or their consequences minimized.

This chapter will consider typical gaps in the reassessment or post-incident analysis phase.

OT risk is not fixed: architectures evolve, vendors change, remote access expands, threat actors adapt. Post-incident analysis needs to take these factors into account to convert the evidence of what happened—including errors, workarounds, and rollbacks—into hard improvements across people, process, and technology. Furthermore, data quality varies; environments drift; causal paths branch; incident reports conflict; and incentives favor quick fixes over root-cause closure.

Post-incident analysis must be repeatable, evidence-based, and consequence-driven.

10.2 REALITY VERSUS ANALYSIS

As this book has noted throughout, the meaning of the term "secure" is not as absolute as we would like it to be. Not only does security in an IT context differ from that in an OT context, but even within the same sector or organization, security can have distinct meanings. This problem is not unique to security.

In their paper, "Revised Approach to Toxicity Test Acceptability Criteria Using a Statistical Performance Assessment," Thursby et al. consider that the answer to the question, "Is the material toxic?" is only truly defensible if a second question, "How good are the data?" is also considered.

The authors go on to describe how statistical significance is relied upon in their work, but that even this statistical analysis has some degree

DOI: 10.4324/9781003610557-10

of error. They represent this error in the form of a matrix showing false positives—statistical results indicate material is toxic, but in reality, it is not—and false negatives—vice versa, as shown in Figure 10.1.[1]

Figure 10.2 shows a variation of this matrix representing security analysis versus reality. This matrix can be viewed from two directions: analysis results to reality, and vice versa.

Following a similar approach to Thursby et al., consider that an assessment is performed to determine the security of an OT system. If the analysis results indicate that the system is secure, this does not mean that

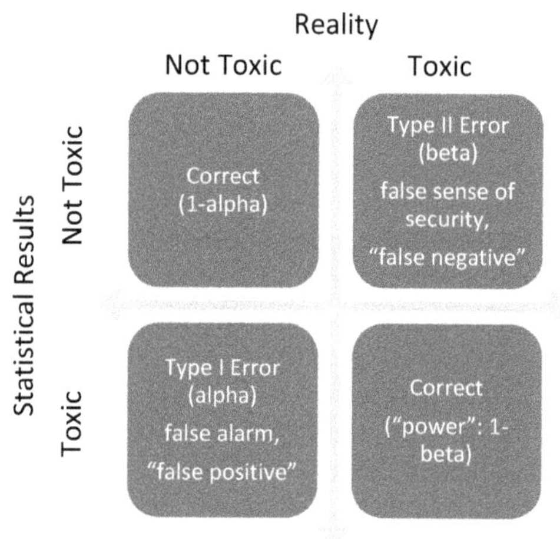

FIGURE 10.1 Relationship between statistical results and reality.

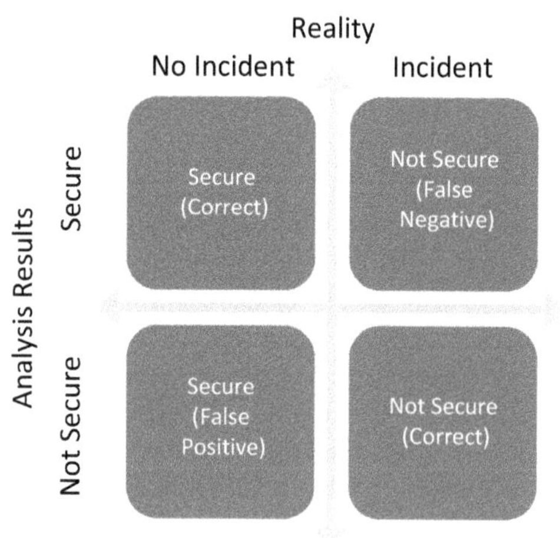

FIGURE 10.2 Graphical comparison of security analysis and reality.

an incident will not occur. This can happen if assessment questions are insufficient or if there is a lack of follow-up questions and verification of answers to assessment questions. For instance, if a user is not prompted to confirm their system's Internet connection, it is impossible to identify potential vulnerabilities related to this scenario. Furthermore, when a user says that their system is not connected to the Internet and there is no follow-up or verification of this fact, the associated vulnerabilities will be missed.

An example of this gap in questioning is the U.S. State of New Jersey, which enacted its Water Quality Accountability Act in 2017. A revision was added to provide an exemption for "water purveyors that do not have an internet-connected control system" from the cybersecurity requirements in the act.[2] Aside from the fact that non-Internet-connected systems are still vulnerable to cybersecurity incidents that could cause operational disruption, this exemption simply allowed users to claim without evidence that their systems were not connected to the Internet. This exemption has since been removed.

Conversely, if the analysis results indicate that the system is not secure, but the proposed remediation is misinformed, it may still leave the system insecure. The Oldsmar incident has been referenced throughout this book, but it provides a good example here. The incident was claimed to be the result of an external attack through an insecure remote access method. The remediation for this involved either removing the insecure method entirely or replacing it with a secure method.

Subsequent investigations were unable to substantiate the claim of an external actor, meaning the most likely cause was human error. The controls required to deal with human error are very different from those to deal with insecure remote access. This is not to say that Oldsmar should have ignored the insecure remote access problem. Still, once the investigation was completed it is unclear if they re-analyzed their controls and made other changes—for example, implementing limits on setpoint values or independent validation of changes.

Viewing the matrix from the other direction is equally revealing. If there are no security incidents, this could confirm the analysis results that the system is secure or disprove the analysis results that the system was not secure. Neither situation is desirable.

The first case is a form of survivorship bias. Just because there are no incidents does not mean a system is secure. In addition, security is only valid at a point in time. Since so many other aspects change, there is no guarantee that a currently secure system will still be secure. This is why continuous assessment is essential.

The second case can cause a lack of trust in the analysis method. In many cases, organizations that have never observed a security incident will remain skeptical when told they are operating insecurely. In large part, this explains why so many organizations fail to act and end up paying the price when they have to deal with the consequences of an incident.

In both cases the result is likely to be that no further analysis is performed. This is not uncommon. Many organizations initiate a cybersecurity management program, identify risks, deploy controls, and then never revisit their risk posture, despite all the factors that can impact it. This continuous improvement aspect will be considered in the next chapter.

10.3 COLLECTING INCIDENT DATA

The matrix in Figure 10.2 also highlights the need for thorough incident reporting. For post-incident analysis to be effective, this should include more revealing data such as:

- Safeguard performance—Which controls worked, and which didn't?
- Latency—A measure of delays in detection, diagnosis, decision, dispatch, and restoration.
- Human-system interaction—How did operators handle the situation?
- Unknown vulnerabilities—Including "shadow" remote access paths, ad hoc vendor accounts, and flat networks that are revealed by emergency workarounds.
- Exception debt—Temporary bypasses and emergency accesses that have accumulated over time.
- Consequence evidence—how close did these consequences match the analysis results?

The need for capturing near-miss incidents was discussed in Chapter 9. These incidents are often overlooked—for a variety of reasons—or called something else, less severe-sounding—for example, "events." As shown in the security triangle in Chapter 9, there is a direct correlation between near-miss incidents and major security incidents, just as there is between safety near misses and major accidents in the safety triangle.

If near misses are not recorded as incidents, the organization experiences a false sense of security. Over time, near misses increase. This happens as employees and contractors forget their training, together with a lack of oversight and management buy-in, causing an erosion of the security culture. Eventually, a major security incident will occur. In many cases, the organization will address the specific incident. They may instigate some security training, but eventually, over time, the same erosion of security culture will occur. Figure 10.3 shows this in graphical form.

In addition to near misses, incidents may not be declared as cyber-related. This is common for hardware failures and human error. In fact,

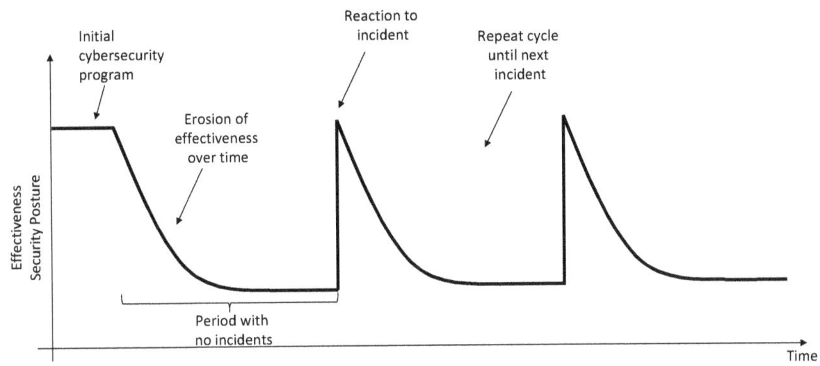

FIGURE 10.3 The erosion of security effectiveness over time.

both cases should be included in the analysis. As discussed in this book, the primary objective of OT cybersecurity management is to maintain safe and reliable operations. Controls that should be in place to manage cybersecurity incidents, if implemented correctly, will mitigate the consequences of human error and hardware failure.

Even real incidents can be downplayed or attributed to the wrong vulnerability. The towns of Hale Center and Lockney suffered repeated attacks on their infrastructure from a nation-state actor, and both towns claimed that the disruption was minimal and the incidents were contained. This desire to report a positive outcome could understate the amount of effort required at the time and may understate the continued risk these towns carry. Appendix B discusses these incidents in more detail.

When accurately reporting and tracking incidents, organizations are likely to experience different results from those expected. One major factor is that controls behave differently when under stress. For example, when sitting around a table discussing incident scenarios, it is easy to say what everyone will do. However, in the heat of the moment during a real scenario, those involved may react very differently. This is why it is essential to not only perform exercises—to build "muscle memory"—but also to incorporate real-world applications into these exercises. Tabletop formats are better than no exercise at all, but they lack the sense of realism needed to improve actual response performance.

10.4 REVISITING INCIDENTS

In many cases, early reports of cybersecurity incidents prove to be wrong or incomplete. The 2011 report of an attack on a pump in the Curran-Gardner Public Water District in Springfield, an Illinois utility. This began with a report titled "Public Water District Cyber Intrusion" that was picked up by media. It was called the "first successful target of a cyber-attack on a computer of a public utility." After detailed analysis, DHS and the FBI said they had "found no evidence of a cyber intrusion."[3] This highlights the importance of revisiting cybersecurity incidents. As previously noted, remediations that have been implemented may need to be revised in light of new information. In addition, organizations should regularly review incidents (including near misses and "non-cyber" incidents) because changes to infrastructure, threats, organization, or regulations may change the risk profile.

Organizations that have utilized methods such as DBT should update their results with observed realities (e.g., hacktivist spill-over, supply chain targeting, insider-adjacent access) to help improve the quality of the recommendations.

10.5 CONCLUSION

Post-incident analysis is not a luxury or an optional final step in incident response; it is a critical link between *what happened* and *how we prevent it from happening again*. As this chapter has demonstrated, organizations often fall into the trap of treating incident closure as the end of the story, when in fact it should be the beginning of learning. Whether through incomplete questioning, survivorship bias, or premature assumptions, failures in reassessment distort the true risk picture and leave organizations exposed.

The examples presented—from Oldsmar to New Jersey's now-removed exemption for "non-internet-connected" systems, to the Illinois pump case—illustrate the dangers of relying on early or incomplete narratives. Real incidents often reveal that safeguards behave differently under stress, that early attributions may be incorrect, and that unverified assumptions can persist long after evidence disproves them. Equally, near misses and "non-cyber" events, if ignored, silently erode security culture until a major incident occurs.

Effective post-incident analysis must therefore be evidence-driven, repeatable, and consequence-focused. It requires disciplined reporting of safeguards, latency, human-system interaction, exception debt, and consequence evidence. It also demands acknowledgment that no analysis method is flawless, that reality may deviate from expectation, and that the absence of incidents does not prove security.

The core lesson is that learning must be continuous. Controls must be revisited as architectures evolve, vendors change, remote access expands, and threat actors adapt. Design-basis threat models should be updated with observed realities, not frozen in time. Above all, organizations must commit to reassessment not as an afterthought but as an embedded practice of operational culture.

Only by treating every incident, near miss, and misattribution as a source of learning can OT environments move beyond reactive fixes toward true resilience. The next chapter will extend this theme by examining how continuous improvement can be structured, measured, and sustained across the lifecycle of cybersecurity risk management.

NOTES

1 Hazard/Risk Assessment, Revised Approach To Toxicity Test Acceptability Criteria Using A Statistical Performance Assessment, Glen B. Thursby, James Heltshe, K. John Scott, received Aug 12, 1996, accepted Oct 31, 1996, p. 1323; URL: https://www.waterboards.ca.gov/water_issues/programs/tmdl/records/region_2/2008/ref2416.pdf.
2 https://www.rivernetwork.org/policy/water-quality-accountability-act-n-j-s-a-5831-1 (alt URL: http://riskbook.infracritical.com/book1/chapter10/ch10ref1.pdf [initial law] and http://riskbook.infracritical.com/book1/chapter10/ch10ref2.pdf [modified law with rescinded provisioning).
3 https://krebsonsecurity.com/2011/11/dhs-blasts-reports-of-illinois-water-station-hack/?utm_source=chatgpt.com

CHAPTER 11

Continuous Improvement in OT Cybersecurity

11.1 INTRODUCTION

In dynamic environments, where threats evolve and systems change over time, the principle of continuous improvement must be embedded into every aspect of OT cybersecurity risk management.

Threats evolve, systems change, and operational states are updated. Continuous improvement ensures risk management strategies remain relevant, effective, and aligned with operational, safety, and regulatory requirements.

Many organizations rely on automated systems for OT cybersecurity. While this can be advantageous in some situations, it can also create a false sense of security, leading to dangerous blind spots. Automation provides speed, consistency of response, and is excellent at handling repetitive tasks. These characteristics mean it can contribute positively to cybersecurity risk management. However, automation lacks the contextual awareness and judgment that human oversight provides—particularly in complex OT environments where process safety, equipment behavior, and operational priorities are deeply intertwined.

This chapter explores key dimensions of this principle, focusing on continuous risk assessment, after-action reviews (AAR), and the critical challenge of oversight in automated monitoring systems.

11.2 THE MYTH OF CONTINUOUS IMPROVEMENT

Every standard, framework, and guide on risk management refers to the importance of the continuous nature of the process. For example, the NIST Cybersecurity Framework says, "Cybersecurity risks are expanding constantly, and managing those risks must be a continuous process."[1] ISA/IEC 62443-2-1 says that "an effective and comprehensive

DOI: 10.4324/9781003610557-11

risk management process that includes cybersecurity should be employed seamlessly throughout the organization with overall objectives of continuous improvement."[2]

Figure 11.1 shows how this continuous risk management lifecycle is often represented.

However, despite claiming to follow this principle, most organizations implement a process like that shown in Figure 11.2.

In this case, the organization might initiate a program to develop a cybersecurity management system, implement the specified controls, and

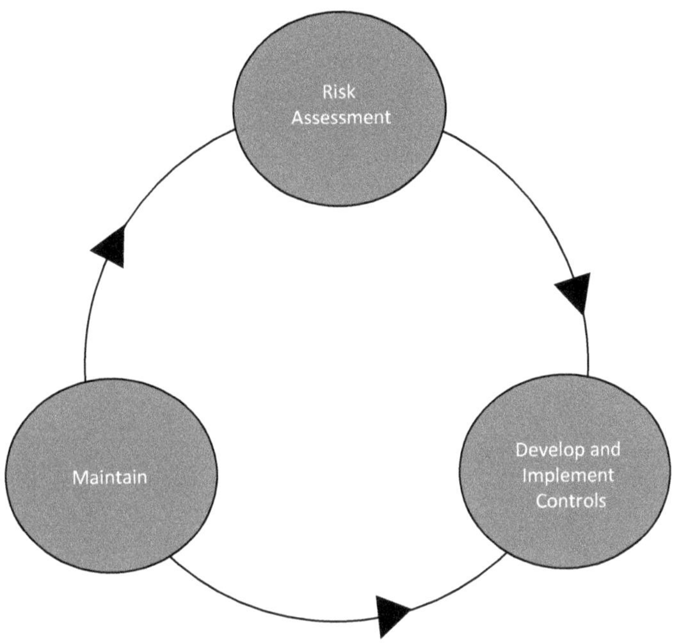

FIGURE 11.1 The most common representation of the continuous risk assessment process.

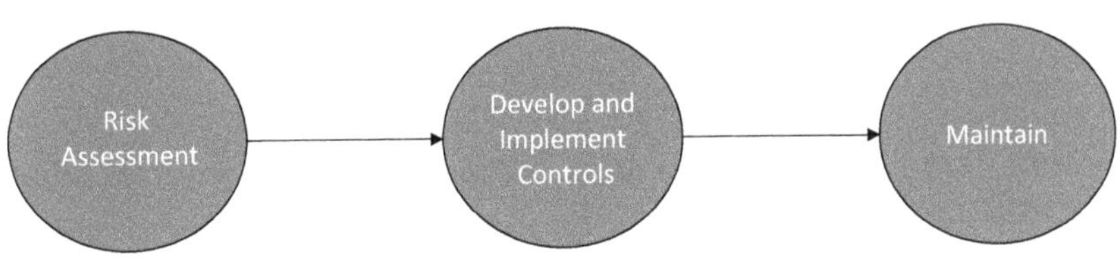

FIGURE 11.2 The most common form of risk assessment process.

then maintain these controls. When audits occur, the organization may find that controls have become ineffective, or their application has lapsed due to a lack of oversight. When an incident occurs, it may be due to gaps in the required controls. The organization then remediates these gaps and returns to the same reactive posture, awaiting the next audit or incident finding.

Figure 11.1, however, is not an accurate representation of how continuous risk management needs to be implemented. A state transition diagram, or state machine, best represents continuous risk assessment. In these diagrams, the circles or ovals represent specific states that the system is in, and it will be in only one state at any point in time. Arrows between states represent transitions, initiated because of the action described in the arrow.

Figure 11.3 shows such a diagram. The steady state—"maintain"—is interrupted for a variety of reasons. Changes—to systems, organization, regulations, threats, or vulnerabilities—should result in a risk assessment and subsequent changes or updates to controls, before returning to the maintain state. Actions and findings from audits, incidents, and incident response exercises may result in updates or changes to controls. These are typically a result of discovering a gap in existing controls.

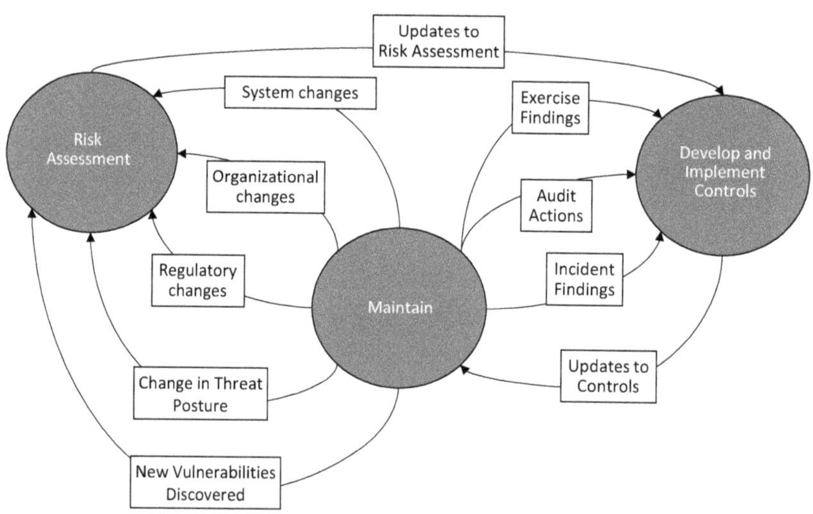

FIGURE 11.3 State transition diagram representation of the continuous risk assessment process.

11.3 CONTINUOUS RISK ASSESSMENT AND OPERATIONAL REVIEW

As noted, even when performed correctly, a risk assessment is only valid at a particular point in time. It can become outdated by changes in the threat landscape, system configuration, or operational changes.

Continuous risk assessment is essential to ensure that organizations respond to:

- Changes in system topology.
- Shifts in threat behavior or adversary tactics.
- Drifts in configuration.
- Vulnerabilities in firmware versions.
- Changing user roles.

New PLCs, human-machine interfaces (HMIs), or remote access points introduce new vectors and, along with that, new vulnerabilities. During the COVID-19 pandemic, organizations added remote access capabilities to allow their businesses to operate.

Many of these capabilities will still be in place today. No doubt many have not been subject to any type of risk assessment that would ensure controls are introduced to manage the risk of these capabilities.

Prior to Stuxnet, no one seriously considered the possibility that someone could create malware that would modify the integrity of control system data. Prior to TRISIS no one seriously considered the possibility that someone could modify a safety controller program.

Each new tactic requires organizations to reconsider the controls they have in place. For instance, procedures to independently verify control system data and procedures to keep controller key switches in their run position.

Since it is easy to add new firewall rules or change switch configurations, the paperwork or process may take significantly longer than the actual change. As a result, organizations might inadvertently encourage the bypassing of procedures if it means the benefit can be realized quickly.

Over time, this can encourage individuals to make increasingly significant changes without oversight, and this will inevitably result in some unforeseen vulnerability.

At the same time, electronic programmable equipment vulnerabilities are reported and these need patching. Often these individual vulnerabilities may seem innocuous.

Again, the desire to maximize operational time may discourage the right behavior, in this case to patch a seemingly minor vulnerability, and so the behavior continues until the environment is rife with known vulnerabilities.

Joiners, movers, and leavers create churn in an organization. While the principles of removing access to users who leave or change their role are well understood, they may not be universally enforced.

Even in IT systems where authorization and access are centrally controlled (e.g., Microsoft Entra ID), organizations may leave accounts active for several days, weeks, or even months after someone leaves.

In OT systems, this problem is compounded through the frequent use of:

- Default, and in some cases, hard-coded passwords in devices.
- Workgroup security on workstations and servers.
- Generic accounts for operators or engineers.
- Commonly used vendor default accounts.

Together with little or no audit logging, this situation leaves organizations wide open to insider threat as well as through unauthorized access.

By integrating risk monitoring into daily operations reviews—including alarms, logs, change control records, and control system diagnostics—teams can detect early indicators of risk that static assessments would miss. This fusion of cybersecurity and operational awareness forms the backbone of a proactive defense strategy.

11.4 LESSONS LEARNED AND AAR

No cybersecurity program is perfect. Incidents will occur, whether minor anomalies or significant events. The true differentiator of a mature organization is how it learns from these moments.

A Lessons Learned or AAR is the structured analysis of an event to identify:

- What happened.
- Why it happened.
- What worked, what failed.
- What changes are needed to prevent recurrence.

These reviews must be:

- Timely, conducted soon after the event.
- Blameless, to encourage honesty and transparency.
- Actionable, producing specific improvements in procedures, controls, or training.

Chapter 9 describes the five whys process, which can be an excellent way to drill down into the real reason for an incident, instead of focusing on the observable cause.

For OT environments, this might include:

- Revisiting network segmentation strategies.
- Reassessing alert thresholds for anomaly detection.
- Updating procedures for HMI operations.

Regularly scheduled reviews, even of near-misses or anomalies, drive a culture of continuous learning and refinement.

11.5 METRICS AND KEY PERFORMANCE INDICATORS (KPIS)

Continuous improvement in OT cybersecurity requires measurable evidence that security efforts are working. Metrics and KPIs transform qualitative objectives into quantitative data points, allowing organizations to track progress, identify weak points, and justify investments.

When applied correctly, metrics and KPIs act as an early warning system, a decision-making tool, and a benchmarking mechanism, all rolled into one. They help answer the essential question: "Are we actually getting better?" by considering:

- Effectiveness—Confirm that controls are reducing risk or improving resilience.
- Trend analysis—Show whether threats, vulnerabilities, or incidents are increasing or decreasing over time.
- Compliance—Provide documented proof for regulators, auditors, and internal governance bodies.
- Investment—Help leadership decide where resources will deliver the most impact.

Unlike IT environments, OT systems prioritize safety, reliability, and uptime over rapid technological change. This means that improvements in OT cybersecurity are often incremental and must be carefully measured over longer time horizons.

For KPIs to be useful, they must be:

- Relevant—Tied to business and operational objectives, not just generic IT security targets.
- Actionable—Providing data that can drive decisions, not just "nice to know" information.

- Consistent—Measured in the same way over time to ensure trend accuracy.
- Balanced—Including both leading indicators (predictive of future performance) and lagging indicators (measuring past results). Leading Indicator: percentage of control system network segments with active anomaly detection sensors. Lagging Indicator: number of OT system downtime incidents caused by cyber-related events in the past quarter. By tracking both, an organization can anticipate potential issues (leading) and measure the real-world impact of past improvements (lagging).

Table 11.1 shows categories of OT cybersecurity metrics with some examples.

TABLE 11.1 Categories of OT Cybersecurity Metrics

Metric Category	Purpose	Examples
Operational	Indicators tied to daily system performance and security hygiene.	Number of unpatched critical vulnerabilities in OT assets. Percentage of OT devices with up-to-date firmware and security configurations. Mean Time Between Failures for security-critical components.
Incident	Measures related to detection, response, and recovery from security events.	Mean Time to Detect and Mean Time to Respond for OT-specific incidents. Number of unauthorized access attempts detected per month. Ratio of successful mitigations to total incidents.
Compliance	Evidence of adherence to applicable standards and regulations.	Percentage of security controls meeting ISA/IEC 62443, NERC CIP, or NIST CSF requirements. Frequency of successful internal/external audit results without major findings.
Resilience Metrics	Indicators that measure the ability to withstand and recover from disruption.	Percentage of critical OT systems with tested disaster recovery plans. Time to restore operations after a simulated cyber incident.

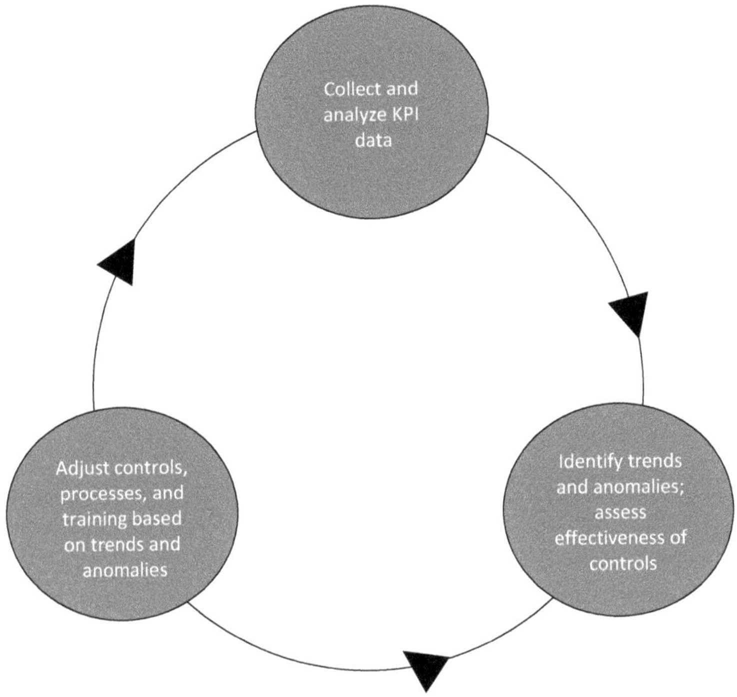

FIGURE 11.4 Continuous KPI monitoring.

Metrics and KPIs are not the end of the process—they are feedback mechanisms that inform adjustments in another continuous lifecycle, as shown in Figure 11.4.

When KPIs are thoughtfully designed, regularly reviewed, and tied directly to the organization's risk management strategy, they become one of the most powerful tools for driving real improvement in OT cybersecurity performance.

For example, The UK National Cyber Security Centre (NCSC) began its Active Cyber Defence program in 2016 and provides various publicly available reports. In one report, it notes,

> Our rationale for producing the report has remained constant during this time: a commitment to transparency, and basing our interventions on unbiased data and evidence to better understand better the reality of cyber attacks, as well as **the efficacy of our products and services.**

The report goes on to note improvements in various measures as a result of proactive actions based on data collected. For example, the NCSC started using honeypots to expose commonly attacked protocols and to discover more targets for takedowns.[3] This sort of targeted action would not be possible without the collection and analysis of data to identify trends and patterns.

11.6 CHANGE MANAGEMENT AS A SECURITY CONTROL

In OT environments, change is often treated with caution—and for good reason. Industrial control systems are purpose-built to meet specific operational and safety requirements, and even minor, untested modifications can introduce instability that can, in turn, result in serious operational consequences.

Many high-profile OT security incidents have stemmed from poorly controlled changes, such as:

- Applying patches to control systems without testing, causing process disruptions.
- Adding network connectivity to legacy devices without reviewing security implications.
- Replacing or upgrading hardware without verifying compatibility with existing safety and cybersecurity controls.

In each case, the lack of a structured review process allowed changes to create exploitable weaknesses or reduce the effectiveness of existing defenses. A disciplined change management program ensures that every proposed modification—whether technical, procedural, or configuration-related—is reviewed for potential cybersecurity impact before it is implemented.

Effective change management is not just an operational best practice—it is a critical security control that protects both system integrity and organizational resilience.

Table 11.2 shows the core elements of a secure change management process.

Assessing the security impact of a change has traditionally been a challenge due to the lack of rigorous development practices. As noted in Chapter 1, product vulnerabilities are introduced early in the product lifecycle by vendors who lack secure development practices. The lack of demand from asset owners for secure products has resulted in vast quantities of insecure products in OT environments. Asset owners are often dependent on independent security researchers discovering vulnerabilities so that they can be addressed. For example, in 2012, a researcher found a hard-coded username and password for administrative access to a ruggedized switch commonly used in OT environments. This was

TABLE 11.2 Core Elements of Secure Change Management

Element	Requirements
Formal Approval Process	Changes must be documented, risk-assessed, and approved by designated authorities, including OT security personnel, before implementation.
Security Impact Assessment	For each change, determine whether it affects safety, integrity, availability, or confidentiality.
Testing and Validation	Test changes in a non-production or simulated OT environment to confirm they work as intended without introducing security vulnerabilities.
Rollback Procedures	Maintain a tested contingency plan for quickly reversing changes that produce negative operational or security effects.
Audit Trail	Keep detailed records of what was changed, who authorized it, when it occurred, and why—enabling forensic analysis if incidents arise later.

the manufacturer's "back door," known to them but not publicized.[4] This knowledge would be critical in a change management process, perhaps resulting in the selection of another product or the removal and replacement of existing vulnerable devices.

To be effective, change management must be seen as an enabler of secure and reliable operations, not as bureaucratic red tape. This requires:

- Leadership Support—Executives must reinforce that no change bypasses the process, regardless of urgency.
- Operator Engagement—Field and engineering teams must be trained to recognize the security implications of even small changes.
- Policy Integration—Change management should be tied to all relevant policies and procedures so that security considerations are baked into operational requirements.

By treating change management as a security control rather than just a maintenance process, organizations can significantly reduce their exposure to both accidental and deliberate threats, strengthening the overall resilience of their OT environment.

11.7 THREAT INTELLIGENCE AND EMERGING RISK MONITORING

The threat landscape evolves constantly as adversaries develop new tactics, adapt to defenses, and exploit technological change. For asset-intensive industries, the speed at which threats evolve can easily outpace traditional risk assessment cycles if there is no mechanism for actively monitoring emerging risks. Integrating threat intelligence into the continuous improvement process, as shown in Figure 11.3, ensures that security measures remain relevant, timely, and proportionate to current and anticipated threats.

Unlike IT environments, OT systems operate with legacy equipment and proprietary protocols. Threat intelligence, therefore, needs to be tailored to OT to provide:

- Contextual relevance—Focusing on vulnerabilities, exploits, and attack vectors that directly affect OT environments.
- Early warning—Identifying attack campaigns, malware strains, or adversary behaviors before they reach the organization's sector or geography.
- Operational insights—Translating technical threat data into actionable process and safety recommendations.

Sources of OT-specific intelligence include Information Sharing and Analysis Centers, CERT advisories, industry peer networks, and vendor security bulletins.

Emerging risks are not limited to active threats. They also include technology-driven changes—such as the introduction of AI-enabled tools, the adoption of cloud-connected OT systems, or the integration of Internet of Things (IoT) devices into control networks. Monitoring for these risks involves:

- Technology trend scanning—Tracking developments in hardware, software, and connectivity that may expand the attack surface.
- Regulatory horizon scanning—Identifying pending regulations—such as Network and Information Security Directive 2 in the EU and the Cyber Incident Reporting for Critical Infrastructure Act of 2022 in the United States[5]—that may alter compliance obligations.
- Sector-specific developments—Understanding how changes in supply chains, energy markets, or environmental factors could introduce new operational vulnerabilities.

Threat intelligence is most valuable when it drives decisions, not just awareness. ENISA defines a cybersecurity threat landscape methodology that it uses to provide threat intelligence to its stakeholders.[6] This methodology can be customized for any organization. It includes six main steps:

- Direction, defining the objectives, stakeholders, and other criteria for the process.
- Collection, including the identification and validation of data sources, and planning to collect the data.
- Processing, converting the acquired data into a usable format for analysis.
- Analysis and production, putting the data into context and applying analytical methods and models.
- Dissemination, delivering the results to the appropriate stakeholders.
- Feedback, collecting and acting on comments from stakeholders.

In 2022, Ukrainian energy infrastructure was targeted with Industroyer2 malware—an evolution of the Industroyer malware used in the 2016 grid attack. Thanks to alerts from CERT-UA, the Ukrainian Computer Emergency Response Team, the attempt was detected and mitigated before causing significant outages such as had been seen in 2016.[7]

When embedded into the continuous improvement process in Figure 11.3, threat intelligence shifts OT cybersecurity from a reactive stance to a proactive, anticipatory defense posture—closing the gap between threat emergence and defensive adaptation.

11.8 TRAINING, SKILLS DEVELOPMENT, AND KNOWLEDGE RETENTION

In OT cybersecurity, where the intersection of safety, reliability, and security demands precision, human capability is a decisive factor in risk management. Continuous risk management improvement depends on the organization's ability not only to train its personnel but also to retain and evolve that knowledge over time.

Cybersecurity awareness training ensures that operators, engineers, IT/OT security teams, vendors, and executive leadership understand:

- Threat awareness—How adversaries might exploit OT vulnerabilities.
- Operational context—How security measures impact physical processes and equipment.

- Incident response protocols—What to do when systems are compromised or fail unexpectedly.

As noted in Chapter 1, everyone must understand the context. Cybersecurity training is often generic and may be focused on IT systems rather than OT. While everyone must understand the risks of clicking on insecure links in phishing emails or protecting their identity online, they must also be educated on the link between these issues and the possible consequences in the operational environment. For those working in the operational environment (operators, engineers, etc.) this is easy, as they already require extensive training on safety and reliability issues and how to manage them. However, the training must show the link for them to understand that they play a part in keeping operations safe by managing cybersecurity risk.

As Figure 11.3 shows, many triggers cause a reassessment of risk and/or an update to security controls, including policies and procedures. As a result, training must follow these updates if personnel are to keep up with changes in threats, vulnerabilities, and organizational and system changes.

Regular training sessions should also help ensure that existing security controls, especially procedural controls, are not forgotten or outdated. Organizations need to avoid the slow erosion of controls over time, only to have them flagged during audits, corrected, and then slip back afterward. Investing in skills development enables teams to participate actively in improvement initiatives, rather than passively following procedures created by others.

For example, a poor password management practice involves using labels on workstations to show user account details. Without regular training in enforcing proper password management, the organization will only discover this gap during an audit. At that time, the operators may comply with the audit action and remove the labels, only to add them back later.

Another significant factor in knowledge retention is the high turnover of contractors and an aging workforce. Without formal mechanisms for capturing institutional knowledge, valuable insights—such as the operational quirks of legacy systems or lessons from past incidents—can vanish when personnel leave.

Best practices for knowledge retention include:

- Structured documentation—Standard operating procedures, configuration records, and incident logs stored in centralized, accessible repositories.
- Mentorship programs—Pairing experienced staff with newer hires to transfer tacit knowledge that cannot be easily documented.
- Post-incident reviews—Capturing lessons learned and integrating them into future training.

Continuous improvement thrives when learning becomes a cultural expectation rather than a compliance task. This means:

- Linking training objectives to individual performance evaluations.
- Encouraging staff to propose security enhancements based on training takeaways.
- Recognizing and rewarding those who apply lessons from training to improve operational resilience.

11.9 AUDITS, ASSESSMENTS, AND EXTERNAL REVIEWS

Continuous improvement in OT cybersecurity depends on the ability to verify that security controls, processes, and governance structures are not only in place but remain effective over time. Independent validation—through audits, assessments, and external reviews—provides the objective scrutiny needed to detect blind spots, validate compliance, and build stakeholder confidence. Audits and external assessments serve three primary purposes:

- Verification—Confirming that implemented measures meet regulatory requirements, organizational policies, and industry standards (e.g., ISA/IEC 62443, NIST CSF, ISO 27001).
- Validation—Determining whether the security controls are operating as intended under realistic conditions.
- Improvement Identification—Revealing gaps, inefficiencies, or emerging risks that internal teams may overlook due to familiarity bias or operational silos.

Table 11.3 shows the types of audits that may be conducted. For OT environments—where security, safety, and reliability are tightly intertwined—external validation is critical. Even minor oversights can lead to significant operational disruptions or safety hazards if left uncorrected.

The ACSSA inspection and certification scheme is a form of third-party audit and offers a common industry-vetted method for evaluating conformity to ISA/IEC 62443 for an IACS, which includes all policies and procedures, service providers, and technical security controls. This is part of a wider program that also includes:

- Product Supplier Security Development Lifecycle Assurance—Ensures secure development practices of vendors.
- Component Security Assurance—Verifies the security of individual system components, including IIoT devices, as off-the-shelf products.

TABLE 11.3 Types of Audits

Type	Format
Internal Audits	Conducted by in-house compliance or cybersecurity teams to ensure adherence to documented processes. These are useful for routine health checks but can be biased by internal assumptions or competing priorities.
Third-Party Audits	Independent organizations, such as accredited certification bodies or consulting firms, perform a structured evaluation against specific standards or regulatory frameworks.
Peer Reviews	Specialists from outside the organization but within the same industry review architecture, incident response procedures, or control configurations to share lessons learned and highlight sector-specific risks.
Regulatory Inspections	Formal examinations by government or industry regulators, often tied to licensing or operational certification. Failure to pass can have legal, financial, and reputational consequences.

- System Security Assurance—Validates the security of integrated systems and configurations, as off-the-shelf products.
- ISA offers a cybersecurity expert certificate program, providing individuals working for product suppliers, system integrators, maintenance providers, or asset owners with the skills and knowledge necessary to manage ACS cybersecurity risk.

The ISASecure ACSSA evaluates conformity to the ISA/IEC 62443 requirements as follows:

- Verify the asset owner's risk assessment process and the results of that process. This is performed against ISA/IEC 62443-3-2, Security for industrial automation and control systems Part 3-2: Security risk assessment for system design.
- Verify that the asset owner has policies and procedures in place for their security program for the IACS that meet the requirements for asset owners in ISA/IEC 62443-2-1, Security for industrial automation and control systems Part 2-1: Security program requirements for IACS asset owners.
- Identify cases where a service provider is responsible for processes that deliver capabilities described in this standard, for the

IACS under evaluation. In these cases, the evaluator will verify that these processes, as applied for this IACS, conform to ISA/IEC 62443-2-4, Security for industrial automation and control systems Part 2-4: Security program requirements for IACS service providers.
- Verify that the asset owner has configured and is utilizing technical capabilities described in ISA/IEC 62443-3-3, Security for industrial automation and control systems Part 3-3: System security requirements and security levels, provided by the hardware and software control system for the IACS.[8]

Audits and external reviews should not be viewed as compliance hurdles but as catalysts for continuous improvement.

Findings feed directly into the improvement cycle shown in Figure 11.3:

- Assessment Results—Update processes, controls, and documentation.
- Identified Gaps—Trigger targeted training, investment, or redesign efforts.
- Recommendations—Shape future technology deployments and governance policies.

11.10 AUTOMATION IN CONTINUOUS IMPROVEMENT

When carefully integrated into the continuous improvement loop in Figure 11.3, automation accelerates detection, reduces human error, and frees skilled staff to focus on higher-value analysis and decision-making. However, automation is not a substitute for expertise, and its role should be to augment, not replace, informed human judgment.

The following are areas where automation can augment human efforts:

- Automating Data Collection and Monitoring—One of the most effective uses of automation is in consolidating security data from across disparate systems. Monitoring tools can gather logs and security events in real time, reducing the time spent on manual data retrieval.
- Streamlining Gap Identification and Prioritization—Automation can assist in identifying known vulnerabilities and misconfigurations by comparing system states against baselines or regulatory checklists.

- Supporting Change Implementation—In the implementation stage, automation helps enforce consistency and reduce human error in applying security configurations, patching, or updating systems. Changing orchestration tools can apply updates across multiple devices in a controlled sequence, maintaining availability while minimizing exposure.
- Measuring Results in Real Time—Automation supports continuous measurement by generating KPI dashboards that track patch compliance, backup statistics, and the number of recurring incidents. These metrics provide evidence-based progress tracking.
- Learning and Adapting Faster—Automated correlation and analytics tools can help identify recurring patterns in incident data, highlighting systemic weaknesses. When coupled with machine learning, these systems can detect emerging risks before they become critical.

While automation delivers speed and scale and removes humans from mundane tasks, it can also magnify mistakes if poorly configured, overlooked, or exploited by adversaries. Over-reliance on automation without proper oversight may result in blind spots—especially in OT environments where context, process safety, and operational continuity must be factored into every decision.

For example:

- Automated data collection is only as good as the data that has been designated for collection. There may be system limitations preventing some data from being collected automatically.
- Many devices in OT environments are incompatible with automated vulnerability analysis tools. Manual procedures may still be necessary to check for vulnerable devices such as protocol converters or legacy PLCs or RTUs with limited network protocol support.
- Likewise, change orchestration tools may only be useful when updating compatible devices. Manual procedures may still be necessary for legacy devices.
- Analysis of data may be tailored toward identifying unauthorized access and usage and may miss early warning of insider threats.

Overall, organizations must take care with automation tools. As Carl Sagan noted in his 1995 book *The Demon-Haunted World*:

> Appeal to ignorance—the claim that whatever has not been proved false must be true, and vice versa (e.g., There is no compelling evidence

> that UFOs are not visiting the Earth; therefore UFOs exist—and there is intelligent life elsewhere in the Universe. Or: There may be seventy kazillion other worlds, but not one is known to have the moral advancement of the Earth, so we're still central to the Universe.) This impatience with ambiguity can be criticized in the phrase: absence of evidence is not evidence of absence.[9]

To avoid this over-reliance on automated tools, governance should require:

- Validation: Regular testing of alert systems, dashboards, and logs to confirm that they reflect accurate, up-to-date information.
- Red teaming: Simulated attacks (including insider threats) to test whether monitoring systems detect and respond appropriately.
- Meta-monitoring: The use of independent tools or audit processes to verify the performance of core monitoring systems.
- Human oversight: Skilled analysts who can question automated conclusions and spot anomalies that the tools may miss or misinterpret.

11.11 GOVERNANCE, OVERSIGHT, AND ACCOUNTABILITY

Governance, oversight, and accountability transform risk management from abstract discussions into measurable commitments that are funded, monitored, and validated over time.

Governance establishes the policies, roles, and structures that guide how OT cybersecurity risk management decisions are made. In a strong governance model, security responsibilities are clearly defined across all levels—from frontline operators maintaining control systems to executive leadership making investment decisions. Governance documents should specify who owns each part of the continuous improvement loop in Figure 11.3, how decisions are escalated, and which metrics are reported to stakeholders.

Oversight ensures that governance policies are being followed and that improvement commitments are progressing as planned. This may involve regular reviews by internal audit teams, board-level committees, or independent third-party assessors. Effective oversight is proactive, looking for gaps before they turn into incidents.

Accountability ties governance and oversight together by ensuring there are clear consequences—positive and negative—for how security responsibilities are carried out. This doesn't mean punishing individuals for incidents. Still, it does mean holding people accountable for whether known improvements are implemented, whether documented procedures are followed, and whether lessons learned from past events are put into practice. In the most mature organizations, accountability is reinforced by measurable performance objectives linked to security outcomes, making continuous improvement a shared, tangible goal.

The North American bulk power system offers a high-profile example of governance, oversight, and accountability in action. Under the NERC Critical Infrastructure Protection (CIP) standards, registered entities must implement strict governance structures for their OT environments, maintain oversight through documented audits and self-certifications, and demonstrate accountability through penalties for non-compliance, which can reach up to $1 million per day, per violation. While the program is sometimes criticized for being compliance-driven, it has raised the baseline level of governance and reporting across the sector, making continuous improvement a visible and enforceable expectation.

Table 11.4 provides guidance on the key activities for governance, oversight, and accountability as applied to the continuous improvement cycle shown in Figure 11.3.

Embedding governance, oversight, and accountability into the culture of an OT organization means that a few dedicated security practitioners do not just champion improvement efforts but are part of the organization's operations. When leaders regularly review cybersecurity performance, when oversight functions provide timely and actionable feedback, and when individuals know their security contributions are recognized and measured, continuous improvement moves from aspiration to daily reality.

11.12 EMBEDDING IMPROVEMENT INTO CULTURE

Processes, tools, and frameworks may define how improvements are identified and implemented. Still, culture determines whether they are consistently acted upon—and whether lessons learned survive beyond the next budget cycle or personnel change.

Closing the loop means more than ticking a box after an incident review or risk assessment. It means ensuring that insights from monitoring, incidents, and near misses are actively converted into updated processes, refined controls, and informed people. This requires three cultural elements:

- **Ownership at All Levels**—From operators on the plant floor to executives in the boardroom, everyone has a role in OT security. When operators see a procedural change emerge from their own

TABLE 11.4 Governance, Oversight, and Accountability in the Continuous Improvement Process

Continuous Improvement Stage	Governance Role	Oversight Function	Accountability Mechanism
Risk Assessment	• Define assessment scope, objectives, and methodology • Approve criteria for prioritizing risks based on operational impact, safety, and compliance requirements	• Verify that assessments follow documented procedures • Review risk registers for completeness	• Hold assessment leads accountable for completeness, accuracy, and timely delivery of reports • Require documented justification for risk prioritization decisions
Develop and Implement Controls	• Set improvement goals and align them with budget, resources, and regulatory obligations • Approve change management process and technical control implementation plans	• Evaluate proposed improvement plans for feasibility, cost-effectiveness, and compliance • Conduct audits or peer reviews during change execution	• Link improvement milestones to responsible managers' performance objectives • Require sign-off by accountable managers before changes are marked complete
Maintain	• Establish KPIs and performance metrics for evaluating improvement success • Mandate after-action reviews and formal lessons-learned documentation	• Independently verify KPI data • Review lessons-learned reports for actionable recommendations	• Hold metric owners accountable for providing accurate, timely data and corrective action plans if targets are missed • Require evidence that identified lessons have been incorporated into policies, training, or procedures

feedback, or when executives visibly support lessons-learned initiatives, it reinforces that improvement is valued, not optional.

- **Transparency Over Blame**—Fear of repercussions can suppress the very information needed to improve. Organizations that normalize open, blame-free reporting of security concerns—like the safety-reporting cultures in aviation and nuclear power—see faster detection of emerging risks and more meaningful post-incident insights.
- **Integration into Daily Operations**—Continuous improvement cannot be something "done" only after a major incident or during an annual audit. Embedding improvement into shift handovers, maintenance planning, and project design reviews ensures the loop is always turning, even during normal operations.

A strong improvement culture also recognizes the value of visible wins. When a post-incident change leads to faster recovery from the next outage, or when a training update prevents a phishing attempt from escalating, those successes should be shared widely. They build momentum, foster pride in secure operations, and make continuous improvement part of the organization's identity.

In essence, closing the loop is about making improvement reflexive—a natural response to new information, rather than a reaction triggered only by crisis or compliance pressure. When an organization reaches the point where every team instinctively asks, "How can we make this better?" after any operational or security event, continuous improvement has truly become part of its operational culture.

11.13 CONCLUSION

Continuous improvement in OT cybersecurity is not a luxury—it is a necessity for effective risk management. The threat landscape confronting operational technology is constantly evolving, with critical infrastructure remaining a prime target for both nation-state adversaries and opportunistic criminal groups. New vulnerabilities are discovered every day, while asset owners simultaneously modernize their environments with new technologies that bring both benefits and risks.

Recognizing that continuous improvement is essential is the first step. Organizations must move away from the reactive, linear, risk management process. Organizations need to acknowledge that continuous improvement is not even a constant circular process, but is in fact best visualized as a state machine, with reactions to various internal and external stimuli.

Strong governance, oversight, and accountability are what transform continuous improvement from theory into practice. When combined with meaningful metrics and lessons learned, these elements ensure that progress is not only measurable but also sustainable. Embedding feedback loops and vigilance into daily operations shifts organizations away from reactive firefighting and toward a proactive, forward-looking security posture.

Ultimately, continuous improvement is the foundation for building trust—not only in the strength of OT cybersecurity but also in the ongoing reliability, safety, and resilience of industrial operations.

NOTES

1 NIST Cybersecurity Framework (CSF) 2.0, pp iv, https://csrc.nist.gov/pubs/cswp/29/the-nist-cybersecurity-framework-csf-20/final (alt URL: http://riskbook.infracritical.com/book1/chapter11/ch11ref1.pdf).
2 ISA/IEC 62443-2-1, pp. 87.
3 Active Cyber Defence, The Sixth Year, National Cyber Security Centre. https://www.ncsc.gov.uk/report/acd-the-sixth-year ((alt URL: http://riskbook.infracritical.com/book1/chapter11/ch11ref2.pdf).
4 Zetter, Kim. Equipment Maker Caught Installing Backdoor Account in Control System Code, Wired, April 25, 2021, https://www.wired.com/2012/04/ruggedcom-backdoor/
5 https://www.cisa.gov/topics/cyber-threats-and-advisories/information-sharing/cyber-incident-reporting-critical-infrastructure-act-2022-circia (alt URLs: http://riskbook.infracritical.com/book1/chapter11/ch11ref3a.pdf, http://riskbook.infracritical.com/book1/chapter11/ch11ref3b.pdf, and http://riskbook.infracritical.com/book1/chapter11/ch11ref3c.pdf).
6 https://www.enisa.europa.eu/publications/enisa-threat-landscape-methodology#contentList (alt URL: http://riskbook.infracritical.com/book1/chapter11/ch11ref4.pdf).
7 Greenberg, Andy. Russia's Sandworm Hackers Attempted a Third Blackout in Ukraine, Wired, April 12, 2022, https://www.wired.com/story/sandworm-russia-ukraine-blackout-gru
8 https://isasecure.org/isasecure-site-assessment
9 Sagan, Carl. The Demon-Haunted World: Science as a Candle in the Dark (1st ed.). New York: Ballantine. p. 213. ISBN 0-345-40946-9. OCLC 32855551.

CHAPTER 12

Closing Thoughts

12.1 REFLECTING ON THE JOURNEY

This book has traced a comprehensive path through the evolving discipline of OT cybersecurity risk assessment. From clarifying what risk means in industrial environments to detailing methods of measurement, governance, training, intelligence, and continuous improvement, each chapter has built toward a single premise: OT cybersecurity risk management is not a one-time activity, but an ongoing commitment to safety and resilience.

We began by establishing that cybersecurity risk in OT is context-dependent. A disruption in OT technology could have catastrophic implications in the facility. This framing underscored the importance of tailoring assessments to operational realities, rather than applying generic IT-driven approaches. Subsequent chapters showed how combining qualitative insights with quantitative models enables both practical decision-making and executive-level justification.

12.2 CORE LESSONS AND THEMES

Several key themes run throughout the book:

- **Integration into Enterprise Risk Management.** OT cybersecurity cannot remain an isolated technical concern. Its risks affect safety, reliability, and continuity of operations, demanding integration into broader enterprise risk frameworks and board-level oversight.
- **Frameworks and Standards as Guides, Not Checklists.** Standards such as NIST CSF, ISA/IEC 62443, and ISO 27001 provide a framework, but effective programs adapt them to the organizational context rather than mechanically applying controls.

DOI: 10.4324/9781003610557-12

- **People and Culture as Critical Controls.** Training, knowledge retention, and cross-functional communication consistently emerged as key factors. Technology alone cannot defend OT; the competence and vigilance of operators, engineers, and managers form the real frontline.
- **Change as Both a Risk and an Opportunity.** Every upgrade, integration, or modernization introduces potential vulnerabilities. Yet with robust change management, these same activities can strengthen resilience by embedding better practices and technologies.
- **Continuous Improvement and Metrics.** Measuring progress through meaningful KPIs and using lessons learned to refine processes ensures risk management evolves in step with both the threat landscape and operational change.
- **Threat Intelligence and Proactive Monitoring.** Case studies, from Stuxnet to Industroyer2, illustrate that adversaries are adaptive and patient. Organizations that subscribe to intelligence sharing, monitor anomalies, and stress-test defenses gain a decisive advantage.

12.3 THE ROAD AHEAD

Looking forward, the convergence of IT and OT will only continue. Emerging technologies, such as AI, digital twins, and advanced analytics, will create opportunities to strengthen predictive defenses, but they will also expand the attack surface. The core challenge remains unchanged: ensuring that critical technology used in asset-intensive industries and critical infrastructure—such as water, energy, manufacturing, and transportation—remains safe and reliable despite relentless adversaries.

Organizations that succeed will be those that embrace governance, foster a culture of continuous improvement, and leverage both technology and people as complementary defenses. They will understand that resilience is not built overnight, but through steady cycles of assessment, learning, and adaptation.

12.4 FINAL THOUGHTS

The message of this book is ultimately one of cautious optimism. OT cybersecurity risk management is complex, but it is not insurmountable. By aligning practices with operational realities, integrating cybersecurity into enterprise risk, and cultivating a culture of vigilance and accountability, organizations can not only withstand today's threats but also build the adaptive capacity to face tomorrow's unknowns.

Continuous improvement, grounded in risk-informed practice, will remain the cornerstone of resilience. In the end, protecting critical infrastructure is not just about technology—it is about safeguarding the people, communities, and economies that depend upon it every day.

APPENDIX A

Risk Framework Models, Standards, and Guidelines

A.1 TERMINOLOGY

TABLE A.1 Terms and Abbreviations

Term or Abbreviation	Definition
AAA	Authentication, Authorization, and Accounting
AAD	Azure Active Directory
ACL	Access Control List
AD	Active Directory
ALARP	As Low As Reasonably Practicable, a definition of the point where risk is being managed as well as possible
ANSI	American National Standards Institute
AV	Antivirus
Availability	The probability that the system is operating properly when it is required. Availability is measured as a percentage over a defined period
AWIA	America's Water Infrastructure Act
AWWA	American Water Works Association
Barrier	A technical or procedural element that minimizes the likelihood or consequence of an incident. Also known as a control
Bowtie	A diagrammatic method used to show the relationship between threats, causes, consequences, controls, and escalation factors
BYOD	Bring Your Own Device
CCTV	Closed-Circuit Television
CCU	Critical Care Unit

(*Continued*)

TABLE A.1 (Continued)

Term or Abbreviation	Definition
CERT	Computer Emergency Response Team
CIA	Confidentiality, Integrity, Availability (security triad)
CISA	Cybersecurity and Infrastructure Security Agency
CMMS	Computerized Maintenance Management System
Consequence	The result of an incident. For instance, ransomware on a computer system can result in a loss of business operations
Control	Another term for barrier, a technical or procedural element that minimizes the likelihood or consequence of an incident
CPG	Cybersecurity Performance Goal
CSIRT	Computer Security Incident Response Team
CVE	Common Vulnerabilities and Exposures
DHCP	Dynamic Host Configuration Protocol
DHS	Department of Homeland Security
DLP	Data Loss Prevention
DMZ	Demilitarized Zone
DNS	Domain Name System
EDR	Endpoint Detection and Response
Encryption	A method of protecting sensitive information by converting it into an unreadable form
EPP	Endpoint Protection Platform
Escalation Factor	A way in which the effectiveness of a barrier or control can be degraded
Exploit	A means to use a vulnerability to create a cybersecurity incident
Failsafe	A type of barrier or control that is in place to minimize the consequences of an incident. For example, a pressure relief valve
FBI	Federal Bureau of Investigation
FIDO	Fast Identity Online, an open standard and a set of technology specifications designed to improve online authentication and enhance digital security
Firewall	Network Security Device
Four-eyes	A practice that requires the involvement of at least two individuals in a critical action or decision. It is a control mechanism to reduce the risk of fraud or errors

(*Continued*)

TABLE A.1 (Continued)

Term or Abbreviation	Definition
Geofencing	Geofencing uses location data to define boundaries that can be used to trigger actions, notifications, or apply policies
GIS	Geospatial Information System
GPS	Global Positioning System
Hash	A unique representation of data that can be used to validate that data is not compromised during transmission
HIDS/NIDS	Host-based Intrusion Detection System/Network-based Intrusion Detection System
HiPo	High Potential, a type of incident (usually safety but can apply to cybersecurity)
HTTP	Hypertext Transfer Protocol
HTTPS	Hypertext Transfer Protocol Secure
IACS	Industrial Automation and Control System
IAM	Identity and Access Management
ICS	Industrial Control System
IDS	Intrusion Detection System
IEC	International Electrotechnical Commission
IoT	Internet of Things
IPS	Intrusion Prevention System
ISA	International Society of Automation
ISO	International Standards Organization
IT	Information Technology
Key	Data used in an encryption algorithm, combined with the original data to make the encrypted form
KPI	Key Performance Indicator
LAN	Local Area Network
LDAP	Lightweight Directory Access Protocol
Likelihood	The probability that an event will occur
MAC	Media Access Control
Maintainability	The ease with which a product can be maintained and is an essential element for successful operations
MDM	Mobile Device Management
MFA	Multi-factor Authentication
MITM	Man-in-the-Middle

(Continued)

TABLE A.1 (Continued)

Term or Abbreviation	Definition
MS-ISAC	Multi-State Information Sharing and Analysis Center, a U.S.-based organization that focuses on enhancing the cybersecurity resilience of state, local, tribal, and territorial governments
NAC	Network Access Control
NIST	National Institute of Standards and Technology
NRWA	National Rural Water Association
NTP	Network Time Protocol
OAUTH	Open Authorization, an open standard authentication and authorization framework
OSINT	Open-Source Intelligence
OT	Operational Technology
PCI DSS	Payment Card Industry Data Security Standard
PII	Personally Identifiable Information
PIN	Personal Identification Number
PLC	Programmable Logic Controller
PoLP	Principle of Least Privilege
RAT	Remote Access Trojan
RBAC	Role-Based Access Control
RCE	Remote Code Execution
Red Team	A red team is a group that pretends to be an adversary. They attempt a physical or electronic intrusion in an organization at the direction of that organization, with limits on what they may or may not do. For more information, see https://csrc.nist.gov/glossary/term/red_team
Redundancy	Achieving high availability by replicating hardware so that if one device fails, another can take over
Reliability	The probability of a component or system to perform a required function in a specific environment for a specific period without failure
Risk	The result of exposure to a hazard or threat. Risk is typically determined from the product of likelihood and consequence
RTU	Remote Telemetry Unit or Remote Terminal Unit
SCADA	Supervisory Control and Data Acquisition
SIEM	Security Information and Event Management
SOP	Standard Operating Procedure
SSO	Single Sign-On

(*Continued*)

TABLE A.1 (Continued)

Term or Abbreviation	Definition
Threat	Also known as a hazard, it could be environmental-based, such as flooding or earthquake, or infrastructure-based, such as loss of power or communications, or others, such as cybersecurity-related (hacker, nation-state, etc.)
TLS/SSL	Transport Layer Security/Secure Sockets Layer
USB	Universal Serial Bus
U.S. EPA	U.S. Environmental and Protection Agency
VLAN	Virtual Local Area Network
VPN	Virtual Private Network
Vulnerability	A flaw in software or hardware, a configuration error, or a failure in a process or procedure
WaterISAC	Water Information Sharing and Analysis Center, an organization that focuses on enhancing the cybersecurity and physical security resilience of the water and wastewater sector in the United States
WEF	Water Environment Federation
WEP	Wired Equivalent Privacy
WPA	Wi-Fi Protected Access
WWV	NIST radio station that broadcasts time and frequency information 24 hours per day, 7 days per week
Zero Day	Vulnerability exploited before it is known to the vendor

A.2 RISK FRAMEWORK MODELS

A.2.1 Bowtie Analysis

1. BowtieXP by CGE Risk
   Website: https://www.cgerisk.com
   (Offers software, methodology, and white papers tailored to industrial risk assessment.)
2. *CCPS—Guidelines for Hazard Evaluation Procedures* (3rd Edition)
   Publisher: AIChE/Center for Chemical Process Safety
   ISBN: 978-0-470-16569-0

3. Energy Institute (UK)—Bowtie Analysis Guidance
   Title: "Bowtie Analysis: Guidance on Use"
   Free download: https://www.energyinst.org

A.2.2 Cyber PHA/HAZOP

4. ISA—"Conducting Cybersecurity Risk Assessments for IACS"
   Technical Report: ISA-TR84.00.09-2017
   (Applies traditional HAZOP-style methods to cybersecurity.)
5. ISA—"*Security PHA Review for Consequence-Based Cybersecurity*"
   Authors: Edward Marzal/Jim McGlone
   Publisher: International Society of Automation
   ISBN: 3: 978-1-64331-002-2
6. Dragos—"Cyber PHA/HAZOP: Assessing Cyber Risk in OT Environments"
   Authors: Dragos Inc./ex-ICS-CERT experts
   https://www.dragos.com
7. ICS Security Risk Assessment Methodology (NIST)
   NIST SP 800-82 Rev. 2—Guide to Industrial Control Systems Security
   https://csrc.nist.gov/publications/detail/sp/800-82/rev-2/final

A.2.3 Fault Tree Analysis

8. Ericson, Clifton A.—*Hazard Analysis Techniques for System Safety*
   Publisher: Wiley, 2nd Edition
   ISBN: 978-1118940382
   (Excellent resource on FTA and related techniques.)
9. IEC 61025—Fault Tree Analysis (FTA)
   Standard defining methodology and application of FTA in safety systems.
10. CCPS—Guidelines for Hazard Evaluation Procedures (see above)
    (Includes FTA as part of hazard assessment toolset.)

A.2.4 LOPA

11. CCPS—*Layer of Protection Analysis: Simplified Process Risk Assessment*

Publisher: AIChE/CCPS
ISBN: 978-0-8169-0811-2
(The definitive guide.)
12. IEC 61511—Functional Safety for the Process Industry Sector
(LOPA is referenced as a method for SIL determination.)
13. Exida—LOPA white papers
https://www.exida.com/resources

A.2.5 FAIR (Factor Analysis of Information Risk)

14. The FAIR Institute
Website: https://www.fairinstitute.org
(Includes standards, training, tools, and a free FAIR risk taxonomy.)
15. Jones, Jack—*Measuring and Managing Information Risk: A FAIR Approach*
Publisher: Butterworth-Heinemann
ISBN: 978-0124202313
(Written by the FAIR model creator.)
16. NIST IR 8286—Integrating Cybersecurity and Enterprise Risk Management (ERM)
(Mentions FAIR as a recommended risk model.)

A.2.6 OCTAVE

17. OCTAVE Allegro Implementation Guide—Carnegie Mellon/SEI
https://resources.sei.cmu.edu/library/asset-view.cfm?assetid=297720
18. CMU/SEI Website—OCTAVE Methodology Resources
https://www.sei.cmu.edu/octave
19. NIST IR 8183—Cybersecurity Framework Manufacturing Profile
(Mentions OCTAVE in context of cyber risk assessment.)

A.2.7 Cyber-Informed Engineering (CIE)

20. Idaho National Laboratory (INL)—CIE Strategy White Paper
Title: "Cyber-Informed Engineering: Strategy for Cybersecurity in the Energy Sector"
https://inl.gov/cie/

21. U.S. DOE—Cyber-Informed Engineering Program Resources
https://www.energy.gov/ceser/cyber-informed-engineering
22. Idaho Falls CIE Playbook
Title: "A Framework for Integrating Cybersecurity into Engineering Practices"
(Developed by INL and used in U.S. national labs and utilities.)

A.3 STANDARDS, REGULATIONS, AND GUIDELINES

A.3.1 NERC CIP

23. Official NERC CIP Standards Page:
https://www.nerc.com/pa/Stand/Pages/CIPStandards.aspx
(Includes all current and historical CIP standards, like CIP-002 to CIP-014.)
24. NERC—CIP Standards Guidance
Title: CIP Standards: Summary and Intent
https://www.nerc.com/pa/CI/
25. NERC Reliability Guidelines:
https://www.nerc.com/comm/OC/Pages/Reliability-Guidelines.aspx
(Helpful for implementation examples.)

A.3.2 NIS2

26. Official NIS2 Directive Text:
https://eur-lex.europa.eu/eli/dir/2022/2555/oj
(Directive (EU) 2022/2555 of December 14, 2022.)
27. ENISA—NIS2 Implementation Guidelines & Sectoral Guidance
https://www.enisa.europa.eu/topics/cybersecurity-policy/nis-directive/nis2-directive
28. European Commission—NIS2 Overview:
https://digital-strategy.ec.europa.eu/en/policies/nis2-directive

A.3.3 CRA

29. Official Proposal Text (EC):
https://eur-lex.europa.eu/legal-content/EN/TXT/?uri=CELEX%3A52022PC0454

30. European Commission Q&A:
https://digital-strategy.ec.europa.eu/en/faqs/questions-and-answers-cyber-resilience-act
31. ENISA CRA Impact Study (2022):
https://www.enisa.europa.eu/publications/preparatory-study-for-the-cyber-resilience-act
32. EU Council & Parliament Legislative Updates:
https://oeil.secure.europarl.europa.eu/oeil/popups/ficheprocedure.do?reference=2022/0272(COD)
33. Analysis by Law Firms and Think Tanks:
https://www.cliffordchance.com/insights/resources/blogs/regulatory-investigations-blog/2023/01/the-eus-cyber-resilience-act.html
https://www.ceps.eu/ceps-publications/eus-cyber-resilience-act/

A.3.4 America's Water Infrastructure Act Risk and Resilience Assessments and Emergency Response Plans

34. U.S. EPA AWIA Resources Page:
https://www.epa.gov/waterresilience/americas-water-infrastructure-act-awia
(Covers RRA/ERP requirements under AWIA Section 2013.)
35. EPA AWIA Tools and Templates (for utilities):
https://www.epa.gov/waterresilience/tools-and-templates-risk-assessments-and-emergency-response-plans

A.3.5 National Institute of Standards and Technology Cybersecurity Framework

36. Official Framework for Improving Critical Infrastructure Cybersecurity (v1.1/v2.0):
https://www.nist.gov/cyberframework
37. NIST CSF 2.0—Official Launch Page:
https://www.nist.gov/news-events/news/2024/02/nist-launches-cybersecurity-framework-version-20
38. NIST Cybersecurity Practice Guides (NCCoE):
https://www.nccoe.nist.gov

A.3.6 International Society of Automation/International Electro Technical Commission 62443

39. ISA 62443 Series Overview (via ISA.org):
https://www.isa.org/standards-and-publications/isa-standards/isa-62443-series-of-standards
(Includes technical reports and standards like 62443-2-1, 62443-3-2, 62443-4-2, etc.)
40. IEC 62443 Series (via IEC):
https://webstore.iec.ch/publication/7028
(Primary reference point for international versions.)
41. ISA Global Cybersecurity Alliance Resources:
https://gca.isa.org/resources
(Guidance on implementation of the standards.)
42. ISASecure:
https://www.isasecure.org
(ISA/IEC62443 certification programs related to products, systems, and facilities.)

A.3.7 International Standards Organization/International Electro Technical Commission 27001

43. ISO/IEC 27001:2022 Standard (via ISO):
https://www.iso.org/standard/82875.html
44. ISO/IEC 27000 Series Overview:
https://www.iso.org/isoiec-27001-information-security.html
45. Free ISO 27001 Implementation Guidance (e.g., IT Governance):
https://www.itgovernanceusa.com/iso27001

A.3.8 Center for Internet Security Critical Security Controls

46. Center for Internet Security (CIS)—Official Controls List:
https://www.cisecurity.org/controls
47. CIS Controls v8 PDF & Implementation Groups (IGs):
https://www.cisecurity.org/white-papers/cis-controls-v8
48. Implementation Guide for ICS/OT Environments:
https://www.cisecurity.org/insights/blog/securing-ot-with-the-cis-controls-v8

A.3.9 Cross-Sector Cybersecurity Performance Goals

49. CISA Official CPG Resource Page:
    https://www.cisa.gov/resources-tools/resources/cross-sector-cybersecurity-performance-goals
50. CPG Checklist for Critical Infrastructure Operators:
    https://www.cisa.gov/sites/default/files/2022-10/cpg-checklist.xlsx

A.3.10 NIST Special Publication 800 Series

51. NIST 800 Series Master Index:
    https://csrc.nist.gov/publications/sp800
    (Includes SP 800-30 (Risk Assessment), 800-53 (Controls), 800-82 (ICS security), 800-171 (contractor data), and more.)

A.3.11 American National Standards Institute/American Water Works Association Risk Management Standards

52. Available from: https://www.awwa.org/Store
    a. G430-14(R20): Security Practices for Operation and Management—Focuses on physical and cyber protection for water utilities.
    b. G440-17: Emergency Preparedness Practice—Defines ERP requirements for utilities.
    c. J100-21: Risk and Resilience Management of Water and Wastewater Systems—Integrates resilience and cybersecurity under AWIA; based on EPA's VSAT methodology.
    d. G300-14: Source Water Protection—Addresses upstream risk reduction and source vulnerability management.

A.3.12 ISO/IEC 27005

53. ISO/IEC 27005:2022 Standard (via ISO):
    https://www.iso.org/standard/80585.html
    (Provides guidance for implementing risk management aligned with ISO/IEC 27001.)
54. Overview & Application of ISO 27005:
    Official guidance document available via ISO member bodies or standards libraries.
    Also referenced in NIST RMF and other sector-specific frameworks.

A.4 OTHER RESOURCES

National Rural Water Association—NRWA (https://nrwa.org/issues/cybersecurity) The National Rural Water Association is a non-profit organization dedicated to training, supporting, and promoting the water and wastewater professionals that serve small and rural communities across the country. The NRWA focuses on simple guidance and practical steps that will help all members better manage their cybersecurity risk: The NRWA is developing a plan for a comprehensive continuous cyber education program that will help all small and rural water and wastewater systems better manage their cybersecurity risk, by • Creating a multi-stage training program that targets guidance based on risk along with the technical ability and capacity of systems; • Focusing on training Circuit Riders, the key NRWA field experts who are best placed to sustain the ongoing effort needed to manage the cybersecurity risk; and • Integrating with other initiatives around water sector cybersecurity to ensure that time, effort, and funds are used to best effect.
Water Information Sharing and Analysis Center—WaterISAC (https://www.waterisac.org) WaterISAC is the designated information sharing and operations arm of the Water Sector Coordinating Council. WaterISAC has established secure and close contact with partners in government to access sensitive and classified security information. WaterISAC maintains two-way communication with the CISA, the Federal Bureau of Investigation (FBI), the U.S. EPA, state intelligence fusion centers, and other federal and state agencies. Through the National Council of ISACs, WaterISAC also collaborates with more than two dozen other ISACs, particularly with the Electricity ISAC. They also amass intelligence and resources from selected security experts, water and wastewater industry partners, news media, and their own members.
American Water Works Association—AWWA (https://www.awwa.org/Resources-Tools/Resource-Topics/Risk-Resilience/Cybersecurity-Guidance) The AWWA is an international, non-profit, scientific and educational society dedicated to providing total water solutions ensuring the effective management of water. In addition to sector-specific risk management standards that address cybersecurity and a cybersecurity assessment tool, AWWA provides reports and other guidance to support the water and wastewater sector's management of cybersecurity.

(*Continued*)

Infracritical (http://infracritical.com/)

Infracritical is an organization founded by Bob Radvanovsky and Jake Brodsky, internationally recognized experts in the field of industrial cybersecurity.

Infracritical provides two resources:

- The Systems and Cyber Impact Database Markup (SCIDMARK) (directly available at http://scidmark.com/). This site provides a register of industrial cybersecurity incidents.
- The SCADASEC mailing list, free to join, share knowledge and discuss industrial cybersecurity issues with experts around the world (https://scadasec.groups.io/).

Top 20 secure PLC coding practices (https://www.plc-security.com/)

A project to provide guidelines to engineers who are creating software used in industrial control systems.

ICS Advisory Project (https://www.icsadvisoryproject.com/)

The ICS Advisory Project provides smaller operational technology asset owners, CISOs, cybersecurity analysts, and researchers with an analysis tool that allows them to quickly identify threats and vulnerabilities by product, vendor, and by critical infrastructure sector. Interactive dashboards collate publicly available threat and vulnerability data such as CISA ICS Advisories, CVEs, and MITRE ATT&CK.

Mitre (https://www.mitre.org/focus-areas/cybersecurity)

The MITRE Corporation was founded in 1958 as a not-for-profit company to serve as advisers in systems engineering to government agencies, both military and civilian. They maintain a database of vulnerabilities called CVE, the Common Vulnerabilities and Exposures database, and also provide cybersecurity guidance and frameworks.

$(CS)^2$AI (https://www.cs2ai.org/)

Founded by Derek Harp and Bengt Gregory-Brown, $(CS)^2$AI is a global, not-for-profit, workforce-development organization supporting professionals of all levels charged with securing control systems. They provide a platform for members to help members foster meaningful peer-to-peer exchange, continue professional education, and directly support cybersecurity professional development.

InfraGard (https://www.infragard.org/)

InfraGard is a partnership between the FBI and members of the private sector for the protection of U.S. Critical Infrastructure. InfraGard connects owners and operators within critical infrastructure to the FBI, to provide education, information sharing, networking, and workshops on emerging technologies and threats.

InfraGard's membership includes business executives, entrepreneurs, lawyers, security personnel, military and government officials, information technology professionals, academia, and state and local law enforcement.

(*Continued*)

Vulnerability Self-Assessment Tool (VSAT) for water and wastewater risk assessment (https://www.epa.gov/waterriskassessment/vulnerability-self-assessment-tool-conduct-drinking-water-or-wastewater-utility)
U.S. EPA recommends that the quantitative risk assessment be limited to a small number of the assets and threats that present the highest risk.

Attempting to analyze a high number of asset/threat pairs in a single assessment will render the assessment difficult to complete and make the interpretation of results challenging. Strategies to reduce the number of asset/threat pairs including grouping similar assets into a single asset category and limiting threats to those with the highest likelihood of occurrence.

Cyber Security Evaluation Tool (CSET)
(https://www.cisa.gov/downloading-and-installing-cset)

CSET is a desktop software tool that guides asset owners and operators through a step-by-step process to evaluate industrial control system (ICS) and information technology (IT) network security practices. Users can evaluate their own cybersecurity stance using many recognized government and industry standards and recommendations. CSET v11.5 includes a Cyber Performance Goals (CPG) Assessment.

AWWA Cybersecurity Risk Management Tool
(https://cybersecurity.awwa.org/)

The AWWA Water Sector Cybersecurity Risk Management Tool is an online tool to support utilities in developing their cybersecurity risk management strategy. The tool is aligned with the NIST CSF.

APPENDIX B

Case Studies

B.1 INTRODUCTION

This set of case studies has been selected to highlight many of the key issues discussed in this book, particularly how the focus on risk needs to look beyond the cyber aspects.

The examples chosen are all in the water/wastewater sector. This helps with the comparisons between incidents, but it does not imply that the water/wastewater sector is unique in its issues.

This appendix compares several well-documented events—including Oldsmar, Spencer, Muleshoe, and Forest Park—to highlight how different causes can produce similar outcomes, and how organizational response shapes resilience.

A recurring question underlies these cases: *are they truly "attacks," or failures of process, design, and oversight that allowed an event to escalate into a potential safety or reliability concern?* Regardless of classification, the consequences in terms of operational disruption and public confidence are strikingly similar.

B.2 CITY OF OLDSMAR (2021)

It was reported that on February 5, 2021, unidentified cyber actors obtained unauthorized access to the supervisory control and data acquisition (SCADA) system at a U.S. drinking water treatment facility.[1] The report stated that these unidentified actors used the SCADA system's software to increase the amount of sodium hydroxide, also known as lye, a caustic chemical, as part of the water treatment process. Water treatment plant personnel immediately noticed the change in dosing amounts and corrected the issue before the SCADA system's software detected the manipulation and alarmed due to the unauthorized change. As a result, the water treatment process remained unaffected and continued to operate as normal. The cyber actors likely accessed the system by exploiting cybersecurity weaknesses, including poor password security, and an outdated operating system. Through the course of the subsequent investigation, the FBI could not confirm that a targeted cyber intrusion initiated this incident.

- Cause—The original cause was identified as an insecure remote access connection that was exploited by an unauthorized party. After a two-year FBI investigation identifying no external attacker, the conclusion is that the increase in sodium hydroxide level was a result of human error by an authorized operator.[2]
- Impact—There was no impact as the extremely high setpoint for injected sodium hydroxide was quickly adjusted before toxic levels of the chemical entered the water system.
- Response—The error was noted and reversed before it could result in toxic levels in the potable water supply. Law enforcement was engaged.

Consequence—No physical harm occurred, but the incident revealed the presence of insecure remote access (although it was not the vector through which the incident occurred), along with more concerning news that the software used on the SCADA system had lack of restriction on setting potentially dangerous setpoint levels, either extremely high or low.

B.3 SPENCER, MASSACHUSETTS (2007)

On April 25, 2007, city officials discovered that there was a malfunction at one of the town's water treatment facilities, where an extremely dangerous amount of sodium hydroxide was released into the town's water supply. The official statement indicated that it was a malfunction by the computer system controlling the amount of sodium hydroxide released into the town's water supply due to operator error. The incident resulted in approximately 145 residents suffering skin burns and irritations resulting from exposure to and ingestion of water with an elevated pH level.[3,4]

The cause of the incident appeared to have been operator error, along with the failure of alarm systems to notify the operators of the problem when those operators were off-site. Based on interviews, MassDEP believes that the incident began because of the operators placing the sodium hydroxide feed system in "manual operation mode" as part of maintenance and repair of one of the lines. Sodium hydroxide commonly is used to treat the water to prevent the leaching of lead and copper into the drinking water from domestic plumbing. The sodium hydroxide feed was normally in automatic operation, meaning an electronic control provided the proper dose of chemical into the water distribution line. In a regular, automated operation, sodium hydroxide only flowed into the system when a pump moving water out of the treatment plant was operating. The sodium hydroxide feed would shut down when the pump turned off. This would ensure the proper dosage and adequate dilution of the sodium hydroxide into the water supply.[5]

- Cause—An operator was making repairs to one of the water lines on April 24, 2007, and switched the controlling pump to "manual operation" in order to make repairs to a leaking line. Once repairs were completed, the operator failed to switch the controlling pump back to "automated operation." This resulted in the release of approximately 34 gallons of sodium hydroxide into the water supply from April 24 to April 25, 2007, for a period of approximately 12.5 hours—without proper dilution.
- Impact—Approximately 145 residents suffered skin burns and irritations due to the elevated pH levels in the town's water supply. Additionally, the serviced equipment suffered undisclosed damage and was repaired later.
- Response—Recovery was rapid, with local personnel restoring systems and operations within hours.
- Consequence—Damage appeared to be isolated to the Town of Spencer only; however, as there were multiple residents affected by the tainted water, multiple fire districts were contacted to alleviate the overwhelming number of residents requiring immediate medical attention. The serviced equipment suffered some damage resulting from the operator error and was replaced at an unknown date; additionally, the alarm system was remediated as well, also at an unknown date.

B.4 ABERNATHY, MULESHOE, HALE CENTER, AND LOCKNEY (2024)

A reported cyber intrusion attributed to Russian threat actor known as Cyber Army of Russia Reborn (referred to as both CAR and CARR through multiple sources; however, for sake of clarity, we use the U.S. federal government's abbreviation as "CARR")[6] targeted utilities in four small rural towns in Texas, all within 100 miles of each other.[7] In July of 2024, the United States Department of State sanctioned two members of a Russian activist group known as the CARR for their involvement in attacks on water facilities in Abernathy, Muleshoe, Hale Center, and Lockney, Texas.[8,9]

The Water, Agriculture, and Rural Affairs Committee invited three witnesses to testify on a panel regarding cybersecurity issues in Texas water systems during its May 15, 2024, hearing. Those three witnesses represented the City of Muleshoe, the Texas Department of Information Resources, and the Texas Public Policy Foundation (TPPF), respectively.[10]

IN the testimony, officials indicated that CARR changed settings in Muleshoe's system, causing a water tower to overflow.[11] The CARR was able to access the water systems of several communities in the Panhandle region using the same hacking method it deployed against Muleshoe.[12] As indicated by the report, "there was no release of any private data and no interruption of service resulting from the breach of Muleshoe's firewall."[13] Nonetheless, Muleshoe testified that the community was "rattled" by the incident, particularly after national media drew attention to the situation.[14] Muleshoe responded to the situation by: replacing compromised equipment; replacing old passwords with newer, stronger ones; implementing multi-factor authentication protocols for system users; and reducing the general Internet exposure of its water system.[15]

TPPF characterized the Russian cyberattacks on Muleshoe and neighboring cities in West Texas[16] as "Russian cyber-terroris[m]" and an example of the "new digital warfare landscape that [the United States is] seeing."[17] To emphasize the scale of the cyberattacks in West Texas, TPPF pointed out that approximately 37,000 attempts were made to penetrate the firewall for the City of Hale Center before Russian actors were able to successfully break through.[18] Perhaps most concerning of all, TPPF characterized the Russian cyberattacks as "prepositioning"—in other words, practice attempts that equipped the Russians with "new insights on vulnerabilities [with which to] refine their tactics, techniques, and protocols for future attacks."[19]

It should be noted that The Honorable Mr. Kevin Sparks, State Senator of District 31 for The Senate of Texas, discussed about several state bills, of which Senate Bill (SB) No. 1034, titled "Water Cybersecurity Measures For Retail Public Utilities" was one of them.[20] However, the bill, which was introduced on January 31, 2025, did not proceed any further and "died" in its initial stages; thus, it was not sent to a dedicated committee for further review or discussion, or passed by the State Senate. As its progression was listed as 25%, this means that it was introduced but did not progress further to other legislative steps such as a committee review or any floor debate.[21]

Abernathy, Texas (2024)

- Not much data is available specific to the incident at the Town of Abernathy, other than that they had experienced similar attacks to that of Muleshoe, Texas. Details as to what systems were impacted, and what the eventual consequence(s) were, remain unknown.

Muleshoe, Texas (2024)

- Cause—According to officials, external adversaries accessed the water plant's network of Muleshoe, Texas, on January 18, 2024; the site's control system, which allows access to communicate and manage the local primary water tank, was infiltrated and setpoints were modified.
- Response—Officials quickly disconnected their control system, reverting to manual operations.
- Impact—Muleshoe services approximately 5,000 residents. Although water availability was not interrupted, the water system required flushing due to overflow of its local primary water tank for approximately 30–45 minutes before city officials acted by shutting down their HMI. The event posed no threat to public safety or water quality.[22] The impact was considered as minor to the public.[23]
- Consequence—Disruption was contained with minimal customer impact; confidence shaken but restored through rapid communications.

Hale Center (2024)

- Cause—The city experienced an aggressive cyber intrusion—roughly 37,000 login attempts were made against its firewall over a span of four days.
- Impact—Hale Center services approximately 2,000 residents; however, none of its customer base was impacted due to the removal of access to the water plant's control system. There was no impact to the public.
- Response—Officials responded by disconnecting (unplugging) remote access to their control system that manages and communicates with their water systems, as well as switching to manual operations, successfully avoiding any disruption to water service. Further network hardening efforts were performed following the attempted breach.
- Consequence—The consequence was considered minor due to minimal impacts to their network infrastructure.

Lockney (2024)

- Cause—Intrusion was attempted but was thwarted before any access was gained.
- Impact—Lockney services approximately 1,500 residents. The town reacted quickly by removing remote access, further

preventing any future attacks that could affect or impact the town's water supply. There was no impact to the public.[24]

- Response—There was no operational impact—only a nuisance to the town personnel.
- Consequence—There appeared to be no consequences resulting from this incident as it had little to no impact to their network infrastructure.

B.5 FOREST PARK, ILLINOIS (2025)

On May 15, 2025, a resident of Forest Park, located near the Howard Mohr Community Center at the intersection of Des Plaines and Jackson, reported water flowing from the building to a local street. The situation prompted the Forest Park Police to notify the village's public works department. Upon arrival, individuals discovered that water was streaming from the underground million-gallon reservoir, an underground facility that supplies drinking water to the community, located directly below the community center.

The village's primary reservoir is a million-gallon concrete storage tank, located directly underneath the community center. Additionally, another reservoir with a capacity of 350,000 gallons at another location also holds potable water.

The flooding was attributed to a computer malfunction at the public works department. This caused the valve controlling the main pump from the City of Chicago to fault and open completely, overfilling the reservoir. The excessive water flowing from the community center was due to excessive water flowing from an already full reservoir. The failure of the computer system meant that no alarms were triggered to alert staff. As a result, the overflow not only inundated the community center but also impacted the pumping station responsible for distributing water from the reservoir out and throughout the village. Additionally, the pumping station was also flooded due the computer malfunction.

- Cause—Computer malfunction, resulting in full opening of the primary intake valve from the City of Chicago to replenish the underground water tank facility, resulting in flooding of the community center and adjacent pumping station, as the reservoir was completely full at the time of the incident.
- Impact—The local community center was completely flooded, and thus, carpeting, staff offices, and other areas were damaged and required repair. Though the pumping station was flooded, there were no statements as to any detail of any damages to equipment inside the pumping station.

- Response—Although there were no indications of converting to manual operation, the authors surmise that the water system would be operated manually to perform diagnostics and conduct further forensics of the incident.
- Consequence—Operations continued, but reliance on manual backup would have resulted in additional costs and inefficiencies.

Comparison

All examples exhibit the same themes:

- Operators intervened quickly, preventing service issues and, in the case of Oldsmar, potential harm to the public.
- Manual operations are the ultimate fallback. This is particularly true for several critical infrastructure organizations, such as the electricity industry (distribution, transmission, and especially, generation), the railroad industry (contingency plans involve manual switching and bonfires manned by railroad personnel using two-way communications), and the water industry (also manned by water utility personnel). Although it may be costly, the infrastructure will continue to operate safely.
- Recovery and remediation processes required improvisation under pressure and scrutiny. None of the organizations had an incident response plan—none was mentioned in any reports—to cover such situations, so they relied on the initiative of personnel.
- The fragility of operations without appropriate safeguards. If not for the prompt action of operators, the consequence(s) could have been more severe. In the case of Oldsmar, the County Sheriff Bob Gualtieri said in a press conference days after the incident that, "It would have taken 24–36 hours for the water to reach the system, and that there are several redundancies in place that would have alerted that the levels were too high before that happened."[25] It is unclear what those redundancies were or how effective they would have been.

B.6 KEY TAKEAWAYS

- At the time that this book was written, lawmakers are becoming acutely aware of the threat of cyberattacks within the water industry. However, utilizing law as a measure of securing an operation may not necessarily be the best method of ensuring safe and reliable operations.

- The common question when discussing OT cybersecurity is, "Is this really an attack?" Ultimately, these examples demonstrate that it is irrelevant whether the threat actor is a nation-state, a disgruntled contractor, or an authorized employee acting in error. The consequences can be identical. The Oldsmar case is a perfect example. Initially believed to be an external, intentionally malicious attack, it was eventually concluded to be human error from an authorized individual; the result was unchanged—potable water was at risk of containing a dangerous level of sodium hydroxide.
- Cause is less critical than consequence. Whether intentional or accidental, the trigger matters less than a utility's ability to detect, respond, and recover.
- Key elements of the responses in these case studies were the employees' critical thinking skills and their institutional knowledge. However, these cannot be the primary basis for response. In many of the examples, the quick thinking and responsiveness are portrayed heroically. Organizations don't need heroic individuals, modern-day "MacGyvers," or people who can solve any problem with the most improbable solutions.[26] Instead, they need tried and tested response plans that are regularly updated in light of changes.
- Risk management must address the consequences of an incident, intentional or otherwise. Relying on operators to react is not an acceptable mitigation on its own—although it should form part of a layered response.
- Rapid, coordinated shutdown and transitional actions to manually switch from an automated to manual mode are often the safest path for small utilities—but this should be part of a preplanned resilience strategy, not an improvised emergency measure. Differences are not measured based solely on the eventual consequence(s), but are based on the utility's preparedness and decisiveness, not by an attacker's capability.
- Preparedness—The efforts of preparing for any consequence(s), regardless of attack or accident, are paramount. Response playbooks, operator training, and manual fallback procedures are crucial.
- Resilience—The resilience of any critical infrastructure organization is demonstrated by well-thought-out and carefully planned actions to mitigate the consequences of an incident. Utilities that acted decisively minimized disruption; those that hesitated suffered significantly greater impacts.

NOTES

1 http://scid.infracritical.com/pages/archived/scid-00113
2 "Compromise of U.S. Water Treatment Facility", Joint Cybersecurity Advisory, TLP:WHITE, CISA, February 11, 2021; URL: https://www.cisa.gov/sites/default/files/2023-04/AA21-042A_Joint_Cybersecurity_Advisory_Cyber_Actors_Compromise_U.S._Water_Treatment_Facility.pdf (alt URL: http://riskbook.infracritical.com/book1/appendixb/ap_bref1.pdf)
3 "Statement by MassDEP of Preliminary Findings Regarding the Water Supply Incident in Spencer, Massachusetts April 25-27, 2007"; MassDEP; dated 2-May-2007
4 http://scid.infracritical.com/pages/archived/scid-00115
5 "Spencer Water Crisis April 25-27, 2007 – After Action Report / Improvement Plan, September, 2007"; URL: https://www.spencerma.gov/sites/g/files/vyhlif1246/f/uploads/wateremergency.pdf (alt URL: http://riskbook.infracritical.com/book1/appendixb/ap_bref2.pdf)
6 Interim Hearing, The Texas Senate Committee on Water, Agriculture, and Rural Affairs Interim Report to the Senate of the 89 th Texas Legislature (statement of Ramon Sanchez, City Manager, City of Muleshoe, Tex).
7 https://www.texastribune.org/2024/04/19/texas-cyberattacks-russia/
8 Interim Report to the Eighty-Ninth Texas Legislature, House Select Committee on Securing Texas from Hostile Foreign organizations, December 4, 2024, p.24; URL: https://www.house.texas.gov/pdfs/committees/reports/interim/88interim/House-Select-Committee-on-Securing-Texas-From-Hostile-Foreign-Organizations-Interim-Report-2024.pdf (alt URL: http://riskbook.infracritical.com/book1/appendixb/ap_bref3.pdf)
9 Interim Report to the Eighty-Ninth Texas Legislature, House Select Committee on Securing Texas from Hostile Foreign organizations, December 4, 2024, p.24; URL: https://www.house.texas.gov/pdfs/committees/reports/interim/88interim/House-Select-Committee-on-Securing-Texas-From-Hostile-Foreign-Organizations-Interim-Report-2024.pdf (alt URL: http://riskbook.infracritical.com/book1/appendixb/ap_bref3.pdf)
10 The Texas Senate Committee on Water, Agriculture, and Rural Affairs, Interim Report to the Senate of the 89th Texas Legislature, December 1, 2024, p.12; URL: https://senate.texas.gov/cmtes/88/c700/c700_InterimReport_2024.pdf (alt URL: http://riskbook.infracritical.com/book1/appendixb/ap_bref4.pdf)

11 The Texas Senate Committee on Water, Agriculture, and Rural Affairs, Interim Report to the Senate of the 89th Texas Legislature, December 1, 2024, p.12; URL: https://senate.texas.gov/cmtes/88/c700/c700_InterimReport_2024.pdf (alt URL: http://riskbook.infracritical.com/book1/appendixb/ap_bref4.pdf)

12 The Texas Senate Committee on Water, Agriculture, and Rural Affairs, Interim Report to the Senate of the 89th Texas Legislature, December 1, 2024, p.12; URL: https://senate.texas.gov/cmtes/88/c700/c700_InterimReport_2024.pdf (alt URL: http://riskbook.infracritical.com/book1/appendixb/ap_bref4.pdf)

13 The Texas Senate Committee on Water, Agriculture, and Rural Affairs, Interim Report to the Senate of the 89th Texas Legislature, December 1, 2024, p.12; URL: https://senate.texas.gov/cmtes/88/c700/c700_InterimReport_2024.pdf (alt URL: http://riskbook.infracritical.com/book1/appendixb/ap_bref4.pdf)

14 The Texas Senate Committee on Water, Agriculture, and Rural Affairs, Interim Report to the Senate of the 89th Texas Legislature, December 1, 2024, p.12; URL: https://senate.texas.gov/cmtes/88/c700/c700_InterimReport_2024.pdf (alt URL: http://riskbook.infracritical.com/book1/appendixb/ap_bref4.pdf)

15 The Texas Senate Committee on Water, Agriculture, and Rural Affairs, Interim Report to the Senate of the 89th Texas Legislature, December 1, 2024, p.12; URL: https://senate.texas.gov/cmtes/88/c700/c700_InterimReport_2024.pdf (alt URL: http://riskbook.infracritical.com/book1/appendixb/ap_bref4.pdf)

16 The Texas Senate Committee on Water, Agriculture, and Rural Affairs, Interim Report to the Senate of the 89th Texas Legislature, December 1, 2024, p.12; URL: https://senate.texas.gov/cmtes/88/c700/c700_InterimReport_2024.pdf (alt URL: http://riskbook.infracritical.com/book1/appendixb/ap_bref4.pdf)

17 Interim Hearing, The Texas Senate Committee on Water, Agriculture, and Rural Affairs Interim Report to the Senate of the 89 th Texas Legislature (statement of David Dunmoyer, Campaign Dir. for Tech. Pol'y, Tex. Pub. Pol'y Found.).

The Texas Senate Committee on Water, Agriculture, and Rural Affairs, Interim Report to the Senate of the 89th Texas Legislature, December 1, 2024, p.12; URL: https://senate.texas.gov/cmtes/88/c700/c700_InterimReport_2024.pdf (alt URL: http://riskbook.infracritical.com/book1/appendixb/ap_bref4.pdf)

18 Interim Hearing, The Texas Senate Committee on Water, Agriculture, and Rural Affairs Interim Report to the Senate of the 89 th Texas Legislature (statement of David Dunmoyer, Campaign Dir. for Tech. Pol'y, Tex. Pub. Pol'y Found.).

The Texas Senate Committee on Water, Agriculture, and Rural Affairs, Interim Report to the Senate of the 89th Texas Legislature, December 1, 2024, p.12; URL: https://senate.texas.gov/cmtes/88/c700/c700_InterimReport_2024.pdf (alt URL: http://riskbook.infracritical.com/book1/appendixb/ap_bref4.pdf)

19 Interim Hearing, The Texas Senate Committee on Water, Agriculture, and Rural Affairs Interim Report to the Senate of the 89 th Texas Legislature (statement of David Dunmoyer, Campaign Dir. for Tech. Pol'y, Tex. Pub. Pol'y Found.).

The Texas Senate Committee on Water, Agriculture, and Rural Affairs, Interim Report to the Senate of the 89th Texas Legislature, December 1, 2024, p.12; URL: https://senate.texas.gov/cmtes/88/c700/c700_InterimReport_2024.pdf (alt URL: http://riskbook.infracritical.com/book1/appendixb/ap_bref4.pdf)

20 The Honorable State Senator Mr. Kevin Sparks of District 31, The Senate of Texas, "STATE SENATOR SPARKS FILES FIFTH 89th PRIORITY LEGISLATIVE PACKAGE ON WATER ACCESS & SUPPLY", p.3; URL: https://senate.texas.gov/members/d31/press/en/p20250226a.pdf (alt URL: http://riskbook.infracritical.com/book1/appendixb/ap_bref5.pdf)

21 TX SB1034 | 2025-2026 | 89th Legislature; URL: https://legiscan.com/TX/bill/SB1034/2025.

22 Interim Report to the Eighty-Ninth Texas Legislature, House Select Committee on Securing Texas from Hostile Foreign organizations, December 4, 2024, p.29; URL: https://www.house.texas.gov/pdfs/committees/reports/interim/88interim/House-Select-Committee-on-Securing-Texas-From-Hostile-Foreign-Organizations-Interim-Report-2024.pdf (alt URL: http://riskbook.infracritical.com/book1/appendixb/ap_bref4.pdf)

23 "Report: Russian-linked hackers carry out cyberattack on Texas town's water system", CNN, April 17, 2024; URL: https://www.cnn.com/2024/04/17/politics/russia-hacking-group-suspected-texas-water-cyberattack/index.html

24 "Rural Texas towns report cyberattacks that caused one water system to overflow", The Texas Tribune, April 19, 2024; URL: https://www.texastribune.org/2024/04/19/texas-cyberattacks-russia.

25 https://edition.cnn.com/2021/02/08/us/oldsmar-florida-hack-water-poison

26 The U.S. television show "MacGyver" ran between 1985 and 1992.

Index

Please note that page numbers in *italics* denote figures, those in **bold** denote tables, while n indicates a note.

For Product Safety Concerns and Information please contact our EU representative GPSR@taylorandfrancis.com
Taylor & Francis Verlag GmbH, Kaufingerstraße 24, 80331 München, Germany

www.ingramcontent.com/pod-product-compliance
Ingram Content Group UK Ltd.
Pitfield, Milton Keynes, MK11 3LW, UK
UKHW052051230926
475702UK00025B/1100

* 9 7 8 1 0 4 1 0 0 6 8 2 4 *